T0270559

UP IN ARMS

UP IN ARMS

ARMS

HOW MILITARY AID STABILIZES — AND DESTABILIZES — FOREIGN AUTOCRATS

ADAM E. CASEY

BASIC BOOKS

New York

Basic Books
Hachette Book Group
1290 Avenue of the Americas, New York, NY 10104
www.basicbooks.com

Printed in the United States of America

First Edition: April 2024

Published by Basic Books, an imprint of Hachette Book Group, Inc. The Basic Books name and logo is a registered trademark of the Hachette Book Group.

The Hachette Speakers Bureau provides a wide range of authors for speaking events. To find out more, go to hachettespeakersbureau.com or email HachetteSpeakers@hbgusa.com.

Basic books may be purchased in bulk for business, educational, or promotional use. For more information, please contact your local bookseller or the Hachette Book Group Special Markets Department at special.markets@hbgusa.com.

The publisher is not responsible for websites (or their content) that are not owned by the publisher.

Graphs produced by the author and designed by Tanner Uselmann.

Print book interior design by Bart Dawson.

Library of Congress Cataloging-in-Publication Data has been applied for.

ISBNs: 9781541604018 (hardcover), 9781541604025 (ebook)

LSC-C

Printing 1, 2024

To Tayla

CONTENTS

INTRODUCTION

FRIENDLY TYRANTS

When thousands of Iranians took to the streets in late 1978, they did not just rise up to denounce their authoritarian monarch, Mohammad Reza Pahlavi. The shah was indeed an autocrat, and his repressive rule featured centrally in the protests. But he was not the only source of revolutionary ire. In addition to chants of "Death to the shah," protesters exclaimed "Yankee go home!" Demonstrators repeatedly tied their dictator to distant America. American policy was highlighted so prominently by protesters because the United States was viewed by all sides as a central player in Iranian politics. To supporters, the monarch was a stalwart American ally bolstered by American support. To detractors, he was an American puppet. It was presumed by both that his survival in office was the product of US military and economic aid. For many protesters, it was believed that in order to overthrow the shah the revolutionaries would need to break his support not only in Tehran but also in Washington.[1]

It was not only protesters in Iran who decried their authoritarian leader as a stooge of a foreign power. Opposition activists in Ngo Dinh Diem's South Vietnam, Hosni Mubarak's Egypt, and both Fidel Castro and Fulgencio Batista's Cuba all claimed their ruling regimes to be puppets propped up by a foreign power. It is not only in the cries of those seeking the overthrow of the regime where one finds the claim that the government remains in office thanks to external aid. Very diverse actors tend to agree that many dictatorships are kept in power thanks to the assistance of foreign countries. Opposition activists, foreign adversaries, and even policymakers in the state offering the support often presume that certain regimes are propped up by foreign aid.

No period in recent history would seem to illustrate these dynamics more than the Cold War. This climactic battle of wills between the communist Soviet Union and capitalist United States pitted two competing worldviews and superpowers against each other in a contest over the fate of the global order. In this competition for global supremacy, Moscow and Washington each cultivated a network of allies arrayed against its competitor. These alliances were vulnerable to reversal if the ruling governments were to fall. A central dynamic of this Cold War therefore involved efforts to ensure aligned regimes did not collapse, lest their replacement realign to the rival superpower. Aid, arms, and advisers poured into friendly governments to bolster their rule. Like the shah, not all of these allies were particularly savory.

While the US had many democratic allies in the so-called Free World, it also aligned itself repeatedly with anticommunist authoritarian leaders. To many analysts, these dictators were propped up by American aid. Prominent critics of American foreign policy like Noam Chomsky argue that in Guatemala the US overthrew the democratic government in 1954 and has "maintained the rule of murderous gangsters ever since." Other governments too lobbed such criticism against US-supported regimes, describing Chiang

Kai-shek in Taiwan as a "puppet propped up by American bayonets" and Ngo Dinh Diem as an American lackey. US Senator Jacob
Javits bemoaned aid for the anticommunist junta in Cambodia as
another effort at "propping up incompetent or unpopular governments." Leading accounts of American foreign policy offer that
during the Cold War the United States broadly supported "reactionary political elites" who "survived only with American support." American officials installed "despots in their place abroad
as strategic weapons" to be used against Soviet geopolitical rivals.[2]

Propping up friendly dictators was not a behavior apparently
limited to the United States. France, China, the United Kingdom,
and the Soviet Union were all accused of ensuring the survival of
allied autocrats through military and economic aid in the Cold
War. The argument that US support stabilizes friendly dictatorships is not unique to the critics of such policies. Supporters of
aid for autocrats agree that American assistance helped entrench
friendly regimes who served core foreign policy interests.[3]

The accepted wisdom that American aid stabilized authoritarian regimes generated considerable discomfort for policymakers.
The "friendly tyrants" dilemma emerged from the tension between
America's own democracy and any embrace of foreign autocrats.
Detractors claimed that as a democracy the US should not ally
with authoritarians. Supporters contended that however distaste-
ful these foreign tyrants, these alliances served core American
foreign policy interests. It was a dilemma nested in a larger debate
about the goals that ought to guide American foreign policy, pit-
ting self-described "realists" who advocated the passionless pursuit
of America's national interests against "idealists" who argued the
US had a duty to promote the expansion of liberty and equality
abroad.[4]

These debates have shaped American foreign policy since the
founding. In the early years of the republic, the US government
agonized over whether to provide aid to the French revolutionaries

3

who rose up for many of the same principles that had motivated America's own revolution. As the US rose to international prominence, it came to expand its reach into Central and Latin America and experienced dilemmas over whether to support democratic movements or retrograde regimes that promised stability and pro-American orientation. While many American administrations reconciled themselves with the need to enter into temporary alliances with foreign despots, most have also maintained that America has a duty to support the expansion of democracy beyond its borders. In the evocative formulation of President Woodrow Wilson, America's mission was "to make the world safe for democracy." The clash of dictatorships against democracies in the World Wars of the twentieth century reinforced American officials' conviction that the nation was to serve as the vanguard of democracy, spreading liberty worldwide.[5]

But the tension between pursuing interests and values in foreign policy only became more acute after the US rose to a position of unprecedented global power. At the conclusion of the Second World War, Washington emerged as the undisputed center of Western power. The British and French empires were irreparably damaged by the war and would never return to their prewar dominance.

By midcentury, only the Soviet Union rivaled America in power and influence. Moscow's rise to global power was perhaps even more remarkable than America's, given its position as it entered the twentieth century. Russia had gone from a backwater of Europe to a state riven by revolutionary ferment and near total collapse. When the Bolshevik revolutionaries seized power in 1917, they inaugurated the first successful communist revolution. After years of intense and bloody struggle the Bolsheviks consolidated a brutally effective authoritarian regime in Moscow. Besieged on all sides by foreign powers and counterrevolutionaries intent on crushing their revolution, the Bolsheviks constructed a paranoid and repressive regime. Despite its inauspicious origins and the attendant almost unimaginable violence, the Soviet Union experienced rapid industrialization and modernization, although at tremendous cost to human life.[6]

After the existential war against Nazi Germany, the Soviet Red Army straddled a landmass that rivaled some of the greatest empires in history. Soviet troops stood from the Elbe River in Germany to halfway down the Korean peninsula. At the same time, communist revolutionaries seized power in the Balkans and were on the offensive in Greece. Meanwhile, French and Italian communist parties seemed poised to reap major election victories. It appeared communism was on the march. The debilitating economic inefficiencies that would later plague the Union of Soviet Socialist Republics (USSR) were not yet readily apparent, and the Soviet Union experienced rapid postwar industrial growth.[7]

In response, America came to embrace its newfound responsibility as the leader of the Free World arrayed against the growing communist menace. Communism had posed a *subversive* threat to American interests before the US-Soviet competition that would soon be called the Cold War. But it was the newfound superpower status of the Soviet Union that rendered the spread of communism a *strategic* threat after 1945. Communist governments would not just challenge the new American-led economic system but could join the Soviet Union as military allies in a war to come. The task of stopping the spread of communism by bolstering noncommunist governments fell to the United States.[8]

At its core, the Cold War was a superpower rivalry that pitted two very different political and economic systems against each other. Ideologically, it featured a clash between the democratic, capitalist United States and the authoritarian, communist Soviet Union. As a geopolitical rivalry, it prompted both the US and the USSR to build a network of allies to seek a favorable correlation of forces. These competing power blocs emerged as a shifting patchwork of allies and aligned states that, with varying degrees of consistency, supported one superpower against the other. As starkly as the political and economic systems of the two superpowers differed, their allies in the Cold War proved a far more heterogeneous group.

This was most apparent in the US-led Free World. "Free" proved a capacious category that came to include many regimes with highly circumscribed freedoms for their own populations. Most notably, it included many anticommunist dictatorships, some of whom—like Thailand—had even allied with the former fascist powers. These were unappealing friends who presided over governmental systems that were often "repugnant" to the "basic ideals" of Americans.[9]

Supporting friendly tyrants was not a decision made lightly by Cold War–era US administrations. Nevertheless, anticommunism ultimately trumped enduring discomfort toward autocracies seeking American support during the Cold War. Where autocrats were considered sufficiently geopolitically important and potentially vulnerable to communist subversion, they found a willing patron in the United States.

For those seeking to understand how the US came to support anticommunist dictatorships, many have offered the apocryphal quote attributed to President Franklin D. Roosevelt, variously applied in reference to dictators in either Nicaragua or the Dominican Republic: "He may be a son of a bitch, but he is our son of a bitch." In addition to its dubious veracity, this quote does a poor job capturing the dynamics of American support for foreign dictators during the Cold War. A statement that more accurately encapsulates the feelings of American government officials was provided by avid cold warrior John F. Kennedy. President Kennedy was remarkably frank about the priorities of his administration in regard to the Dominican Republic when he offered that "there are three possibilities in descending order of preference: a decent, democratic regime, a continuation of the Trujillo regime, or a Castro regime. We ought to aim for the first, but we really can't renounce the second until we are sure that we can avoid the third." It was not that the US preferred the rule of a despot, but only that it preferred a despot to a communist.[10]

In short, the rivalry with the Soviet Union was a looming exigency that dampened American preferences for promoting democracy. Policymakers believed that "while it would be best to allow free institutions and governments to struggle to take hold, there did not appear to be time." Just as World War II had brought the United States to embrace some unsavory allies, from Central American military juntas to the Soviet Union itself, the superpower contest unfolding between Washington and Moscow pushed many American officials to accept a need to widen the coalition of allies to include anticommunist governments of many political stripes. In some cases, this meant merely a passive toleration of pro-American autocrats. In others, the US role was far more extensive: some dictatorships received covert and overt American assistance in seizing and consolidating power. The US poured aid, arms, and advisers into a range of friendly dictatorships to bolster the rule of anticommunist regimes.[11]

The US reconciled the tensions between democratic ideals and an embrace of friendly anticommunist dictatorships in several ways. American aid was intended to ensure the conservative leadership necessary to guarantee domestic stability, pursue reliable anticommunist polices, and usher in responsible political development that would even bring eventual democratization. Moreover, while their democratic credentials were far from impeccable, these regimes were usually freer than the "totalitarian" communist regimes in the Soviet bloc. With quiet American pressure, autocratic allies might be pushed to embrace formal democratic institutions like multicandidate elections, representative legislatures, and reasonably free rights of assembly for noncommunist groups.

Military strongmen would trade their fatigues for business suits and hold managed plebiscites to rest a fig leaf of democratic legitimacy on their rule. The authoritarian nature of the regime could also be excused by a racist paternalism on the part of the US that viewed societies in the postcolonial world as too politically immature to sustain fully free elections, which they might use to elect communists.[12]

The geopolitical benefits provided by these friendly tyrants were vulnerable to reversal if regimes were overthrown. For the United States, the primary threat came from the violent revolutionary ouster of its allied governments. Marxist-Leninist insurgents defeating anticommunist regimes on the battlefield and seizing control of the capital haunted American policymakers. The reverse held true for the Soviet Union. For Moscow's communist allies, the primary threat was posed by the counter-revolutionary overthrow of leftist incumbents. The forces of reaction—landowners, the clergy, military officers—lurked in the shadows of vulnerable revolutionary governments and threatened to oust Soviet allies from power through coups d'état or war. Therefore, for each superpower the domestic rule of friendly regimes had to be sustained with aid, arms, and advisers. Keeping a sovereign-friendly foreign government in power was no small task. Formal sovereignty reduced the levers available to foreign powers to guarantee continued rule by loyal clients. Local allies were vulnerable to overthrow by domestic forces yet had no desire to be dominated in neocolonial relationships with former metropolitan powers or the new superpowers.

Despite the practical and moral challenges posed by aid for friendly autocrats, the conventional wisdom is that the United States and other foreign powers broadly succeeded in entrenching friendly regimes in power. Much of the debate hinges on the morality of this policy and whether such interventions served broader foreign policy interests. Yet arguments both in favor of and opposed to support for friendly tyrants rest on untested assumptions about the actual effects of American aid for autocrats. Whether the US should have propped up dictators during the Cold War rests on an antecedent question: did the US really prop up dictators? Autocrats really did receive military supplies, economic aid, and advice designed to ensure their rule remained stable. But was external aid really so helpful for dictators? The conventional wisdom that external assistance ensures authoritarian survival stands on surprisingly shaky ground.

The question of whether aid really does stabilize dictatorships is not of mere historical significance. A growing American rivalry with China has resuscitated the debate over aid for friendly autocrats. Any argument over support for friendly tyrants in the future would benefit significantly from a serious examination of the history of foreign assistance for dictatorships in the first Cold War. What lessons do we learn by reexamining past American and Soviet support for authoritarian regimes?

We have learned much from particular cases of foreign aid for particular dictatorships. Scholars and practitioners have spilled much ink detailing the provision of economic aid, military supplies, and foreign advisers to help bolster the rule of individual authoritarian regimes. Yet without placing these behaviors in their comparative context, we lack insight into how common any one experience is.

Thanks to the declassification of government records and the work of political scientists and historians, we are now able to answer these questions. With an increasingly comprehensive picture of the history of foreign security and economic assistance during the Cold War, we are able to place particular dictatorships and specific actions of support in their proper comparative context. Using hundreds of books, intelligence reports, and diplomatic cables, I created an original measure of the foreign support available to every autocracy in every year from 1946 to 2010. Not only did this require the availability of hitherto unavailable records, it also required the generation of high-quality data on authoritarian regimes. Luckily, political scientists such as Barbara Geddes, Joseph Wright, and Erica Frantz have released data on the origins and tenure of all authoritarian regimes since the Second World War. By merging this data with information on foreign support, I was able to generate the highest-quality data to date on foreign aid for autocrats.[13]

Identifying autocrats that foreign powers sought to prop up presents conceptual difficulties in addition to the challenge of finding relevant data. Autocracies that do not receive military supplies or economic aid of any kind from foreign powers are rare. Yet the intensity and exclusivity of these connections vary considerably. Some regimes, like that of Julius Nyerere and his Party of the Revolution in Tanzania, deftly balanced competing global power blocs by hosting advisers and receiving aid from countries as varied as China and Canada. This kind of balanced foreign policy was relatively rare, however. Many regimes primarily aligned with one bloc in the bifurcated superpower struggle. Yet many of these alignments came with surprisingly sparse connections.[14]

Paraguay under Alfredo Stroessner (1954–1989) offers a useful illustration. Stroessner was an avowed anticommunist military dictator who explicitly and repeatedly aligned himself with the United States. However, the limited communist threat to his regime brought little reciprocal American interest. Contrary to popular assertion, American policymakers did not simply bankroll every anticommunist dictatorship. Aid was conditioned heavily on the perceived threat of communist subversion. The United States continued to provide Stroessner's government with nominal military aid, sell him a modest supply of weapons, and dole out limited economic assistance, but the connections were relatively minimal and heavy subsidies nonexistent. Stroessner was staunchly pro-American, but there was no real American investment in his regime. Over the course of his tenure, American policy amounted to an orientation that vacillated between intermittent pressure for democratization and passive toleration of his personalized dictatorship.[15]

In other cases, relations were primarily commercial. Libya under Mu'ammar al-Gaddhafi purchased billions in Soviet weaponry with revenue from oil exports, and advisers were deployed to service the advanced armaments. This was not military aid to entrench the erratic Libyan autocrat's rule but instead was a mutually beneficial financial relationship. Moscow received hard currency, and Libya overcame its international isolation to receive sophisticated weaponry. It would be misleading to investigate such transactional relations as attempts to prop up a regime, given the primarily commercial motivations and relatively sparse foreign investment in the survival of the government.[16]

Finally, formal alliances did not always accompany extensive efforts to protect regimes from internal or external threats. Beijing provided the Khmer Rouge government (1975–1979) with extensive military and economic aid yet never maintained a formal alliance with Phnom Penh. Discerning the true nature of international relationships requires a deeper investigation than merely noting the formal structures tying two states together or the volume of weapons sales.[17]

Just as the US was wrongfully accused of propping up all anticommunist dictators, the Soviet Union was not always behind avowedly Marxist Leninist governments. In 1974–1975, Marxist-Leninist guerrilla groups seized power across Portuguese Africa. These liberation movements had all received important support from the Soviet Union during their struggles for independence, yet the postcolonial revolutionary regimes generated widely varying Soviet interest and support. Angola and Mozambique were the objects of considerable Soviet efforts to support their independence movements both before and after they became ruling regimes. In Angola and Mozambique, the Soviet Union deployed advisers and provided key aid in reorganizing the army, building the secret police, and planning combat operations against insurgent groups. By contrast, Soviet interest and investment in Guinea-Bissau was marginal in both absolute and relative terms. Angola and Mozambique both hosted thousands of Soviet advisers and, in the case of Angola, tens of thousands of Cuban combat troops. By contrast, Guinea-Bissau never maintained more than one hundred Soviet military advisers.[18]

Of course, the muted reception of the United States toward military rule in Paraguay does not mean the US did not support any anticommunist dictatorships. Other regimes received considerable American investments to strengthen their governments. For some autocracies, this even involved US help with the seizure

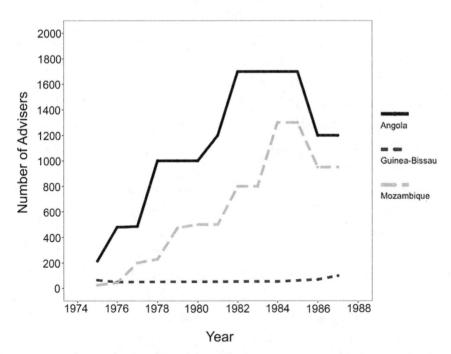

Figure 1. Soviet military advisers in revolutionary regimes in Lusophone Africa (*Source:* Declassified CIA documents)

of power. The United States helped organize the intervention that brought former army officer Carlos Castillo Armas into power in Guatemala in 1954. Once ensconced in Guatemala City, Castillo Armas received millions in new military aid; US intelligence helped identify alleged communists; military and police advisers arrived to train their Guatemalan counterparts; and, in June 1955, a mutual defense treaty committed the United States to Guatemala's defense. In other cases, aid was slower to materialize. In Nicaragua, significant US assistance for the regime of Anastasio Somoza García began to arrive only after the beginning of the small-scale guerrilla war by the Sandinista National Liberation Front in 1961. This was many years after the avowed anticommunist cold warrior Somoza had sought US aid. He had secured the resumption of military sales in 1950 and modest military aid four years later. But it took the sixty-three or so Sandinista fighters sharing around thirty weapons to bring serious American support for Somoza. After this tiny guerrilla column set up operations near the Honduran border, US military aid increased sevenfold, and military advisers were deployed. Therefore, while Somoza was not always an American client, he did become one.[19]

This same pattern holds for the Soviet Union. Moscow too provided enormous resources to some foreign authoritarian regimes. Some of these are well-known cases like Cuba, or the regimes imposed in Eastern Europe after World War II. Others have received scanter attention, like the Soviet efforts to support regimes in Ethiopia, Mozambique, South Yemen, and Somalia. Like their American counterparts, some Soviet allies received support on their road to power or immediately once they had seized control of the state. Moscow provided aid to the Angolan and Mozambican insurgent movements and to clandestine communist parties in places like Afghanistan long before these movements seized power. Others found Soviet support slower to arrive. In Cuba, the turn to Moscow for succor did not happen until the collapse in relations with the United States, some eighteen months into Castro's tenure. In South Yemen, Soviet aid, arms, and advisers began to arrive in large quantities in the early 1970s, several years after the National Front had seized power.

In short, the actual pattern of military and economic aid for dictatorships in the Cold War was highly complex. As a truly global superpower competition, the Cold War touched all corners of the globe in some way. American and Soviet arms reached nearly everywhere, but the biggest battlegrounds featured far more intense involvement. Some autocracies received American or Soviet help building new armies from scratch, organizing intelligence agencies, paying and staffing government bureaucracies, drafting and executing economic policies, and identifying potential sources of opposition. These intense bilateral relations sought to entrench the rule of friendly regimes, with decidedly mixed results.

The accumulation of data on foreign military and economic support that underpins the findings in this book grapples directly with these complexities in international relationships. To build a measure of foreign support, I examined all 280 authoritarian regimes in this period. I compiled information on economic and military aid as well as the role of military and security advisers in organizing security forces in client autocracies. I operated using a high threshold for what constituted a client regime, to only compare autocracies with broadly similar intensity of foreign support. These data allow us to compare autocracies that a foreign sponsor makes serious efforts to protect from potential internal or external threats to those that do not enjoy such foreign backing.

Armed with systematic data on aid for autocrats in the Cold War, we are able to assess the effects of assistance on authoritarian survival. At first glance, the conventional wisdom that great powers propped up dictators appears well supported by a more

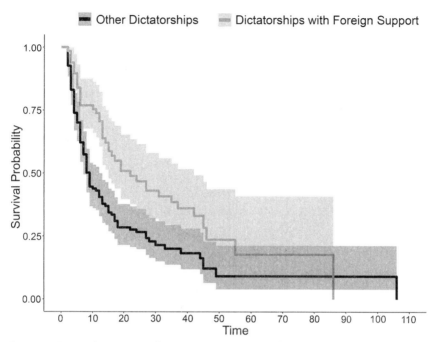

Figure 2. Survival curves: Authoritarian regimes with foreign support, 1946–1989

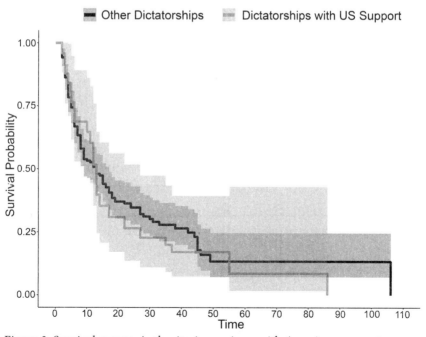

Figure 3. Survival curves: Authoritarian regimes with American support, 1946–1989

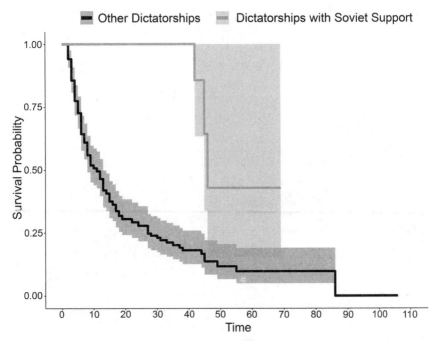

Figure 4. Survival curves: Authoritarian regimes with Soviet support, 1946–1989

(Source for data in Figures 2–4: Adam E. Casey, "The Durability of Client Regimes: Foreign Sponsorship and Military Loyalty, 1946–2010," World Politics *72, no. 3 (2020): 411–447, https://doi.org/10.1017/S0043887120000039)*

systematic investigation. Throughout the Cold War, dictatorships that received foreign support over the course of their existence lasted on average a decade longer than other autocracies.

However, if we split our analysis by who is supporting the dictatorships, we see that this relationship was driven almost entirely by the Soviet Union. Soviet client regimes lasted twice as long as their American counterparts. In any given year, American-backed dictatorships had almost the same risk of collapse as typical autocracies, while Soviet clients were seven times less likely to fall. The same story holds for the United Kingdom and France, whose support was also not associated with longer regime tenures. This means not only that Soviet-supported dictatorships were longer lasting than their American-backed rivals, but that they were some of the most resilient dictatorships in the twentieth century.[20]

What accounts for this stark variation? The answer lies not in the popularity, economic performance, or amount of aid granted to Soviet-backed dictators over their American counterparts. Both superpowers provided comparably enormous sums of military and economic aid to their clients. Despite their much greater resilience, Soviet-backed regimes presided over even worse economic outcomes than their US-backed counterparts. The variation we observe is not coincidental. Instead, it is the product of the intended and unintended impacts of strategies of support on the distribution of power within dictatorships.[21]

Aid, arms, and advisers do not just bolster dictatorships, they also transform them. These transformations are not always beneficial for the stability of authoritarian regimes. To understand why American support did not stabilize autocracies, while Soviet aid entrenched highly durable dictatorships, we must understand both how each superpower actually supported friendly regimes and how autocracies work. US and Soviet military and economic aid did have many similarities: both superpowers bankrolled the expansion of armies, paid government salaries, and offered advice for how to organize security forces and defeat enemies of the regime. Yet the advice for how to organize security forces differed in critically important ways. The models of military organization promoted by each superpower diverged starkly. Washington and Moscow each exported its own model of political-military relations, with very different consequences for their allied autocracies. The United States promoted the establishment of autonomous militaries that separated the army from autocratic politics. The Soviet Union sponsored the subordination of the army to the ruling regime by thoroughly politicizing the military.

American military aid strengthened the autonomy and position of the army within allied authoritarian regimes. While this served US goals for bolstering the single most important institution for preventing communist takeover, it proved a decidedly mixed blessing for the allied rulers themselves. In practice, it created a powerful internal rival to American-backed dictators. Contrary to the claims of protesters, America's friendly tyrants were no puppets and recognized the threat their newly ascendant armies posed to their regimes. US-backed dictators bucked American advice and consistently sought to subvert this process by interfering in the army to keep it under their control. The regime's American-trained military officers often reacted to this political meddling by attempting to overthrow their regimes in coups d'état. Confident the army would produce another anticommunist and pro-US leader, the United States largely accepted these coups.

When these coups failed, America's friendly tyrants, aiming to reduce the threat of future coups, proceeded to cannibalize their own armed forces, steadily hollowing out the very state institutions the US sought to strengthen. The result was an increasingly weakened state apparatus that subverted American aid in the interests of regime survival and often dragged the United States further into interventions to sustain the beleaguered government.

By contrast, Soviet military aid did not strengthen the domestic position of the army in its client states. Instead, the very opposite happened: Soviet aid helped subordinate the army to the control of the ruling regime. With Soviet aid and advice, allied regimes embedded highly effective mechanisms of control within their armed forces that rendered military coups too difficult to carry out. This resulted in politically docile armed forces that were incapable of ousting Soviet client regimes in coups d'état. Not a single Soviet client regime fell to a military coup. As coups are the most common way authoritarian regimes collapse, this invulnerability accounted for the remarkably long tenures of Soviet client regimes even in the context of mass unrest, war, famine, economic collapse, and extreme state violence. By inoculating themselves from the threat of military coups, Soviet-backed regimes were able to survive in office far longer than most other autocracies.

In short, the common story about aid for autocrats in the Cold War is in need of retelling. Critics of American and Soviet foreign policy were not wrong that Washington and Moscow poured billions into friendly regimes to sustain their rule. But the actual effects of this aid on the internal stability of dictatorships is a much less known story. This book offers the first comprehensive attempt to tell this story. It is a history that is more urgent than it might seem.

INTEREST IN THE FRIENDLY-TYRANTS DILEMMA LARGELY DISSIpated with the end of the Cold War. In part, this reflected the considerable decline in foreign support for autocrats. The collapse of the Soviet Union removed one major source of aid and engendered a profound change in American attitudes toward dictatorships. With the communist superpower gone, anticommunist dictatorships now inhabited a world markedly less threatening to American strategic interests. Washington's newfound security brought a greater emphasis on promoting liberal reforms abroad. Dictators from Mobutu Sese Seko in Zaire to Samuel Doe in Liberia found that whatever vestiges remained of their appeal were markedly diminished with the end of the Cold War. The new global order was not lost on ruling regimes. Multiparty elections spread rapidly through much of the developing world in the early 1990s not because demands for democracy by citizens had sharply increased or entrenched dictators were suddenly converted into democrats. Instead, authoritarian regimes now inhabited a unipolar American world with a superpower that proved willing to use a muscular approach to promoting democracy. In the memorable explanation for a transition to multiparty rule offered by Tanzanian autocrat Julius Nyerere, "When you see your neighbor being shaved, you should wet your beard. Otherwise, you will get a rough shave."[22]

In extreme cases like Panama (1989) or Haiti (1994), the United States engaged in direct military interventions to topple dictators. Elsewhere the US enacted coercive measures to restrict access to international financing and isolate recalcitrant autocrats who refused to liberalize their political systems. Reliant on American goodwill to access international financial institutions and devoid of a justification for support based on countering Soviet-backed communism, autocracy after autocracy ushered in liberalization to adjust to the new international system. Professed Marxist-Leninists like Yoweri Museveni in Uganda and Sam Nujoma in Namibia were apparent born-again liberals. Of course, autocrats proved adept in adopting the more visible trappings of democracy—elections and multiparty legislatures—while working behind the scenes to hobble the capacity of opposition to mount successful electoral campaigns. Yet amid the constraints of the new international system, even these insincere domestic reforms had real consequences. Autocrats had to work hard to manipulate competitive elections and frequently lost power. There were a few notable exceptions to this trend. For authoritarian regimes in Saudi Arabia, Jordan, and Pakistan, continued or renewed geopolitical relevance would ensure uninterrupted American support. But for other dictatorships, like Myanmar and Eritrea, forgone democratic reforms meant pariah status.[23]

This post–Cold War period of unrivaled American hegemony is ending. Over the past decade, proclamations of a "new Cold War" between China and the United States have become commonplace. While explicitly disavowing this designation, American officials frequently mention a need to counter the threat posed by their "near peer competitor" in Beijing. Like its twentieth-century predecessor, this contest embodies another clash of systems. US Secretary of State Anthony Blinken characterized China as the only country with the intention and means "to advance a different vision of international order." The 2022 National Security Strategy released by the White House named China as "America's most consequential geopolitical challenge." In his State of the Union speech earlier that year, President Joseph R. Biden Jr. described a "battle between democracy and autocracies" taking place in the world. According to the White House, autocracies in this new era seek to "export" their own governance models abroad.[24]

Whether or not one agrees that the US–China contest constitutes a new Cold War, it is increasingly clear that, at the very least, the American unipolar moment is ending. In the view of the Biden administration, the post–Cold War era, a period of unrivaled American power, is "definitely over." The friendly-tyrants dilemma has resurfaced with this return to great power competition. Some commentators have already called for the United States to embrace friendly autocracies to sustain its global position against China and Russia. Commentators noted that the first American-held "Summit for Democracy" in late 2021 included autocratic regimes like Angola and notable democratic backsliders like India and the Philippines. The latter two invitees were viewed by many as hardly accidental: both countries are destined to play an important role in countering China in America's "pivot" to Asia. In the most recent National Security Strategy, the US partnership with the consolidated autocracy in the United Arab Emirates was cited as an example of a partnership with "democracies and other like-minded states."[25]

The "new Cold War" is leading the United States in a search for potential allies, not all of whom are particularly politically palatable. In some cases, this has been a re-embrace of existing, if estranged, autocratic allies. The September 11, 2001, terrorist attacks against the United States brought an increased toleration of and support for authoritarian regimes in the Middle East just after the turn of the century. While President Donald J. Trump was perhaps unusually explicit in his embrace of his "favorite dictator" in Egypt, the military coup that brought Abdel Fattah el-Sisi to power had been quietly—if awkwardly—accepted by the Obama administration. As a candidate, Joe Biden vowed to make Saudi Arabia a "pariah." The new US administration did notably distance itself from America's longtime autocratic clients in Riyadh by declassifying intelligence linking the crown prince and de facto ruler Mohammed bin Salman to the murder and dismemberment of the journalist Jamal Khashoggi in 2018 and by leveling sanctions against some of those involved in the killing. However, in June 2022 it was announced that in efforts to secure greater Saudi cooperation with American foreign policy goals, Biden would be making a volte-face and visiting Riyadh. While in Saudi Arabia, Biden greeted Mohammed bin Salman and declared that the United States would "not walk away and leave a vacuum to be filled by China, Russia, or Iran." Just months later, however, tensions over Saudi cooperation with Russia to cut oil production led the United States to declare it was "reviewing" its relations with Saudi Arabia.[26]

America's often tortured relationship with Saudi Arabia is a remnant of the first Cold War, yet there is evidence that a growing US tolerance toward authoritarian-leaning leaders is already underway in regions more central to the Sino-American rivalry. In the Philippines, the response by the United States to democratic backsliding under President Rodrigo Duterte was decidedly muted. In part, this reflected American fears that he would make good on his pledge to abrogate the US military basing agreement and continue his rapprochement with China. While Duterte opted not to remain in office, it is difficult to imagine strong American pressure against his regime if he were to have tried. Given continued fears of warming Filipino-Chinese relations, it is also hard to imagine strong pressure against any continued backsliding under Duterte's successor, Ferdinand Marcos Jr. In February 2023, it was announced that the United States would be expanding its military facilities in the Philippines.[27]

The quiet warming of US-Thai relations despite continued rule by the military junta also demonstrates an increasing wariness of China and a desire to reestablish close links with the Thai defense establishment. While Thailand was once a key ally, the end of the Cold War reduced American willingness to tolerate continued military rule in Bangkok. The United States was dismayed and embarrassed when the Thai military, one week after senior US officials expressed confidence the armed forces would exercise restraint, declared martial law and seized power in May 2014. Secretary of State John Kerry stated plainly that the coup had "no justification" and would have "negative implications" for the US-Thai military and political relationships. Accordingly, the coup was quickly followed by sanctions. The Chinese reaction was much more permissive and brought military sales that further alarmed American policymakers. Despite notable snubs of the Thai junta—including its exclusion from the Summits for Democracy and from high-level regional visits—US military ties quickly recovered, especially after Thailand's nominal return to democracy in 2019.[28]

Perhaps the most remarkable new alignment is with Hanoi. Vietnam is ruled by the same communist regime the United States fought in a long and bloody war. The Vietnamese security establishment unsurprisingly harbors considerable suspicion of the United States, and some Vietnamese war veterans apparently "vowed to go to Iraq to fight for Saddam Hussein" back in 2003. Nevertheless, concerns about China in both Vietnam and Washington have spurred a gradual warming of relations between the US and an authoritarian communist regime it lost considerable blood and treasure fighting in the first Cold War.[29]

In short, while this "new Cold War" does plausibly offer a "clash of systems" between the thoroughly authoritarian regime in the People's Republic of China and the democratic United States of America, it would appear the "democracies" arrayed against autocracies may come to be as heterogeneous as their "Free World" predecessors. Unsurprisingly, this seeming return to a more widespread embrace of dictatorships as allies against China and Russia has generated considerable controversy. The contemporary debate between those seeking to place democracy promotion and an alliance of democracies at the center of American foreign policy and those who argue in favor of a "regime-type-blind" foreign policy is largely a rehashing of these Cold War–era disagreements. It remains to be seen whether the rivalry with China will resemble the first Cold War. There is cause for skepticism as to whether it will replicate the intense ideological clash of the US-Soviet contest. As I discuss in the conclusion, the ideological dimension of this rivalry will likely prove important. In any case, it is very likely to bring a return to other elements of the previous superpower rivalry. First and foremost, the Sino-American struggle for global supremacy has already brought an accelerated and broad search for foreign allies.[30]

As the United States reenters this period of great power competition, the same debates about whether Washington ought to offer military and economic aid to foreign dictatorships continue to resurface even as our evidence for the effectiveness of past policies remains woefully underexamined. What do we really know about how attempts to entrench the rule of friendly autocrats affect their domestic politics? Does foreign support really help autocrats remain in power? Were efforts by the United States to support friendly tyrants in the first Cold War successful? What might we learn about the effectiveness of future Chinese efforts to support their own autocratic allies by looking to their Soviet predecessors? This book seeks to answer these questions by systematically examining the history of foreign support for authoritarian regimes.

By reinvestigating the past, we are offered a better window to the future of foreign support for friendly dictatorships.

THE CORE PROPOSITION OF THIS BOOK IS THAT IN ORDER TO understand the effects of efforts to prop up dictatorships we must understand both how the US and the Soviet Union actually went about supporting dictators and the domestic politics of how modern dictatorships work. It is the interaction of the strategies and practices pursued by foreign patrons with the domestic distribution of power inside dictatorships that shapes the survival and demise of foreign-backed autocracies. Beyond taking the behaviors and intentions of both dictators and their external supporters seriously, such an inquiry requires comparing all attempts to prop up friendly dictatorships to ascertain general patterns. Some foreign-backed dictatorships are extremely long-lasting, and others are very fragile. To know how typical a given case is requires a cross-national investigation.

The empirical approach to evaluating these arguments is simultaneously broad and deep. In the following chapters, we move repeatedly from comparative analysis to granular examinations of particular historical moments. We learn about how foreign patrons support autocrats by analyzing this phenomenon from many different angles. It is an inquiry that sits atop a scaffolding of original cross-national data on the foreign support available to autocracies each year. By leveraging recently declassified intelligence reports and historical monographs that access foreign archives, this book offers hitherto unavailable information on the origins and organization of security forces in dictatorships that were previously black boxes. This journey takes us from the hourly deliberations of American officials in Thailand during a coup attempt to the comprehensive record of security institutions set up by Soviet advisers in Afghanistan and Ethiopia. We move back and forth from the deliberations and interests of the superpowers to their allied governments and state institutions.

This work stands on the shoulders of many political scientists and historians who have carefully compiled information on particular instances of foreign aid for authoritarian regimes. By weaving these sources together and properly situating them in the literature on authoritarian politics, this book offers a clearer and more theoretically grounded understanding of how Cold War–era efforts to support friendly tyrants really worked. While every dictatorship is different, the set of policies advocated by foreign patrons was remarkably uniform. Moreover, autocrats themselves maintained surprising commonalities in their strategies to reduce the threats posed by their internal political rivals. This is not a story of a unidirectional flow of commands from superpowers. How such state-building plans were adapted, subverted, and grafted onto local political dynamics is key to understanding how foreign support really affects the durability of authoritarian regimes. By placing these behaviors in their comparative context, we are better able to see why some efforts succeeded and others failed.

To understand why American aid did not bring durable dictatorship and why Soviet assistance entrenched resilient regimes, we must turn to the domestic politics of dictatorships. In particular we must consider how US and Soviet aid shaped the relationship between autocrats and their armies. It is in the starkly different vulnerability to military coups where US-backed and Soviet-backed autocracies diverge. In order to understand why this is the case, we have to understand why coups are such a problem for autocracies.

The loyalty of the coercive apparatus—the army, intelligence agencies, police, and other internal security services—lies at the heart of authoritarian survival. Dictators must retain the support of security forces to survive challenges to their rule. This is true of all dictatorships. Autocrats solve the problem of ensuring military loyalty through a variety of strategies. Many of the most effective means, however, are difficult to achieve. The fundamental dilemma of coup prevention for autocrats is that the very measures that ensure the military cannot carry out a coup also hasten the arrival of coup attempts. Measures that weaken the coup capacity of the army also threaten the privileges and positions of the army's officers, who often resist such measures before they can be fully implemented. It is generally only through considerable luck that autocrats are able to build loyal internal security services. Yet there is another path to subordinating security forces to the ruling regime: external support. The Soviet Union provided assistance in helping its allied regimes reorganize their security sectors to implement the Soviet model of political control over the armed forces. The United States was unwilling to provide such assistance, and in fact the model of military organization provided by American advisers exacerbated rather than reduced the problem of military disloyalty to autocratic governments.

After introducing the centrality of the coercive apparatus to understanding the durability of authoritarian regimes, we consider the origins of the two military models promoted by the US and the Soviet Union. This requires a journey back to the source of these twin political-military systems: the American and Russian revolutions. The United States and the Union of Soviet Socialist Republics were both born of violent revolutions and shared a fear of standing armies. These revolutionaries subsequently set about, in markedly different ways, removing the praetorian threat posed by the army to their nascent republics. Both governments feared that their armies could pose the same challenge the Praetorian Guard posed to the Roman republic, evolving from loyal guardian to principal threat to the regime. For the United States, the solution to the problem of the army was to ensure it would be small and thoroughly depoliticized. For the Soviet Union, it was to tie the army to the ruling regime through thorough politicization. It was these two models of military organization that the US and the Soviet Union exported abroad once they became the twin superpowers at the end of the Second World War.

We then turn to the actual efforts to promote these models through support given to particular autocratic regimes. We examine Soviet efforts to build new regimes in Eastern Europe as well as in South Yemen and Mozambique. For the United States, we examine American efforts to build armies in Korea, South Vietnam, and Cambodia. Once these institutions were built, how did they affect the survival of their regimes? By examining the behavior of authoritarian security structures during coups, we see that the US was willing to accept military coups even in closely allied client regimes. By contrast, the security institutions built to prevent coups in Soviet allies were effective in preventing military takeovers. This discussion takes us to a further consequence of the political dynamics of American military aid for dictatorships. A sustained investigation into the efforts to build the Cambodian military and support the Lon Nol dictatorship (1970–1975) offers a window into how the internal political consequences of military aid and coup prevention paradoxically weakened the Cambodian military. This examination offers considerable parallels to the more recent American efforts to build a new military in Afghanistan.

This discussion of the Cold War is followed by an overview of how military aid from the United States and Russia has changed after the end of the Cold War. Of particular importance have been the decline and possible return of the military coup d'état. This book concludes with an attempt to make sense of the lessons learned from the history of foreign support for dictatorships. In which ways can US and Soviet foreign policy be considered successful or failed? Which of these lessons can be applied to any future Cold War? It is up to the reader to weigh the moral consequences of American and Soviet behavior toward authoritarian regimes in the first Cold War. It is the task of this book to provide an unbiased account of this history and take the goals of each patron and client seriously on their own terms. Only by taking Soviet goals and allied government interests seriously can we accurately account for their observed behavior.

In contrast to much recent work on authoritarian politics, the attention here is focused squarely on the role of the military and internal security services. This may seem unhelpfully retrograde in a world where coups d'état and military rule have declined. Unfortunately, optimism about the decline of the importance of the security apparatus for understanding authoritarian politics is misplaced. The army remains a central actor in the survival of democracies and autocracies alike.

Any return to great power aid for client dictatorships is likely to feature a replay of many of the tragedies and triumphs of the first Cold War. Much has changed since the collapse of the Soviet Union and the end of the Cold War. But much has not. Dictatorships have not fundamentally changed. Even in this modern age, their survival and their demise fundamentally rest on the loyalty of their security services. Military aid in the future will continue to interact with the domestic politics of dictatorships. Without learning lessons from the first Cold War, we risk repeating earlier mistakes.

1 | AUTOCRATS AND ARMIES

Coercion is at the core of authoritarian rule. Autocrats are autocrats because they rule without the consent of the governed. Of course, some authoritarian rulers enjoy real popularity. Dictators who preside over economic growth, provide relative political stability, and minimize corruption do sometimes gain popular support. Yet such efforts are rarely successfully sustained. In order to reward supporters and punish opponents, autocrats distort the economy to divert resources to supporters and provide their subordinates with opportunities to line their pockets. The political stability they provide is ephemeral—dictatorships appear stable until suddenly they are not. President Jimmy Carter described the shah's regime in Iran as an "island of stability" just weeks before mass protests would mark the beginning of the Iranian Revolution that overthrew his regime. Even well-institutionalized authoritarian regimes struggle mightily with leadership succession. The insecurity of the position of members of the inner circle engenders a constant jockeying for power and a pervasive fear of losing out in a factional battle. While repression can keep dissent at bay, it also sows the seeds of future unrest. The prospects of a violent end also haunt all dictatorships. When dictators are overthrown, they face the risk of exile, jail, or death.[1]

As a dictator's reign lengthens, whatever enthusiasm or hope greeted the initial seizure of power tends to dissipate. The lack of a reliable mechanism for accountability through elections virtually ensures that dictators outlive their popularity. Once autocrats face challenges from their fellow governing officials, powerful economic elites, or the masses, they must rely on their security forces. The military, police, internal security, and intelligence services are the institutions of last resort to defend the regime. In infiltrating and monitoring political parties, labor unions, and opposition groups, these security forces seek to preempt challenges from emerging. Police and other internal security forces engage in the quotidian repression that seeks to keep dissidents at bay. The life of an opposition activist in an authoritarian regime entails frequent arrests and harassment from state security agents. In some cases, the repression is highly legalistic, with trumped-up legal charges masking the political nature of the sentence. In others the coercion is more naked. As a last resort, security forces are equipped to use lethal violence to defend the regime from its enemies. Yet the sword that defends the regime is double-edged. The very armed forces who are tasked with protecting the autocracy themselves pose its most potent potential challenge.

We cannot understand how foreign aid affects the survival of autocrats without understanding these internal dynamics. The arrival of a foreign power offering money, guns, and advisers to autocrats facing multiple domestic challengers shapes most of the decisions of those autocrats on the receiving end of the assistance. As we will see, the consequences of external military aid for the relationship between the coercive apparatus and the dictatorship are not always well understood by either the provider or the recipient of this assistance. Of central importance is the relationship between autocrats and their security forces. This is not only because military aid is a central component of foreign assistance for friendly autocrats, but because the military is so central to authoritarian rule.

IT MAY NOT BE OBVIOUS THAT THE MILITARY AND OTHER SECURITY forces stand at the heart of modern authoritarian rule. The conventional popular image of the end of an authoritarian regime is through mass protests. The stylized version features brave protesters weathering repression to sustain mass mobilization that forces the dictator to give up. There is of course much truth to this story, and heroic individual sacrifices are often needed to bring down dictators. But in the end, it is the behavior of the security forces that determines whether an autocrat will fall. When mass protests bring down a dictatorship, it is because the armed forces defect or remove the autocrat themselves. In Algeria in April 2019, octogenarian dictator Abdelaziz Bouteflika resigned after sustained mass protests. But it was not protesters storming into his office that led to his departure. Instead, it was the chief of staff of the powerful Algerian army who ordered him to resign. Once Bouteflika lost the support of those armed to defend the regime, he was done. A very similar sequence of events led to the removal of the genocidal dictator of Sudan, Omar al-Bashir, just nine days after Bouteflika resigned. When Venezuela's Hugo Chávez briefly resigned in April 2002, it was not because the mass of protesters pushed their way into the presidential palace and forced him to step down. Instead, it was the chief of staff of the armed forces who demanded he give up power after he ordered the army to crush mass protests. Unable to rally supporters within the armed forces, Chávez acquiesced and went into military custody. Two days later, disunity within the army would enable him to return with the support of key commanders. It was the army, not the masses in the streets, that proved decisive in both his removal and return to power.[2]

The defection of the army is often a dramatic moment in the life of a protest movement that signals the regime is finished. In Egypt during the Arab Spring, protesters triumphantly proclaimed that "the people and the army are one hand!" The army refused to use force to disperse the protests and, after several weeks of indecision, forced President Hosni Mubarak to resign. During the Iranian Revolution in 1979, protesters placed flowers in the gun barrels of soldiers confronting the mass movement. This fraternization between protesters and the military is common when the army defects from the regime and declines to use force. In other cases, the role of security service defection is more passive. Mass protests against Eduard Shevardnadze in Georgia in 2003 succeeded in ousting his regime during the Rose Revolution, thanks to the passive defection of the army and police. First, the woefully underresourced police did not resist the storming of the parliament by protesters. When Shevardnadze then called for a state of emergency, the military refused to support the declaration. Deprived of any coercive resources to use against the protests, he resigned. In Tunisia in 2011 the army similarly defected from the Zine El Abidine Ben Ali regime. When the chief of staff of the army, General Rachid Ammar, was called on by President Ben Ali to use force against the protesters, he refused and was arrested. In reaction, the army withdrew its forces from Tunis against Ben Ali's wishes, and his regime collapsed.[3]

Yet for all the instances of triumphant crowds cheering the departure of a hated dictator alongside a defecting military there are those in which the armed forces brutally crush the protests. Mass protests in the early 1990s in Togo failed to precipitate the defection of military personnel, who instead reliably used coercion to save the regime. Both the 2009 and the 2022 protests across Iran also failed to bring the defection of state security forces. The two most important coercive pillars of the regime—the Islamic

Revolutionary Guards Corps and the Basij militia—remained loyal to the clerical government. Months of mass protests in Belarus in 2020 similarly failed to secure the defection of the Belarusian army, internal security forces, and intelligence services. Protesters in Cuba, Venezuela, Russia, Syria, and Myanmar have all recently confronted security forces ready and willing to defend their beleaguered regimes, sometimes with brutal violence.[4]

Security force loyalty is also critical in defending regimes from violent challenges that emerge outside the state. Armed rebellions have threatened many dictatorships. To defeat the regime, rebel forces must either defeat the government's army on the battlefield or persuade it to join the rebellion. Student protesters in Myanmar have taken up arms since the coup in 2021 as their peaceful protests faced a hail of bullets from the armed forces. Yet the military has remained largely cohesive and brutal in its defense of the junta. While the odds of these students-turned-rebels defeating the army remain long, insurgencies do regularly defeat dictatorships. They have done so nearly fifty times since 1945, in fact. In Ethiopia, a rebel movement that began with seven students meeting in an Addis Ababa café in 1974 grew into a rebel army that defeated the largest army in sub-Saharan Africa less than seventeen years later. Chad has experienced three successful armed rebellions against dictatorships (1979, 1982, and 1990). To defeat an armed rebellion, dictatorships must secure the backing of a loyal and effective army.[5]

While repressing unarmed protesters depends more on loyalty than military capacity, the army must be competent at executing complex operations to defeat rebels. Unfortunately for dictatorships, such military strength can be used for ends other than countering insurgents. Strengthening the military and other internal security services to defend the regime from these external challenges exacerbates the internal threat posed by the armed forces to the dictatorship. Powerful armies led by competent officers can also lead coups d'état to oust the autocrat they supposedly serve.

This coup threat is in fact even more severe than that posed by mass protests or war. Military coups d'état have been the most common cause of authoritarian regime breakdown since the Second World War. For individual autocratic rulers the picture is even bleaker: more than two-thirds of ousted autocrats were removed by coups. The threat of mass unrest or war means that dictators cannot rule without security forces. Moreover, most autocrats inherit an army built by someone else and which can only be dismantled at great political cost. The problem of the army for autocrats leads authoritarian regimes to engage in a variety of measures to reduce the motivation or capacity of their militaries to carry out coups.[6]

There are three broad strategies that autocrats pursue in trying to reduce the coup threat they face: inducements, fragmentation, and infiltration. Autocrats try to induce their armies not to overthrow their regimes by distributing spoils to the military and by cultivating a loyal crop of senior officers. High wages, opportunities for corruption, and advanced equipment are given to the army in exchange for loyal service to the regime. If officers are happy enough with the current regime, they will be less likely to engage in risky acts of disloyalty. The main constraint on this behavior is fiscal, and the primary political cost is aggravating popular perceptions of corruption. This inducement strategy is not, however, very effective. It is difficult to durably purchase loyalty, and positive inducements leave in place a military capable of ousting the regime at some later date. Officers motivated by material rewards might also calculate that they could get a better deal by simply seizing power for themselves. Moreover, the spoils of command also tend to be unevenly shared, and lavishing senior commanders with opportunities for corruption can exacerbate tensions between junior officers and the generals. This is a problem, as it is the lower-ranked officers—lieutenants, captains, majors—who generally lead the troop commands that provide the muscle behind coups. In Tanzania, the January 1983 coup attempt was motivated by poor living standards for junior officers relative to their senior commanders. Such grievances have motivated many military mutinies.[7]

A riskier but nevertheless common inducement strategy is to manipulate promotions in the military to place allies in key commands. Often these are coethnics, individuals from a leader's home region, preexisting allies, or even family members. Autocratic armies are replete with examples of brothers, nephews, and sons-in-law leading sensitive military commands. In Hafez al-Assad's regime in Syria (1970–2000), his brother-in-law led the Republican Guard, his brother the formidable Defense Companies, and his nephew the Struggle Companies. Such interference in the military hierarchy generates significant grievances among the officers passed over for promotion and has motivated many coups. It is rarely popular among the existing officer corps to place family members or other political cronies in high-ranking commands. It is similarly unpopular to carve out exclusive ethnic enclaves in the upper ranks. While coethnics perhaps make for more loyal military commanders, excluded ethnic groups resent their subordinate position and frequently strike before their status can be successfully lowered.[8]

While the above methods focus on reducing the incentives for a coup, dictators also often attempt to reduce the *capacity* of their militaries to overthrow them in a coup. There are several common strategies. One is through institutional fragmentation: regimes create multiple and often redundant security forces meant to counterbalance the regular military. These are sometimes expanded presidential guards, party militia, paramilitary organizations, or troops from the interior ministry. These internal security forces outside the regular military are not always small: in the late 1960s the People's Militia in Mali outnumbered the army three to one. The Saudi coercive apparatus involves a considerable amount of counterbalancing: the regular army is balanced by both the Royal Guard and the National Guard. The National Guard is not merely a poorly equipped paramilitary adjunct to a superior army but maintains combined arms capabilities and considerable professionalization. The Syrian Defense Companies mentioned above were an elite force with twenty thousand troops, an independent intelligence and security organization, special forces, air defense missile brigades, and the most advanced armored units available to the Syrian army.[9]

Creating counterweights prevents coup attempts from succeeding because counterweights have incentives to fight to defend the regime. Fearing their fate if the army succeeds in seizing power, officers in the alternative internal security organs may fight to defeat the coup. On January 21, 2013, over one hundred soldiers in the Eritrean Defense Force seized control of the Ministry of Information in Asmara. Backed by tanks, the mutinous soldiers broadcast on state-run television demands for political reforms. These soldiers were greeted by Unit 72, the feared special forces arm of the National Security Office, and quickly surrendered. Over the next few days, waves of arrests purged the army of potentially disloyal officers. As we will see in Chapter 6, the Civil Guard in South Vietnam fought desperately to defend Ngo Dinh Diem's regime in South Vietnam from a military coup in 1960. Fragmentation carries its own risks, however. Creating new militarized security organizations to balance against the army is correctly viewed by military officers as a potential threat to their individual and collective interests. Officers see the writing on the wall and have incentives to strike before the new force has reached its full strength. Many coups have been motivated by officers reacting to plans to counterbalance the army with new security services. The 1963 coup in Honduras was motivated by fears that President Villeda Morales's successor would strengthen the paramilitary Civil Guard at the expense of the army, and the 1968 coup in the Congo was motivated by the decision to create a "people's army" separate from the existing military.[10]

The final and most invasive strategy of coup prevention is the penetration of the army by members of the ruling party or intelligence apparatus. The two most common infiltration institutions are political commissars and military counterintelligence officers. As we will see in the following chapter, both were key innovations of the Russian Revolution that soon spread to other states and rebel movements. Political commissars served directly alongside regular military commanders and often had the authority to countersign or overrule the decisions made by professional officers. Their primary responsibility was always to monitor the behavior and political reliability of the officers and enlisted ranks. Military counterintelligence officers were separate from these commissars but duplicated some of the monitoring functions of the commissar. They were even more fearsome, as they were part of a larger security service and were generally responsible for carrying out arrests and purges of disloyal officers. Infiltration was a key component of the Soviet strategy of coup prevention, proving to be a highly effective mechanism for preventing military coups. It too, however, was highly unpopular and risky to implement. Military officers do not like having their orders countersigned by political appointees and their every action monitored by the secret police. This invasive structure of political control is extremely difficult to establish.

Two postcolonial African leaders offer an instructive illustration of the promise and peril of carrying out coup prevention through infiltration. Kwame Nkrumah and Julius Nyerere were both charismatic anticolonial leaders who brought their respective nations to independence from the United Kingdom. Both inherited the institutions of the colonial state more or less intact, and this included the colonial-era army. Nkrumah and Nyerere would ultimately both take similar steps to reduce the threat posed by their own armies to their regimes. In Ghana, these efforts culminated in the very event they sought to prevent: a February 1966 military coup that toppled Nkrumah's regime. In Tanzania, luck would allow Nyerere to institutionalize coup prevention through infiltration after a failed coup that functioned effectively to prevent the military ouster of his regime.

A revered independence leader, Nkrumah betrayed a notable autocratic streak soon after he led the Gold Coast to independence from the United Kingdom. When the Gold Coast gained its independence as Ghana in 1957, it did so with its British-built army intact. Of the 237 commissioned officers in the Ghanian army at independence, only 29 were Ghanaian. The neocolonial arrangement where British officers continued to lead the army of an increasingly vocally anticolonial African state grew too unbearable, and in 1961 the remaining British officers were repatriated. The indigenization of the armed forces was a mixed blessing, however, as the newly empowered officers had few links to Nkrumah and inhabited a sensitive position as commanders of the most formidable armed institution in the country. To counter the threat that Nkrumah perceived to emanate from the army, he began to take measures to reduce its capacity and incentives to launch a coup. He interfered in military promotions, promoted membership in his ruling Convention People's Party, built a new internal security and intelligence service, established a party militia, expanded his praetorian guard, and introduced a plan to install party commissars in the army ranks. Yet these measures generated a considerable and predictable backlash from the army officer corps. Before the commissars could be introduced or the praetorian guard fully expanded, the army struck back. On February 24, 1966, the Ghanaian army violently ousted Nkrumah from power and proceeded to dissolve the new security institutions he had built to forestall this event.[11]

Tanzania (Tanganyika until its merger with Zanzibar in 1964) achieved independence under Nyerere's leadership in 1961. Decolonization left the colonial-era army—the King's African Rifles (KAR)—intact. The new military "changed little aside from its name," and white British officers continued to command the force.

Nyerere and other members of the ruling Tanganyika African National Unity (TANU) party left the management of the army to the remaining British officers and broadly viewed the military as "a refuge for up-country illiterates." In January 1964, the army mutinied over poor officer pay and the slow pace of the Africanization of the officer corps. The mutineers took control of the capital, and Nyerere was forced to flee. After five days, Nyerere requested a British intervention, which quickly put down the uprising. When he returned, Nyerere pledged to dissolve the army. With a contingent of Nigerian troops deployed to maintain order, the government created a new military from scratch. In September 1964, the Tanzania People's Defense Force (TPDF) was born.[12]

In this new army, party membership was encouraged, and political loyalty to TANU was required. Officer appointments were made directly by Nyerere all the way down to battalion commanders. Beyond controlling the initial recruitment, the regime also frequently reshuffled officers. In addition to its discretion over army promotions, the regime created a series of institutional checks on the armed forces. TANU established a system of political commissars embedded in the TPDF. In addition, the regime ran a "pervasive network of informants in the military." The regime also created the Tanzania Intelligence and Security Service (TISS) as well as a party-led People's Militia. Nyerere was able to assemble these invasive structures because he had the opportunity to build a new army from the ground up after his colonial-inherited army nearly ousted his regime. These coup-prevention structures functioned effectively, "easily" putting down the junior officers' coup attempt of January 1983 mentioned above.[13]

The problem of ensuring the loyalty of the colonial-built army to postcolonial regimes was a common story. In Ghana, Nkrumah behaved as one might suggest he should—he undertook several overlapping measures to reduce the praetorian threat posed by his armed forces. Yet these measures caused the very event he sought to prevent. In Tanzania, the army also proved disloyal to the new government. Only thanks to a lucky escape and external intervention was Nyerere able to return and start over again by building a new and much more loyal military from scratch.

Other autocrats have also built formidable and pervasive internal security structures with a heavy dose of luck. Mu'ammar al-Gaddhafi had only been first among equals after he and his fellow officers deposed the UK-backed King Idris of Libya in 1969. After he was lucky enough to survive a coup attempt in 1975 by his erstwhile coconspirators, Gaddhafi was given an opportunity to thoroughly purge the army and establish an extensive web of overlapping security institutions. He infiltrated the army with representatives from the "revolutionary committees." These committees were peculiar institutions that functioned as something of a hybrid between a political party, popular militia, and intelligence service. The committees penetrated army units down at least to the battalion. They had the authority to "overrule senior military officers" and approved all "transfers and promotions" of military personnel. In what was presumably a highly obnoxious affront to officers, the committees even had the responsibility for distributing live ammunition. This last responsibility was not solely theirs, however, and was shared with their own institutional rivals: three different security battalions and Military Intelligence. The primary role of Military Intelligence was not in gathering information on geopolitical rivals or insurgents, but in military counterintelligence. Most of its time was spent monitoring the Libyan military personnel for political unreliability and unearthing incipient acts of disloyalty. MI personnel were present in every military unit and could also overrule army commanders. The security battalions—the Jamahiriya Guards (2,000–4,000 strong in the late 1980s), the aptly named Deterrent Forces (12,000–15,000), and the Al-Sa'di Formation (2,000–4,000)— were internal security units established outside the army chain of command. These three forces were far better equipped than the regular army, and all reported directly to Gaddhafi. Their combined strength of some 16,000 to 23,000 troops was smaller than the army's (90,000), but plenty large to deter a coup. The Libyan army, therefore, had extremely circumscribed authority. It required permission from several separate nonmilitary security services to access ammunition or move troops after dark.[14]

In short, the strategies employed by autocrats to ensure their safety from military coups are highly varied. Some regimes can only placate their powerful armies with spoils and hope for the best. Others are able to utterly and durably subordinate the military to their will. The outcomes of these internal battles of will, resources, and organizational strength between autocrats and their armies are of significant import for the durability of the regime.

However, the internal dynamics of security force design and coup prevention are not entirely internal. External actors can play a key role in the design of security forces and in the strategies autocrats pursue to keep their regimes in power. While some scholars have argued that foreign patrons uniformly prevent military coups against allied regimes,[15] the reality is considerably more complicated. Some foreign powers proved of minimal help to their allied autocrats in either designing coup-proof security institutions or in defending regimes from acts of military insubordination. Others proved helpful on both fronts. The Central African Republic's David Dacko and Angola's Agostinho Neto offer two very different examples of the role played by foreign patrons in the prevention of military coups.

Dacko proved a remarkably unlucky dictator. A former schoolteacher and nephew of Barthélemy Boganda, the leading light of the independence movement in the Central African Republic (CAR), Dacko lived in the shadow of his "veritable prophet" of an uncle. His job in the colonial-era assembly was the product of these family connections. When his esteemed uncle died in an airplane crash, Dacko emerged as the leader of one of the factions to split from Boganda's party. What he lacked in charisma he made up for in political acumen, augmented by the tendency of others to underestimate him. Dacko outmaneuvered and imprisoned his principal rivals and installed himself in office shortly after independence. Two years later the remaining opposition parties were dissolved, and the following year the republic was officially made a one-party state.[16]

Like in most of sub-Saharan Africa, decolonization in the Central African Republic was a gradual process. At independence, the CAR did not even have its own army. Thousands of its citizens had fought in the French army, however, and France led the establishment of a five-hundred-strong army for the newly independent republic based around these veterans. The upper ranks of this force were composed of the dozen or so Central Africans who had trained in France ahead of decolonization. The new CAR army was advised directly by French officers under General Marcel Bigeard, and Paris kept a contingent of its own troops in the capital, Bangui. This small army was outnumbered by the other internal security services, including 450 gendarmes, 330 policemen, and a presidential guard. Just under two years after independence, Dacko elevated his cousin Jean-Bédel Bokassa to command his nascent army. While the family connection was undoubtedly crucial, Bokassa had led a long military career that featured service with Free French forces in World War II and was one of only a handful of commissioned officers upon independence. When he took the helm, the army was an "assemblage of five hundred poorly trained and poorly equipped soldiers."[17]

Oddly enough for a man others had continually underestimated, Dacko committed the same error with his cousin, telling foreign diplomats that "Colonel Bokassa only wants to collect medals" and "is too stupid to pull off a coup d'état." Nevertheless, Dacko did begin to elevate the gendarmerie at the expense of the army to prevent his cousin from threatening his regime, no matter how "stupid" he thought Bokassa was. Consequentially, Bokassa began to worry about his rivals in the police and the security of his own position. As the year 1966 was set to begin—a year that would see the United States deploy a quarter of a million troops to Vietnam and the Soviets accomplish the first soft (unmanned) landing on the moon—a monumental event in the history of the CAR was to occur. The year 1965 ended innocently enough, with an invitation reaching Bokassa imploring him to attend a cocktail party on New Year's Eve hosted by his archrival, the chief of police Jean-Henri Izamo. Convinced the invitation was a ruse to arrest him, Bokassa instead flipped the invitation around. When Izamo arrived at army headquarters, he was arrested, forced into a cellar, and later killed. Four hours later, following a preconceived plan of attack, Bokassa ordered the army to take up positions in the center of Bangui and surround the palace. A brief skirmish with the presidential guard ended with several guards killed by Bokassa's army paratroopers. The coup's target, however, was not at home. Dacko, out dining with friends to celebrate the holiday, heard from partygoers returning from the city that soldiers were surrounding the palace and that he was rumored to have been killed. Dacko decided to return to Bangui and try to rally loyal troops and hopefully the French to defeat the coup. However, on his way into town he was found and arrested by one of Bokassa's officers. At 3:20 in the morning on January 1, 1966, he signed a statement handing off power to his cousin and begged for his life to be spared. Bokassa declared the privileged classes "abolished," the national assembly "dissolved," and the army in power. Soldiers sacked the homes of Dacko's ministers and set piles of looted clothing alight in the street, sending black smoke billowing into the night sky. Lest this chaotic scene and the class warfare rhetoric raise eyebrows in Paris, Bokassa quickly followed these proclamations with a statement that "all previous agreements with foreign countries will be respected."[18]

This later clause was very important. French troops were still in the CAR, and while they had grown estranged from Dacko over his opening of diplomatic relations with communist China, they were taken by surprise by the coup and not overly enthusiastic about the turn of events. Bokassa had feared they might resist the coup, but French troops were nowhere to be found when Dacko's dinner was interrupted by the news that the capital was teeming with soldiers bent on ousting his government. The French reaction to the coup was, to say the least, not what Dacko had hoped for. While Paris made its displeasure known, the principal action of the government of Charles de Gaulle was to demand Dacko not be harmed. After the coup, relations were cool but not hostile, and following a period of aloofness, French recognition came in November. Dacko's French-built army had overthrown his French-supported government, and Paris had done nothing to stop it.

Dacko was down but not out, however. French hesitations to support Bokassa proved to be prescient, as he would turn into one of the more notorious dictators in Cold War Africa. While the more sensational accusations of cannibalism were undoubtedly colored by racism and hard to corroborate, Bokassa was a despotic ruler. The same year that Jimmy Carter took office as US president, Bokassa crowned himself emperor of the self-styled Central African Empire in an ornate ceremony that cost more than the CAR's annual budget. Given the contemporaneous riots over the price of food, Bokassa's golden throne and diamond-encrusted crown were particularly outrageous. The true tipping point, however, was the slaughter in April 1979 of hundreds of children who had protested the requirement they buy expensive school uniforms that featured his visage. While horrified, Paris "equivocated" on the massacre until a report in August directly implicated Bokassa in the atrocity. French aid was terminated, and Bokassa was now "an unacceptable political embarrassment" and a "major blot on France's international reputation."[20]

Convinced it would take a direct military intervention to remove him from power, French officials planned to use their own troops to oust Bokassa. Paris also decided who ought to rule after he was deposed. After considering other alternatives, the French agreed that David Dacko was the best available option. While his health had declined in the interim, and the French viewed him as "weak and ineffectual," Dacko had some domestic legitimacy and was reliably pro-French despite their tepid support for him all those years ago. Happy with his Parisian exile, Dacko took some convincing to agree to the operation. On September 19, 1979, Bokassa and several of his top officials left Bangui for a state visit to Libya. At 9:30 a.m. the next day, several months before the Soviet Union would begin its own intervention in Afghanistan, French intelligence officers picked up Dacko at his apartment in Paris and shuttled the hesitant former president to an airbase, where he joined France's elite paratroopers on military transports. "Operation Barracuda" was underway. Under the cover of darkness, the intervention force of some three hundred elite troops landed at the closed airport and quickly disarmed the "astonished" guards. The French forces fanned out to strategic positions in Bangui and brought Dacko to the radio station. At 11:50 p.m., the deposed president announced his return and that Bokassa's regime was over. As French troops moved through Bangui, Bokassa's soldiers dropped their weapons. His elite imperial guards shed their uniforms on the street and left for their homes.[21]

Dacko's first time in office should have taught him the dangers posed by the army to his government. After Bokassa's fall, this army had essentially "disintegrated." This offered Dacko and his French patrons another chance to build a new and hopefully more loyal military. French forces remained to organize and train this force. But rather than take an active role in the constitution of the new army, Dacko placed the job in the hands of André Kolingba, who had been a brigadier general under Bokassa. Preferring to rely on French paratroopers to protect him, Dacko took little interest in the affairs of the rebuilt army. By 1981 this army had grown to nearly two thousand soldiers, eight generals, and a dozen or so colonels. But the soldiers "received no real training" or budgetary support, and Dacko "treated them with undisguised contempt" and continued to rely on French forces "for his personal security."[22]

When Dacko was asked about his French guards and how long French forces would remain in the CAR, he replied that "they could stay in Centrafrique for a hundred years if they so wished." The French troops were a "ubiquitous" presence in Bangui and were stationed directly outside his palace. French subsidies paid 20 percent of government salaries and covered half the annual budget deficit. Dacko was not a born-again democrat and ruled autocratically the second time around too. In March 1981 he presided over an election "marred by strikes, violent demonstrations, intimidation, and massive fraud," while French soldiers handed out food they advertised as "gifts from Dacko's government." Demonstrations after the election prompted Dacko to impose a ban on opposition parties. Four months later, after explosions in downtown Bangui, Dacko declared a second state of emergency and called on his army chief to restore order. Kolingba did not use his newfound powers to save the regime, however. Instead, he led several hundred of his soldiers from army headquarters to the Palais de la Renaissance. With his soldiers surrounding the palace, Kolingba walked in and demanded Dacko resign.

After this successful coup, Kolingba suspended the constitution, banned political party activity, and named an all-military cabinet. Bokassa gleefully watched the downfall of his cousin for a second time from his exile in the Ivory Coast, gloating that "Dacko is used to quitting." Yet again, Dacko's French patrons were nowhere to be found. The eight hundred French soldiers in the CAR remained confined to their barracks. A mere two years after he had been installed in office by French forces, his well-armed French protectors had taken no action to stop the coup. In Paris, President François Mitterrand described the coup as "an internal matter which concerns only the Central Africans." Dacko's French patrons had built his army, funded his government, and even installed him in power. Yet they did not prevent military coups from ousting him from office on *two* separate occasions.[23]

Not all foreign powers react so passively to coup attempts in their allied regimes. Agostinho Neto, the founding father of independent Angola, arrived in Luanda in February 1975 to jubilant crowds. His political party, the Popular Movement for the Liberation of Angola (Movimento Popular de Libertação de Angola, MPLA), was one of three major liberation movements jockeying for power after the new Portuguese government announced its intention to decolonize Angola following a belated recognition that its brutal war to retain control of the colony was ultimately unwinnable. Neto was a seasoned revolutionary and an accomplished poet. His nationalist activities had long gotten him into trouble, and the founding of the MPLA led to yet another arrest at the hands of Portuguese authorities. The road to liberation in Angola was long and bloody. The arrest of Neto and other top leadership forced the remaining party cadres into what would prove to be a prolonged exile. Party leadership moved among friendly African capitals: first distant Conakry, then Kinshasa, Brazzaville, and ultimately Lusaka. In 1961, the party established the People's Army for the Liberation of Angola (Exército Popular de Libertação de Angola, EPLA). "Army" was a somewhat aspirational description. The EPLA did not even have guns when it began its improbable struggle for independence from Portugal in 1961. After scraping together enough captured guns, the EPLA attacked a military post in the Cabinda exclave and killed nineteen Portuguese soldiers, marking the onset of the prolonged war for liberation.[24]

While the EPLA was engaged in its gradually escalating war for liberation, party leadership remained far from the front. The long distances between Neto and the other exiled party leadership and their military commanders limited their effective control over the armed wing. The largely autonomous EPLA harbored considerable grievances against the MPLA leadership-in-exile. It was as if there were two MPLAs, one inside the country and one outside. Brutal Portuguese counterinsurgency measures hammered the EPLA, and setbacks led the guerrilla commanders to blame the political leadership for their deteriorating position. Tensions culminated in two aborted plots by the EPLA commanders to kill the political leadership, in October 1972 and January 1973.[25]

After the 1974 coup in Portugal, Neto and other MPLA leaders joined other liberation movements to form a transitional government ahead of decolonization. During this time, the EPLA reorganized itself as the People's Armed Forces for the Liberation of Angola (Forças Armadas Populares de Libertação de Angola, FAPLA). An MPLA office was established in the capital of Luanda in August 1974, but the political leadership was so uncertain about FAPLA's reliability and their own security they did not arrive until February of the following year. Fighting between the three liberation movements quickly resumed, but by August 1975 the MPLA was in control of Luanda, and the other two rebel groups regrouped in their rural support areas. Upon the departure of the Portuguese and independence on November 11, the MPLA held Luanda and declared the formation of the People's Republic of Angola (PRA), with FAPLA the official army of the newly independent republic.[26]

While the two rival armed groups posed a serious challenge, "the first conflict with which the MPLA had to contend was that between the fighters from the bush and the ideologues who had comfortably sat out the war in their offices." Neto had only limited control over his own military. This was no minor problem. Neto's military was not a ceremonial force devoid of real combat experience. It was a battle-hardened organization over which he had only nominal control. Its officers and men were bonded by the long and grueling insurgency against the Portuguese and through their shared disdain for the exile politicians who now sought to assert command. Luckily for Neto and the MPLA political leadership, help was coming. In August 1975, Cuban advisers began to arrive in Luanda, followed by thousands of combat troops in October. With the Cubans came the Soviets. Cuban forces allowed Neto and the MPLA to hold Luanda against the combined onslaught of the rival insurgent movements.[27] Perhaps as important for the long-term durability of their new regime, the Soviets and Cubans provided assistance in subordinating the unwieldy army to party rule. FAPLA received significant support from Soviet advisers in transitioning from a "poorly armed rabble" into a modern, conventional military. While its new conventional structure made it more formidable, its new political structure made it more loyal. Soviet advisers helped the MPLA introduce political commissars in every unit for the "institutional penetration and subordination" of the army. With the help of the Soviet secret police, the MPLA established the Directorate of Intelligence and Security (Direção de Informação de Segurança de Angola, DISA), which sought out and repressed regime opposition in the army and society.[28]

While these measures were transforming the party's control over its military, the MPLA still carried considerable wartime political baggage, and its control over the army was not yet complete. At 4:00 a.m. on May 27, 1977, a prominent MPLA leader named Nito Alves led a coup against Neto. Alves was a former field commander who had struggled in isolation from the exiled leadership during the hard days of the war and maintained considerable grievances against Neto and the other political leaders.[29] Over the course of a year, Alves had successfully recruited key members of the army for his putsch. Rebelling units in the army's Eighth Brigade killed the warden of a prison and freed coconspirators who had been imprisoned the previous week. By 7:00 a.m., the putschists had seized the radio station and declared that the government had been overthrown. Neto had been warned by his Cuban supporters that a coup might be imminent a few days prior and was safely in the Ministry of Defense when the coup occurred. As crowds of Alves supporters began to converge on the presidential palace, Neto asked for Cuban help, and unlike the French in the CAR, Cuban forces came to his aid. Deploying their own combat units to the radio station, the Cubans attacked and defeated the rebel troops holding the station. The Cuban commander himself broadcast that the radio station was back in government hands. Around 1:00 p.m., Cuban tanks reached the barracks of the Eighth Brigade and forced the surrender of the mutinous troops but not before the rebels had executed six senior members of the party and army. After the plotters were arrested, Neto led a large-scale purge and arrested hundreds of dissidents, further subordinating the army to regime rule.[30]

Neto's patrons had provided assistance very different from that provided to autocrats backed by Washington, Paris, or London. His advisers had helped him build a thoroughly partisan army and fought back against an attempted coup before the new system was fully institutionalized. These actions helped Neto and the MPLA build a remarkably effective regime from very inauspicious origins. Angola would never again face a coup attempt as it did in 1977, thanks to the pervasive security structure embedded in the army. Though Neto has long since died, his party still rules Angola today.

The way dictators structure their security apparatus to prevent coups is a key dynamic to understanding their durability. Yet how dictators actually get away with their coup prevention strategies is an even more pressing question. Some dictators like Gaddhafi build a "coup-proof" security apparatus with a combination of luck and ruthlessness. But others are like Neto: they enjoy the support of a foreign power. Soviet advisers and Cuban combat troops helped Neto and the MPLA transform their security apparatus to entrench partisan control over a previously autonomous and highly threatening military. In the Cold War, international alliances meant that many autocrats had help in building and reorganizing their security apparatuses. But which foreign country was providing the help really mattered.

Soviet-backed autocrats had remarkably loyal security services. It was not coincidental that not a single Soviet client regime ever fell to a military coup. Concerned that military coups might oust revolutionary pro-Soviet governments and bring to power reactionary US-aligned counterrevolutionaries, Moscow helped its allies like the MPLA in Angola build security institutions under close regime supervision and control. This alignment of interests in preventing coups was very different from American relations with its client autocrats. Mirroring the Soviet Union's own expansive secret police and system of party penetration of state institutions, Soviet-backed autocracies enjoyed Soviet help in infiltrating their militaries with monitoring mechanisms. These internal security services made acts of disloyalty by military officers deadly affairs. Soviet clients imported the Soviet Union's highly effective system of penetrating the army with party officials and military counterintelligence agents and balancing the military with militarized internal security services.

By contrast, American-backed dictators did not enjoy such loyal armed forces. Chiefly concerned with preventing the seizure of power by pro-Soviet communist rebels, Washington pushed regimes to focus not on preventing coups but on building autonomous, professional militaries. More like Dacko's French patrons, the US was concerned with building armies on its own organizational model rather than helping friendly regimes institutionally penetrate and dominate the military. While the US pushed for "apolitical" armies, these efforts rarely resulted in building militaries that avoided praetorian impulses. Instead, in practice they often created a powerful internal challenger to autocrats. American-backed dictators were frequently ousted by their own armies in coups d'état.

The US played a key role in building up new militaries in foreign autocracies but proved unwilling to help these regimes subordinate the armies to party rule and largely stood aside when these armies overthrew their US-supported regimes.

These different methods of regime support had consequences not only for internal challengers but also for external foes. Since American-backed dictators found no help from Washington in preventing a coup, they had to go it alone against the wishes of their patron. America's autocrats were no puppets. These regimes interfered in military promotions and tried their best to weaken their newly powerful armies. Where dictators were lucky enough to succeed in these efforts, coup-proofing strategies meant that despite its massive investment, the United States often found its efforts to build effective militaries severely hobbled by the actions of dictators. US-trained officers may have been the most effective officers, but they also had skills that made them threats to the position of US-backed dictators. This was exacerbated by the suspicion that some of these US-trained officers might be closer to the United States than the ruling regime. Rather than trust such individuals, the regime continued to depend on loyalists to run key commands. This not only generated even more grievances among the capable junior officers in the army but harmed battlefield effectiveness.

Yet this was not the irrational behavior of erratic dictators. It was in fact a rational response to the incentives that arose from American aid. With the United States providing support necessary to counter distant communist rebels, dictators were free to concentrate on the much more proximate threat posed by their American-trained military officers. Frustrated by these dynamics, the United States entertained many coup plots against these capricious dictators. Yet coups rarely brought the stability hoped for by American policymakers. When they failed, they offered dictators a new chance to further purge the army and remove internal rivals.

When they succeeded, military officers rarely consolidated a successful new government. Instead, the cycle of instability often continued: those officers in charge had to contend with the demands of other factions of the armed forces and themselves fell to coups.

It is in the interaction of these two very different models of military organization exported by the rival superpowers and the domestic politics of dictatorships where the stark variation in regime durability originates. Where did these models come from? Both systems of civil-military relations had their origins in revolutions and the reaction of vulnerable postrevolutionary governments to the threat of praetorianism and counterrevolution. The American solution to the problem of the army was to remove it from politics and institutionalize its autonomy. The Soviet solution was to politicize the army and subordinate it to the civilian ruling party. These were the two models that Washington and Moscow promoted abroad, each with important consequences for the survival or demise of allied regimes.

2 | TWO REVOLUTIONS

T he United States of America and the Union of Soviet Socialist Republics were both born of revolution. They emerged out of violent struggles for liberation against regimes they viewed as retrograde and oppressive. Antimonarchism, fear of counterrevolution, and antimilitarism united the two revolutionary republics. They also both sent shockwaves into the world system. The American victory over the British inspired a spasm of revolutionary activity across the Atlantic, from Haiti to France to Spanish America. The Russian Revolution terrified ruling elites and thrilled socialist movements across Europe and Asia. These revolutionary births not only inspired others but also gave the new republics a missionary zeal to remake the world in their respective images.[1]

These were of course very different revolutions. The American Revolution was a liberal revolution that sought to deepen political rights for propertied white men and achieve national sovereignty. The grievances that centered on taxation and autonomy in the colonies grew into a more expansive movement for political equality. Led by the existing elite and not focused on material redistribution or the abolition of slavery, the American Revolution nevertheless contained the seeds of later movements for full equality and democracy. The Russian Revolution was a radical millenarian social revolution, which sought to reorder Russian and global class structures to bring social equality. It was to be the first bold step in a worldwide communist revolution that would triumph over the forces of reaction and build utopia under the banner of the vanguard party.[2]

As they challenged powerful existing elites—loyalists and the British Empire in America and nearly every conceivable foreign and domestic group in Russia—both revolutions shared a fear of counterrevolution. For the American founders, counterrevolutionaries did not just lurk in nearby Canada or on British warships along the coast but also in the institutions of monarchical tyranny that had precipitated their revolt. The Bolsheviks feared many of the same entities: conservative neighboring states as well as the powerful domestic forces of reaction they had deposed in their lightning insurrection in Petrograd.

One institution both revolutionaries feared immensely was the military. Antimilitarism ran deep in both revolutions. Disdain for the armies of an ancien régime as instruments of monarchical despotism had animated revolutionaries in America and Russia before the seizure of power. Yet the revolutionaries did not feel that by defeating the British and tsarist armies they were free from the problems of militarism. Instead, both revolutions feared that their own revolutionary armies might subvert their revolutions. By relying on the force of arms to seize power, both revolutions had to contend with whatever demands those who carried those arms might place on their new governments. Concern over the demands the victorious Continental army might make on their nascent republican government led the American founders to dismantle the very army that had secured their independence. Armed militias of free republican citizens were viewed as the best way to defend this government of the people without falling prey to praetorianism or acting as a prop for monarchical despotism. The Bolsheviks shared this same disdain for standing armies and fear of a Russian Napoleon Bonaparte who might arrive on horseback and destroy the revolution. They too wished to see the army abolished, as it was a hotbed of reactionary politics, aristocratic leadership, and bourgeois values. Like their American counterparts, the Bolsheviks were committed to an armed militia of their key constituents—in this case, proletarian workers—to defend their besieged revolution.

However much both sets of revolutionaries might have hoped to avoid having to contend with a standing army, each government would ultimately feel sufficiently threatened that it would be forced to build a conventional military. To prevent praetorianism, each pursued a different solution to the problem of the army. The Americans would seek to lessen the military threat by keeping the army completely removed from politics. The Bolsheviks would keep the army from destroying the revolution by thoroughly politicizing it. These two models not only had profound consequences for the governments in the US and the USSR but would each spread far beyond the borders of these revolutionary republics through emulation and imposition. It would be these armies that America and Soviet Russia built abroad.

THAT THE UNITED STATES WOULD ONE DAY BE RENOWNED FOR ITS conventional army was far from obvious after the revolution. Fifteen years before the American entry into the First World War, the US military attaché in Imperial Russia complained that there was a "universal belief that our Army is not worthy of serious consideration" by any foreign power. The peacetime weakness of the American army was not an accident. American administrations had feared a large standing army since the revolution. The American solution to preventing the postrevolutionary army from acting as the foundation for despotic rule was to keep it small, spread across American territory, and removed from politics to the greatest extent possible. Rather than tying the army to any ruling party, the American model rested on a nonpartisan and increasingly professional army kept far from the center of power and committed to the Constitution. This model changed over time in important ways. The American army was, for most of its history, a frontier constabulary that was supplemented by volunteer recruits and state militia when engaged in major wars. The building of a permanent peacetime army was a gradual, stepwise process: after each war the army was slightly larger than it had been when the war began.[3]

American fears of the political consequences of standing armies predated the revolution.[4] But it was not just King George III's army that was a threat to democracy. Liberation from Britain was achieved with blood and gunpowder. The army that had forced Britain to surrender its control of the colonies posed an immediate problem to the nascent American republic. In early 1783, as fighting wound down following the American victory two years earlier at Yorktown and peace seemed imminent, the Congress of the Confederation considered plans to demobilize the Continental army in total. This plan was met with the only military coup attempt in American history. The so-called Newburgh Conspiracy, named after the camp in New York that served as base for military operations, involved demands by officers in the Continental army that Congress honor pay promised to the force. The anonymous letters that circulated through the camp on March 10 and March 12 argued the officers must not lay down their arms until they had wrested their just rewards from the ungrateful civilian politicians. The swift reaction of General George Washington, who considered the army "a dangerous instrument to play with," quelled the incipient coup, as did the acquiescence of Congress to paying the promised wages. The concomitant ending of hostilities with Britain enabled Congress to carry out its plan to demobilize the army without further incident. This was a *pronunciamiento* ("proclamation") coup attempt—a declaration by the army meant to achieve its goals by implicitly threatening force. In this case, the plot collapsed before any actual violence. It nevertheless was a major act of insubordination that threatened the new republic.[5]

After safely demobilizing the Continental army, with considerable trepidation, Congress approved the establishment of a much weakened regular army with an authorized strength of only seven hundred. As deliberations over the nature of the postwar American government occupied Congress, delegates debated what to do about the problems posed by the military for a young democracy. At the Federal Convention in June 1787, James Madison warned that "a standing military force, with an overgrown Executive will not long be safe companions to liberty. The means of defense against foreign danger have been always the instruments of tyranny at home." George Washington, the military hero of the revolution, agreed. He too considered a large peacetime army "dangerous to the liberties of a Country," but thought a small force would be safe.[6]

Ultimately, Congress settled on a small peacetime force of regulars that would be supplemented by mobilizing state militia and volunteers in times of war. This regular army was dispersed across the frontier, where it built forts, adjudicated settler-indigenous disputes, and engaged in counterinsurgency against and repression of Native American tribes. This arrangement suited many American political leaders. The secretary of the treasury Albert Gallatin remarked in 1802 that "the distribution of our little army to distant garrisons where hardly any other inhabitant is to be found is the most eligible arrangement of that perhaps necessary evil that can be contrived."[7]

Despite these modest postrevolutionary origins, the peacetime US Army grew gradually into a larger force than many of the founders had intended. The establishment of the Military Academy at West Point in 1802 was a major step in the institutionalization of the regular army. Military Academy graduates slowly came to populate the officer corps in peacetime, though they were far out-numbered by volunteers during war. The War Department that administered the force became better organized and less corrupt. In 1890, physical and professional examinations were introduced for officers seeking promotions, and two years later enlisted men could now apply for commissions. A general staff, widely intro-duced about a century earlier in Europe, was established in 1903. The turn of the twentieth century had witnessed a "managerial rev-olution" in the US military. However, US military modernization lagged far behind its European counterparts, and the professional officer corps and the regular army were not fully ascendant in the American system until World War II.[8]

The US system of civil-military relations centered on keep-ing the military nonpartisan, firmly under civilian control, and removed from participation in politics, in theory if not always in practice. Norms of proper behavior for officers, taught at West Point and reinforced during military service, dictated aloofness from politics, a policy that was generally followed. The army was not penetrated by political party committees, and political con-siderations for promotions were theoretically absent and at least never explicit or uniform. This model of political-military relations has been described in many different ways: "objective control," the "liberal model," the "democratic model," and "professionalism." What these various descriptions share is a focus on the military as a professional institution separate and shielded from partisan poli-tics. If partisan considerations affect promotions, this is a deviation from the model of an apolitical officer corps.[9]

The US military system traded weakness at the beginning of military campaigns for an ability to keep the praetorian impulses down. This is not to suggest that the US military has always avoided politics or even failed to inculcate praetorian officers. Like all militaries, the US Army harbored sentiments hostile to civilian control through various periods. An infamous example was provided by General George B. McClellan, who remarked during the Civil War that he wished to become a dictator in order to save the Union. And of course, traitors such as Robert E. Lee betrayed their country to join the Southern rebellion and preserve the system of slavery. Even some of the army's major reformers and heroes of the Civil War—Lieutenant Colonel Emory Upton, General William T. Sherman, and General Philip H. Sheridan— admired the Prussian military system. Upton in particular harbored "pessimism about the future of an army dominated by civil authority." Nevertheless, major violations of civil-military norms have over the course of American history been met with victory by the civilians. General Douglas MacArthur was fired after he criticized President Truman's policies; and despite the public's propensity for electing former military service members and commanders as president, the US Army has remained a nonpartisan force and has not harbored a serious coup plot or attempted to seize control of the government.[10]

WHEN THE BOLSHEVIKS SEIZED POWER IN RUSSIA, THEY DID SO IN the context of almost total state breakdown. The February Revolution of 1917 (March in the Gregorian calendar) that deposed the tsar led to a shaky provisional government under leftist parties that continued Russian participation in the First World War. The October Revolution (November 7–8) was a lightning insurrection against this interim government by Lenin's Bolsheviks. Tsarist Russia, led by a retrograde absolutist monarchy with highly repressive labor practices that de facto replicated much of the formally abolished serfdom, was home to significant revolutionary ferment. The Bolsheviks, the radical faction of the Russian Social Democratic Party who had styled themselves the "Majoritarians," carried off their power grab thanks to the help of lightly armed party members organized as Red Guards, mutinous soldiers and sailors in

Petrograd, and, most of all, crumbling state capacity that left them largely unopposed.

The Russian imperial army had begun to break down before the twin revolutions in 1917 and played a key role in facilitating the abdication of the tsar and the improbable rise of the Bolsheviks. This twelve-million strong military behemoth had continued to fight German forces across the front after the February Revolution but was near collapse. In Petrograd, sympathetic soldiers in the capital's garrison supported the Bolsheviks in their seizure of power. After the Bolsheviks had established shaky control over the central levers of state power, they were still in dire straits. The radical revolutionary party had few reliable sources of muscle outside its small party paramilitaries. The pro-Bolshevik soldiers were both the saviors and potential scourge of the nascent regime. While they had been critical to the success of the insurrection, only sentiment tied these soldiers to the party. Vladimir Ilyich Lenin and his comrades knew full well that if the soldiers' satisfaction with Bolshevik rule declined, they would pose a potent threat to the revolution.

The anxiety the Bolsheviks felt toward the Imperial Army predated their revolution. Like most Marxists of the time, the Bolsheviks maintained considerable anxieties about standing armies. Military modernization occurring throughout Europe at the time did little to assuage Bolshevik discomfort. While aristocratic officers were beginning to give way to professionals, these new officers were thoroughly bourgeois and therefore harbored antagonistic class interests. The rank and file were little better than "peasants in uniforms," and most Marxists before Mao had a dim view of the revolutionary potential of the peasantry. Marxists of the era concluded that Bonapartism—the gravedigger of revolutionary France—was a threat to all revolutions. They feared what the army might do to their revolution in its vulnerable infancy.[11]

Nevertheless, the Bolsheviks knew they would need coercive muscle to "crush the exploiting classes." This punitive arm of the revolutionary state would need to be built quickly, as the forces of counterrevolution were rapidly regrouping after the stunning Bolshevik victory. Lenin and his comrades faced the daunting prospect of the massive—albeit disorganized, disheartened, and mutinous—tsarist army. It was an army led by officers with much to lose in the new Bolshevik-led social and political order, and staffed by peasant conscripts with their own fears of communist takeover. They also faced an array of hostile foreign states, including especially Germany. The reaction in foreign capitals to the revolution in Russia was swift. Governments from London to Tokyo feared what this communist victory might mean for their own stability. The remarkable success of communist revolution in a backwater like Russia made those in the more industrialized core nervous, just as it made Lenin and his comrades optimistic. Lenin declared in March 1919 that "before the year is out, the whole of Europe will be Soviet." The European leaders were terrified he might be correct. On cue, a wave of revolutionary seizures of power emulating the Bolsheviks spread to Finland (January 1918), Bavaria (November 1918), and Hungary (March 1919).[12]

Even as counterrevolutionary forces gathered, Lenin and his fellow Bolsheviks were committed to destroying the tsarist army. Yet the Bolsheviks faced myriad and far more immediate security problems than their American counterparts had after their own successful revolution. They were a small and radical party with only a smattering of armed supporters. Party leaders quickly concluded they would need a proper army to defend their vulnerable revolution. The military force the Bolsheviks built to meet this challenge would ultimately prove to be one of their most important innovations and organizational exports. On January 28, 1918, Lenin signed a decree that created the Workers' and

Peasants' Red Army. This army would be "both Red and expert": ideologically reliable and militarily competent. While the Soviet Union is understandably known for some of its institutional failures, like the command economy and collective farms, its party army was a remarkably effective and innovative institution of political control that spread far beyond the borders of the Soviet Union.[13]

Lev (Leon) Trotsky, a key Bolshevik leader, was soon put in charge of building this Red Army. Trotsky was the foremost military thinker in the party before the revolution. He had long diagnosed what he saw as the problems of the old tsarist army. Seven years before the revolution, Trotsky wrote that "as long as there exists a standing army that keeps over a million drill-deafened men under arms, and as long as this army remains a blind and dumb instrument in the hands of the Tsar and his black colleagues," so too "will bloody attacks continue to be launched on oppressed classes and weak nations." This royal army had "a ruling apparatus which was constructed, organized, and educated so as to ensure that this army automatically served the ruling class of those days, with the monarchy as its summit."[14]

After the events of 1917, Trotsky quickly agreed that an army would be necessary to defend the revolution. It was, in his view, a "question of life and death for us." He also realized this could not be "an amateur army" built on "some do-it-yourself principle" but instead a "real, centralized army, constructed in accordance with the principles of military science and technique." Trotsky was deeply concerned that such an army might be used by some officer on horseback to oust him and his comrades from power. Therefore, the new army would need to be a "class army" in service of the "proletarian class state." How to build a class army when the Bolsheviks lacked a cadre of proletarian military experts posed a seemingly insurmountable problem. Trotsky lamented that "there are no new military specialists drawn from the working class."

This put the Bolsheviks in a terrible position where they would be forced to enlist the help of former tsarist officers. The Bolsheviks were highly suspicious of these officers, who had only just recently served under the reactionary rule of the tsar. They had suspect class backgrounds and therefore suspect political loyalties and could conceivably destroy the revolution from within.[15]

To contain the counterrevolutionary threat of these officers required, in the view of party leaders, careful "selection and control" of these professional officers. How would these officers be chosen and then regulated to obey and serve the party state? How could the Bolsheviks succeed where their Jacobin predecessors had failed? It would not be enough to simply build a new mass army. Instead, the Bolshevik solution to the military problem was the same as their solution to the problem of proletarian revolution: the vanguard party. If the party could be used to lead the working class to discover their true interests and organize their seizure of power, it would also be central to how that power was exercised. The party could solve the problem of the army by building and maintaining a military that was under thorough party control. The Bolsheviks set out to build the world's first truly *partisan* army. Penetrated by and subservient to the Communist Party, the Red Army would be unable and soon unwilling to act against the revolution. The Red Army would marry the mass party with the mass army in service of the mass revolution.[16]

Concretely, this was achieved by embedding three key institutions *inside* the army. The first key element of this partisan army was the political commissar. Political commissars were political officers who reported to the party and were attached to every unit alongside military officers and given sweeping powers. Commissars countersigned orders under the policy of dual command (*dvoenachalie*). Their formal power in fact exceeded that of the military commander: any order given by the latter had to be countersigned by the former, while the reverse was not the case.

The most important responsibility of the commissars, however, was to report on the political reliability and behavior of the regular military commanders up the party chain of command. They were organized through what would eventually be called the Main Political Administration (Glavnoye politicheskoye upravleniye, GPU). The GPU in turn reported to the Central Committee of the Communist Party. While the precise responsibilities of the commissars changed over time, and the effectiveness of their indoctrination efforts should not be overstated, their monitoring functions remained their primary responsibility throughout Soviet rule.[17]

Commissars were an intrusive and largely unprecedented system of regime control over professional officers in a conventional army. However, the Bolsheviks were not exactly the first to use political commissars. Political officers had been introduced in revolutionary France as the *commissaires du conseil exécutif* in the Ministry of War. These *commissaires* had a similar duty to monitor the political loyalties of military officers. They may also have been present in some Italian mercenary forces a few hundred years earlier. In Russia, the Provisional Government (March–November 1917) had also introduced commissars, but only to the top military brass. What made the Bolshevik use of political commissars innovative was that they all belonged to a single mass party and were introduced at every level of command.[18]

The second institutional innovation the Bolsheviks introduced to ensure a politically reliable army was the creation of a large new security service. It too was an organization later emulated and imposed abroad. Soon after the revolution, the Bolsheviks organized an expansive intelligence and security service to defend the regime against all its perceived enemies: the All-Russian Extraordinary Committee (Vserossiyskaya chrezvichaynaya komissiya), or Cheka. Like the political commissariat, the Cheka was reorganized several times over the course of Soviet rule. Its officers would gain notoriety as the NKVD (People's Commissariat for Internal

Affairs) and later the KGB (Committee for State Security), but it was common to continue to call Soviet security personnel "chekists" in homage to their first organization. As the sword and shield of the revolution, the chekists had many responsibilities. Their primary task was to defend the revolution from counterrevolutionaries and all other internal and external foes.[19]

The Cheka combined many intelligence responsibilities (foreign, domestic, and counterintelligence) as well as operational security forces. Its well-armed security troops were tasked with protecting top party officials. Like the commissars, internal security services that combined policing, intelligence, and regime security functions predated the Russian Revolution. The French revolutionaries had created the Committee of Public Safety (Comité de salut public). It too was created to defend the new republic from the forces of counterrevolution. Political police had also existed in prerevolutionary Russia in the form of the notorious Department for Guarding the Public Security and Order, known commonly as "the Guard" (Okhrana). As with the commissars, it was the size, scope, and partisan nature of the Bolshevik secret police that marked the break from the past.[20]

While a formidable organization on its own, the Cheka also played a critical role in the new army. Starting in December 1918, the security service began to embed special departments (*osobiye otdeli*) of military counterintelligence officers in the Red Army to provide a second check on the behavior of officers. In theory, as counterintelligence officers, these personnel were supposed to monitor the army for the penetration of foreign intelligence services. However, the distinction between foreign and domestic opposition in revolutionary Russia was forever blurred. In practice, nearly all forms of potential opposition to the regime were treated as foreign-inspired or foreign-directed. Paranoid Bolshevik leaders saw fifth columns of imperialist and capitalist agents everywhere in the Soviet state. In the Soviet system, counterintelligence officers would in practice train their gaze on nearly all political opposition even if a foreign hand was not actually present.[21]

The special departments directly penetrated military units with secret police personnel who in turn recruited a network of informants among the ranks. Suspicious even of the loyalty of the commissars, and to prevent any commander-commissar collusion, the special departments also surveilled the political officers. These military counterintelligence officers operated a "very extensive" network of informers and monitored the communications of all military personnel. They operated under "notoriously unconstrained" conditions, striking "fear into all with whom they dealt, no matter what their rank." Just as the political commissars maintained total autonomy from military commanders, the special department officers did not answer to the regular military officers and had their own chain of command to the Communist Party by way of the Cheka. Military counterintelligence officers formed a "closed professional caste" and lived apart from the regular officers. They were permanently based in regular military units, performing regular inspections and investigating the political reliability of officers and troops. In the analysis of a Soviet defector, "they know everyone, and everyone knows them." It was the security service, acting in concert with its military counterintelligence directorate, that carried out the extensive purges of the Red Army that proved a hallmark of early Soviet rule. The military counterintelligence responsibilities of the security service remained a crucial responsibility of the secret police throughout Soviet rule.[22]

The final component of the new army built by the Bolsheviks was the role of party institutions and political reliability in military promotions. The Bolsheviks aggressively promoted party membership among their soldiers and officers at rates higher than in many other state institutions in the Soviet Union. Political reliability was reassessed at each opportunity for promotion, and the secret police and commissars had opportunities to weigh in on the attitudes of the soldier toward Soviet rule when considering advancement. Party membership would ultimately become all but a prerequisite for any successful career in the armed forces.[23]

These three elements—political commissars, military counterintelligence, and party membership—together comprised the *party army*. It was this partisan military structure that the Bolsheviks built to protect their revolution from praetorianism and, eventually, extend Soviet power across an enormous expanse of Eurasia. This model of political-military relations, like the non-partisan American model described above, has been described in many ways: "subjective control," and the "penetration," "totalitarian," or "revolutionary" models. What these descriptions share is an army distinguished from the American model not in its use of formal ranks, emphasis on combined armed operations, or formal subservience to civilian rule—in this sense, the Soviet army was thoroughly conventional. The Red Army truly was the "real" and proper army envisioned by Trotsky. What set the Soviet army apart from its Russian predecessors and Western contemporaries was the ruling regime's considerable effort to penetrate the army. The Red Army married the mass army to the mass party for the first time. As we will see, thanks to Soviet foreign policy and the power of the Bolshevik example, it would not be the last time.[24]

The partisan army severely constrained the opportunities for disloyalty and the capacity to carry out a military coup d'état against Soviet rule. Political commissars were armed, but their threat to officers was through espionage rather than violence. Unlike the security services, commissars didn't prevent coups by organizing violent resistance to coup attempts. Instead, their presence helped deter coup plotting by increasing the fear of discovery. If officers were still not deterred, their disloyalty could be reported up the party chain of command, giving Soviet leadership the time necessary to plan a countercoup using loyal army units or their well-armed chekists. The secret police itself duplicated this monitoring role through the special departments, weighed in on promotion decisions with its extensive records on soldier backgrounds and network of informers, and even had the military capacity, with its security troops, to fight against insubordination. The party committee and requisite membership for promotions incentivized pro-regime behavior by officers or soldiers who sought advancement, career stability, or simply to avoid the violent purges that befell multitudes of their colleagues.

The professional military officers in the Red Army were therefore extremely constrained. Their orders were evaluated and countersigned by party commissars, their behaviors and communications monitored closely by secret police officers and informants, and their political reliability assessed when they applied for party membership and promotions. Unsurprisingly, officers strongly disliked the imposition of these intrusive monitoring mechanisms. Yet the disarray of the tsarist army that had enabled the revolution in the first place allowed the Bolsheviks a critical window of opportunity to embed this radical structure on their new army.[25]

Once imposed, the party army functioned with deadly effectiveness. This interwoven network of monitoring mechanisms severely limited the autonomy of officers and all but eliminated their capacity to organize any resistance to radical Bolshevik rule. Coups require plotters to organize the initial attempt with some degree of secrecy. With potentially dissatisfied officers fearful of discovery from any one of the multiple redundant networks embedded directly in the military, the tremendous violent assaults on the corporate and individual interests of officers in the Red Army went unopposed. It is difficult to conceive of a deadlier assault on a military command than Stalin's Great Purges. Fears of counterrevolution led Stalin and his loyal henchmen to engage in a stunningly expansive purge of the Red Army on the eve of World War II in 1937 and into 1941 that led to the "decimation" of the officer corps.

Sixty-five percent of officers above the rank of brigade commander (*kombrig*, roughly equivalent to brigadier general) in 1936 were executed by the end of the purges. Nevertheless, the army remained passive in the face of this deadly and widespread assault on its officer corps.[26]

Moscow and Washington emerged from their respective revolutions with markedly divergent political, social, and economic systems. These differences were also reflected in their military systems. Both achieved civilian supremacy over the army but in starkly different fashion. These two models did not just affect political-military relations within the borders of the Soviet Union and the United States. Instead, they were the organizational exports of each state as both began to build armies in friendly or conquered states abroad. These models would spread across the world by emulation, assisted transformation, and coerced imposition. Just as they did not always function exactly as intended in the US or the USSR, these models transformed and were transformed by the politics of the new state onto which they were grafted. Despite its imperfect transplantation, the Soviet model proved remarkably effective in removing the threat of military coups in allied regimes. The American model, however, when implemented in weaker states with less legitimate governments, did not successfully achieve apolitical armies devoid of praetorian impulses. Instead, it often exacerbated the problems of military disloyalty.

3 | EXPORTING REVOLUTION

When the Bolshevik revolutionaries seized their precarious grip on power in 1917, they intended it to be the first of many subsequent revolutions. With both Bolshevik aid and their example, communist uprisings would surely topple reactionary governments one after the other. But the weakness of the early Soviet state rendered actual military assistance from the Russian revolutionaries extremely limited. Only in Mongolia did the Bolsheviks play an active role in organizing military, state, and party structures for a friendly revolutionary government they installed in power. It would not be until after the stunning Soviet victory over Nazi Germany in the Second World War that the Soviet Union would be both ready and able to support revolution abroad.

By the time the Soviet Union began to supply socialist-leaning and communist governments with aid, it had its own well-institutionalized matrix of party and state organizations it sought to export to friendly regimes. The revolution that Moscow exported was not just communist ideological principles but also a series of revolutionary institutions. These were the Leninist innovations that had supported the consolidation of a government devoted to radical social transformation and protected it from its real and imagined enemies. The core institutions that guaranteed the survival of the revolutionary cadres—the Leninist ruling party, the partisan army, and the internal security services—were soon promoted abroad with the aid of Soviet advisers.

As local adaptations of a model that had emerged gradually in the Soviet context, these institutions differed along with the local political context of the allied regime. Nevertheless, a remarkably uniform series of ruling-regime institutions patterned closely on the Soviet model spread to Moscow's newfound allies in the emerging Cold War. By the 1970s, the Soviet Union was the developed socialist core of a complex system of alliances and dependencies that stretched from Havana to Ho Chi Minh City. It provided billions in military and economic aid and deployed thousands of military and security advisers to entrench the rule of friendly regimes.

AS WE HAVE ALREADY SEEN, THE EVENTUAL MIGHT OF THE SOVIET empire belies the modest beginnings of the Bolshevik regime. The success of the revolution in Petrograd shocked Europe. Fearing they too might soon face revolution, establishment forces braced for the spread of communist uprisings outside Russia's borders. The Bolsheviks shared the view that the example of their improbable revolution would spur the movement of proletarian forces in Europe's more industrialized core.

The power of the Bolshevik example did inspire revolutionaries in Europe and Asia after their seizure of power. Some three months after the Russian Revolution, workers organized as Red Guards seized power in neighboring Helsinki and other major cities in freshly independent Finland. On January 28, 1918, the revolutionaries declared a new government under the Delegation of People's Commissars of Finland. As Russia's own revolutionary government had only just accepted Finnish independence from

Russia, Russian troops were still garrisoned in Finland. Disorganized pro-Bolshevik troops offered paltry help to the Finnish revolutionaries. With the beleaguered Bolsheviks unable and unwilling to provide serious assistance to the Finnish revolutionaries, the forces of counterrevolution overwhelmed the Delegation of People's Commissars. With German help, right-wing forces in Finland ousted the revolutionaries on April 13 and mopped up the remaining Red Guards in a brutal white terror campaign by mid-May.[1]

The next year brought three more attempted revolutions. In Berlin, a communist uprising in early January was crushed by the far-right *Freikorps*, a paramilitary body established by demobilized officers from the German imperial army. The Hungarian revolution in March initially seemed to fare better, and buoyed Bolshevik spirits and their cause of global revolution. Béla Kun, the Hungarian communist leader, consciously sought to replicate the actions of the Bolsheviks and create a new social order by nationalizing major industries, seizing land, and instituting a proletarian dictatorship. While Moscow looked approvingly on Kun's bellicosity, it was stingier in offering material support. When the Hungarian communists asked for a formal alliance, they were rebuffed and told that the Red Army could spare no troops. Even without Bolshevik protection, the Hungarian revolutionaries took into their own hands the task of spreading revolution. Hungary's army soon invaded Czechoslovakia and installed a Slovak Soviet Republic in Bratislava. Kun tried and failed to instigate a communist uprising in Vienna and declared war on Romania. The incensed authorities in Bucharest organized a counterrevolutionary alliance that marched on Budapest and toppled the regime. Even with this ominous end, a revolutionary movement inspired by Hungary seized control in Munich that April, declaring a Bavarian Soviet Republic until they too were toppled by federal troops and *Freikorps* in May.[2]

In all these cases the Bolsheviks had proven a stingy friend. Soviet power was, at this point, extremely limited. The Red Army was engaged in its own epic struggle to survive against the forces of counterrevolution. Each of these revolutions crumbled and fell to bloody white terror campaigns led by incumbent governments, European powers, and powerful classes that decimated communists and alleged sympathizers. Subsequent communist uprisings in other countries in Central and Eastern Europe ended again in disastrous defeats for the communist parties. Even the revolutions that received Soviet support largely failed. In Spain, extensive Soviet support was not enough to secure the triumph of the communists and their republican allies. Soviet assistance was substantial, with advisers helping their Spanish clients restructure their armed forces along Soviet lines. However, the forces of German-backed counterrevolution again won the day, and General Francisco Franco led the Falangists to a bloody victory. While ultimately successful decades later, Soviet efforts to aid the Chinese Communist Party in the 1920s proved an almost irreparable failure. Advised by Moscow to ally with Chiang Kai-shek and his Nationalist Party (Kuomintang), the Chinese communists were nearly destroyed in a bloody purge in 1927.[3]

Only one pre–World War II Soviet intervention was successful in installing and defending a pro-Soviet regime. In eventual Cold War parlance, Mongolia was the earliest Soviet "satellite." The Mongolian People's Party (MPP) had been formed on June 15, 1920, by urban intelligentsia who had fled to the emerging USSR after Chinese rule was reintroduced in Mongolia the previous year. Chinese control over Outer Mongolia (present day Mongolia) had been lost following the collapse of the Qing dynasty in 1911. The MPP sought Bolshevik assistance to restore Mongol independence under a pro-Soviet regime but was rebuffed by Lenin and his preoccupied comrades. It wasn't until a Russian general from the deposed tsarist regime the Bolsheviks had been fighting set up camp in Mongolia that Moscow changed its mind. In Bolshevik-held territory, Russian cadres began to help the MPP expand its membership and establish the Mongolian People's Revolutionary Army. On July 5, 1921, with the aid of some eight thousand Red Army troops, the MPP was swept into power in Urga, a city the Mongolian communists would rename Ulaanbaatar, or "Red Hero." The Mongolian revolutionaries continued to receive extensive Soviet support after seizing power and imported the Soviet political-military model. The Mongolian armed forces hosted Soviet military advisers, the Soviet security service helped establish a Mongolian counterpart, and Soviet party officials sat in on MPP meetings. A Soviet general even served as chief of the Mongolian army general staff. With Soviet help, Mongolian party control over the army was strengthened with a system of political commissars.[4]

Therefore, conservative fears and Soviet hopes notwithstanding, few revolutions before the Second World War succeeded in seizing and staying in power. While the Mongolian revolution greatly concerned rulers in Tokyo and Beijing, it reverberated much less deeply in European capitals. It appeared that perhaps Russia's improbable revolution would not lead to a cascade of successful communist uprisings after all. This proved false optimism or pessimism, depending on your position. Soviet victory over Nazi Germany and its Axis allies in World War II vaulted the USSR into superpower status and placed Moscow for the first time in a position where it was both willing and able to spread and consolidate revolutionary regimes abroad. The war had exacted an incalculable toll on the Soviet state and society, but Moscow had emerged victorious, and the Red Army had achieved massive prestige. Its influence stretched across a great Eurasian landmass, and its armies had already destroyed a series of Axis-allied regimes in Eastern Europe. While the revolutionary zeal of the Leninist period was gone, the actual power of the Soviet state to spread revolution was now considerable.[5]

The Soviet thrust into Germany brought six new governments in its wake: Bulgaria, East Germany, Hungary, North Korea,

Poland, and Romania. Another communist regime in Czecho-slovakia came to power several years after the war, and with vital Soviet assistance. Yet it was not just in Eastern Europe and North Korea where Moscow helped organize and sustain pro-Soviet regimes after World War II. As a new superpower, the Soviet Union provided aid, arms, and advisers to regimes in Afghanistan, Alba-nia, Angola, China, Cuba, Egypt, Ethiopia, Mozambique, Somalia, South Yemen, Syria, and Vietnam. While some of these regimes had received Soviet support during the struggles that brought them to power, they had seized control on their own accord. These were not Soviet impositions. Moscow nevertheless played a critical role in the consolidation of their rule and the shaping of their institu-tions. One common thread united all these Soviet efforts to sup-port friendly authoritarian governments. They all received Soviet assistance in transforming their security institutions to stave off threats to the pro-Soviet ruling coalitions.

THE LENINIST PARTY WAS ONE OF THE KEY INNOVATIONS OF THE Bolshevik revolution and a major organizational export of Soviet communism. An organized vanguard that supposedly acted in the interests of the working class, the party helped solve the collective action problem at the heart of organizing a proletarian revolution. Featuring mass membership with careful ideological screening and "democratic centralism" that in practice meant rigid hier-archy and often considerable power in the hands of the general secretary and political bureau (politburo), the party was a remark-able tool of authoritarian elite and mass control that formed the basis for many of the most durable autocracies of the twentieth century. The party extended its grip over nearly all aspects of life in communist regimes, from the economy to art. It was an institu-tion that helped regularize life at the apex of authoritarian power through its politburo, and its penetration of the state and society helped stave off challengers emerging outside the government. For Soviet relations with allies, building parties also helped solve the problem of irrational, erratic, or disloyal foreign dictators. With a strong party, the regime could build collective leadership institutions that provided a broader pool of possible alternatives to any one leader. For Moscow, this meant a wider range of potential regime officials who would seek to continue the Soviet alliance. With power resting in top collective leadership institutions in the party such as the central committee and its politburo, capricious client dictators could be removed and replaced by viable alternatives.[6]

While building parties helped solidify the rule of pro-Soviet cadres, building partisan armies helped keep those cadres in power and prevent counterrevolution. To Moscow, the politburo offered not just viable but also *reliable* alternatives. The same could not be said for the barracks. As the preceding chapter discussed, the Soviets had good reason to fear their own army early in the revolution and cast a jaundiced eye on the bourgeois and aristocratic nature of postcolonial militaries in the Third World. These armies were generally the direct descendants of their colonial predecessors and were staffed with officers close to the former colonial metropole. Postcolonial officers had trained alongside European advisers and often shared their strident anticommunism. It was not just in Marxist-Leninist theory where the Soviets found much to fear in reactionary armies: in practice, militaries proved deadly to many regimes that had been sympathetic to the Soviet Union. In West Africa, militaries overthrew Soviet-leaning regimes in Congo (1960), Ghana (1966), and Mali (1968). The coup in Ghana led to the humiliating expulsion of the small Soviet diplomatic and military advisory team. A similar embarrassment occurred in Iraq, where a pro-Soviet military dictatorship was ousted in 1963 and replaced by a much less friendly regime. The new Iraqi leadership inaugurated an immediate bloody crackdown on the local communist party, and the regime change "largely negated the political bene-fits" the modest aid program had provided. While none of these regimes received substantial aid, Moscow had invested some pres-tige, and the coups resulted in the abrupt end of Soviet influence and the realignment of these states back to the West. To Soviet leadership, these coups were a prime example of the problems posed by counterrevolution to Soviet-aligned regimes. By helping allies construct party armies on Soviet lines, Moscow hoped to remove the threat from within posed by counterrevolutionary offi-cers. Embedded mechanisms of party control such as commissars and military counterintelligence officers helped constrain regular officers so severely that coups were either too risky to attempt or swiftly crushed.[7]

These efforts meant that over time Soviet allies came to insti-tutionally resemble the Soviet Union itself. They established Leninist parties, expansive secret police, and partisan militaries. The performance of these Soviet-built institutions of course var-ied considerably. These allies also tended to import less effective Soviet institutions such as those devoted to economic planning. While industrialization was rapid, Soviet economic planning was immensely inefficient, and growth stagnated. Those clients unlucky enough to replicate these economic institutions rarely achieved high economic performance. Soviet allies that pursued collectiv-ization and state control of the economy more generally imported sluggish growth, corruption, and misery for peasant farmers.[8]

The Leninist party often degenerated from the revolutionary zeal of early joiners into an ossified patronage machine. Neverthe-less, even a consolidated patronage machine is an effective tool of authoritarian control. The party's success as an export was some-what uneven, as it rarely constrained individual dictators in the ways Moscow had hoped. It was the security organs and their sys-tem of partisan control that would prove to be Moscow's most suc-cessful institutional export. The party armies and security services built by Soviet advisers proved remarkably effective in preventing military-led counterrevolutions. Again, not a single Soviet client regime was ever ousted in a military coup d'état. This invulnerability to internal rivals in the military was also an extraordinarily durable legacy of Soviet support. These institutions, once built, continued to function effectively even after Soviet advisers themselves departed.[9]

The Soviet Union ultimately supported nineteen foreign autocracies with billions in aid and arms and with thousands of advisers. It did so in three ways: imposing regimes by the force of its own arms, assisting revolutionaries in their fight to power, and aiding existing regimes seeking to transform along Soviet lines.

POSTWAR EASTERN EUROPE OFFERED THE SOVIET UNION CONSIDerable freedom of movement in establishing friendly client governments thanks to the presence of the victorious Red Army. While the UK and the US unevenly sought to restrain Soviet behavior, the rival powers had little leverage. One institution Moscow immediately set its sights on was the armies of the defeated nations. Across Eastern Europe, new armies were built with Soviet help after World War II. How were these new armies actually built? In one sense the answer is easy: the Soviet Union did it. But how did the Soviet Union do it, exactly? How does one build a new army in a foreign country? Did these new armies function effectively? Did they serve their new governments and their Soviet patrons loyally? While the military effectiveness of these new armed forces was never tested, the Soviet Union did achieve their goal of creating pliant militaries that would not overthrow pro-Soviet governments. This was not only because Soviet troops dissuaded coups. The penetration of Eastern Europe by Soviet combat forces was in fact uneven. Yet even in cases like Romania, where the Soviet army and Soviet advisers departed, military rebellion against an increasingly erratic and unpopular dictatorship did not materialize.

As Soviet troops rolled through Eastern Europe on their way to Berlin, the Red Army set up military administrations in conquered territory and began to reshape and remake local states and governments. This process varied in important ways, yet the institutional matrix set up in each new regime was very similar. Even before the Cold War with the United States began to heat up, the Soviets devoted considerable and early attention to building communist parties, party armies, and Soviet-style security services. It was these institutions that would guarantee the new revolutionary governments were safely entrenched in power and remained pro-Soviet. While it is not clear that Stalin had intended to impose full communist regimes in Eastern Europe from the very beginning, building the institutional foundations of Leninist party rule was an early Soviet priority. These communist regimes were, apart from Czechoslovakia, imposed by Soviet arms. Nevertheless, they had real indigenous participation. Eager communists and opportunists alike flocked to the new regimes even as their alien image, punitive Soviet reparations, and radical social and economic policies dampened popular enthusiasm.[10]

As Moscow did not wish to keep its expensive military machine at full strength after the war or use its troops for local security indefinitely, setting up indigenous but thoroughly restructured armies in Eastern Europe and North Korea was an early priority. These armies, with some minor variation, followed the Soviet pattern very closely. In Bulgaria, Moscow gave clear instructions to the military leader of the occupation, Colonel General Sergey Biryuzov, that he was to remove "any obstacles to the path of the B.C.P. [Bulgarian Communist Party] to supreme power," which prompted him to interfere "blatantly in the internal politics of the country and the army." The Soviets pushed two key groups of communists into top commands in the military: wartime guerrilla fighters from the local communist party and émigré communists who had fled to the Soviet Union in the 1920s and survived Stalin's purges. Soviet advisers helped establish a political commissariat, a People's Militia, and a military counterintelligence service to monitor the soldiers and carry out the purges of thousands of soldiers and officers. At the end of 1945, communists comprised only some 40 percent of the top commands in the army. By 1953, 95 percent of the army command was made up of former partisan fighters and exiled BCP members who had arrived with the Red Army.[11]

In Hungary, the Soviet Union organized the new armed forces, and Soviet advisers were embedded throughout the army and security services. The Hungarian Communist Party takeover of the army was gradual, and initially clandestine. An intelligence and security service for the postwar government was established on Soviet territory with exiled Hungarian communists even before the Red Army invaded Hungary. The State Protection Authority (Államvédelmi Hatóság, ÁVH) was used alongside the Soviet's own chekists to hunt down fascists and Nazi collaborators in postwar Hungary. This secret police force also operated the Hungarian Army Political Section, an embedded military counterintelligence service that emulated the role of the special departments in the Soviet Union. The ÁVH was, in the judgment of US intelligence analysts, a "true copy" of the Soviet secret police and acted as the "eye and ear of the Communist Party in Hungary." In the mid-1950s the ÁVH had well-armed security troops organized as seven motorized rifle battalions and provided personal security for party officials.[12]

Poland proved one of the most difficult paths to imposing a communist regime in Eastern Europe. The presence of a noncommunist resistance group (the Home Army) and the weakness of the prewar Polish Communist Party made the consolidation of a pro-Soviet regime in Warsaw both protracted and violent. After Soviet troops had defeated Nazi forces in Poland, the notorious

Soviet security service (NKVD) general Ivan Serov was put in charge of eliminating organized opposition to the Soviet-organized Polish National Liberation Committee. The Polish People's Army (Ludowe Wojsko Polskie) was organized along Soviet lines, with military leadership provided by Polish émigrés and Soviet officers, and political commissars were embedded throughout the organization. Promotions depended on "each individual officer's political behavior and his attitude toward political officers and the Communist Party." The Soviets found Polish communists eager to ensure the reliability of the new army to the party. Jakub Berman, a key member of the politburo, remarked that "we will keep the Soviet personnel in all places where there is even a shadow of doubt about the loyalty of higher officers." Even as late as the early 1950s, the defense minister, chief of the general staff, commander of the ground forces, heads of all service branches, and commanders of all four military districts were former Soviet officers. The Soviet Union devoted early attention to creating and advising counterpart security services to protect the beleaguered regime, including the Department of Security (Urząd Bezpieczeństwa, UB) and the Internal Security Corps (Korpus Bezpieczeństwa Wewnętrznego, KBW).[13]

The North Korean regime was also imposed by force of Soviet arms. The Soviet Union had invaded northern Korea shortly before the capitulation of Japan in the Second World War. In late 1946, the Soviet-backed people's committees began to draw together into an internal security force the various security forces that had emerged after the Japanese surrender. Security cadre training centers were established in December 1946 under the auspices of the Department of Public Security and the Central People's Committee. The Korean People's Army (KPA) was officially established on February 8, 1948. Soviet personnel played a key role in creating the KPA, with Soviet advisers organizing, training, and equipping the force.

The KPA featured the same political and counterintelligence structure as other Soviet-bloc armies.[14]

The special status of Germany as the primary belligerent against the Soviets during the war and the presence of Allied zones of control on the border and in Berlin meant the creation of new state institutions in East Germany was both more gradual and more thorough than in the rest of Eastern Europe. Germany had been split into zones of occupation by the Allied powers after the defeat of Nazi Germany. These temporary occupation zones came to emerge as de facto and eventually de jure sovereign states. The Soviet zone became the German Democratic Republic in 1949. The National People's Army was created in 1956 by reorganizing personnel from the Alert Police, a paramilitary force created by the Soviets in 1948. The Alert Police featured a Soviet-style political apparatus embedded among its ranks in the form of political-cultural (*Polit-kultur*) officers in each unit with equal power to the commanding officer. Moscow also played a major role in the creation of the Ministry for State Security (Ministerium für Staatssicherheit), or Stasi, in 1950. Like its Soviet counterpart, the Stasi maintained a counterintelligence wing in military and police forces.[15]

The Czechoslovak Communist Party (KSČ) had a path to power that featured a much less overt Soviet hand. Soviet troops left Czechoslovakia in December 1945, and the KSČ spent almost three years as just one member of a coalition government. The KSČ spent the period before its coup gradually penetrating government institutions, including the internal security services, intelligence apparatus, and armed forces. The postwar Czechoslovak army emerged principally out of the First Czechoslovak Army Corps. When Hitler occupied Czechoslovakia in 1938–1939, many members of the Czechoslovak government fled to Allied territory, including the Soviet Union. After Germany invaded the Soviet Union in 1941, Moscow began to organize the exiled Czechoslovak soldiers on its territory into the First Corps. By the end of the war, the Corps had grown to some seventy thousand men. It was exclusively trained and equipped by the Soviet army. Under Soviet tutelage, the KSČ membership in Soviet territory began to construct an embryonic party apparatus in the Corps, which was institutionalized as the "enlightenment corps." Party penetration of the Corps was nevertheless still limited when it joined the Red Army in its liberation of Czechoslovak territory in October 1944.

As the Second World War came to an end, the Košice Program granted the Soviet Union broad influence in the building of postwar Czechoslovak military institutions but also brought the departure of Red Army troops. Only five hundred or so Soviet advisers remained in Prague to train the military. KSČ takeover of the postwar military was no small feat. Unlike elsewhere in Eastern Europe, the Czechoslovak military elite had mostly not been tarred with Nazi affiliation. Most officers had retired or fled to London with the exiled government after Hitler's forces marched into Czechoslovakia. The KSČ benefited significantly from the Košice Program decision that the First Czechoslovak Army Corps was to form the "core" of the officers of the postwar military. Yet the relatively small size of the Corps and the limited party penetration of the wartime force meant that by February 1948 only around 15 percent of the most important army posts were held by party members. A military counterintelligence service was created in January 1945 to monitor the mood of officers and investigate subversion in the force. Despite the best efforts of the KSČ and its institutionalized network of political commissars in the Main Department of Enlightenment and Education, the Czechoslovak army was not yet a communist creature.

Communist leadership of the internal security services achieved greater success before the seizure of power in 1948. In part, this was because the hands of the internal security organs were far more bloodied by cooperation with the Nazis. The National

Security Corps (Sbor národní bezpečnosti, SNB) was organized in 1945 after the dissolution of the wartime collaborationist internal security forces. Those individuals who did not desert upon the collapse of the Nazi Protectorate were purged in October 1945. The SNB recruited among the partisan resistance groups that had sprung up toward the end of the war, with some 8,000 of the 30,000 in the service coming from guerrilla backgrounds. By the time the KSČ seized power, the SNB was 150,000 strong. Once the party was in power, the SNB was yet again purged and restructured with the help of Soviet advisers, with a party apparatus introduced in the form of "police commissars," which replicated the military political commissariat. These commissars also reported up an independent chain of command.

While party control over the postwar army was far from ironclad, the KSČ penetrated the force sufficiently to secure its noninterference against their insurrection and seizure of power in February 1948. Ordered by President Edvard Beneš to remain in their barracks during the communist coup, the army neither actively helped nor hindered the overthrow of the government by the KSČ. Of course, this passivity was vitally important. Beneš did not order the army to resist the coup because he and his allies lacked confidence that the communist-penetrated army would obey such an order.

After the communist seizure of power in 1948, the army was purged considerably and reorganized as the Czechoslovak People's Army (ČLA). Soviet advisers arrived after the new regime requested their help in reforming its armed forces. Moscow deployed advisers in the ČLA down to the regiment and in the internal security services. While the Soviet mission had a smaller footprint than elsewhere, it was still somewhere between five hundred and two thousand personnel. In 1950, the Main Department of Enlightenment and Education took on a more orthodox Soviet name as the Main Political Administration. Political commissars mirrored their Soviet counterparts and provided vital information for the regime on the mood and political views of military personnel.

Soviet security personnel also helped establish a counterpart service, the State Security Service (Státní bezpečnost, StB). The StB emerged out of a clandestine intelligence network operated by the KSČ when it was a member of the Beneš-led coalition government. Soviet chekists arrived in September 1949 to convert this informal network into a proper security service. The StB had an expansive counterintelligence function, embedding agents alongside both SNB commanders and army officers. These officers acted with total autonomy from the regular commanders and the political commissars. Therefore, while the seizure of power by the Czechoslovak Communist Party was more gradual and rested only on an implicit threat of Soviet intervention, it nevertheless involved the creation of orthodox communist political and security institutions.[16]

The communist takeover of Romania was a similarly gradual process brought on by eager Romanian communists and backed by the coercive might of the Red Army. The Romanian Communist Party (Partidul Comunist Român, PCR) was founded on May 8, 1921, but prior to the Second World War operated on "the fringes of Romanian politics." State repression and party radicalism brought the PCR to its nadir in 1927 with only three hundred members. When World War II began, its membership was either imprisoned, in exile, or driven underground by state repression. It was the force of Soviet, not Romanian, arms that brought this "small faction-ridden" party "with little or no effective resonance in Romania" into the halls of power in Bucharest. After the Red Army began its offensive against Romania in August 1944, a royalist coup against the fascist-aligned military regime sought to stave off the full Sovietization of Romania. While this action did introduce temporary complications in Moscow's installation of a pliant new government, by war's end the PCR had captured de facto state power.[17]

Romanian Communist Party weakness, the product of decades of repression and unpopular party positions, coupled with the image of a party installed into office by Soviet bayonets, meant the PCR and its Soviet patrons had to compensate by building a formidable security apparatus. There were three principal security institutions that experienced major Soviet reorganization in the early days of the communist takeover: the army, the interior ministry, and the secret police. Each institution would ultimately be reformed closely along Soviet lines and in fully partisan form. Thanks to Soviet advisers, all Romanian security services would feature the same mechanisms of regime penetration and party control: political commissars, party committees, and embedded security service personnel. The Romanian security apparatus emulated the Soviet model par excellence. Not only was the army balanced by formidable and well-armed rivals, but every security service was kept loyal through party penetration. It was a remarkable and seemingly contradictory security apparatus: simultaneously fragmented *and* highly centralized.

Large-scale purges of the Romanian army gradually eliminated officers who had served in the prewar and wartime military. The new army followed the Soviet model closely in nearly all respects. The institutional isomorphism was so extreme, in fact, that US intelligence sources remarked it was "difficult" to "distinguish a Rumanian soldier from a Soviet soldier." The army hosted a considerable Soviet advisory presence, nearly all military equipment was of Soviet origin, and Romanian soldiers even wore Soviet uniforms. The army was organized "according to the instructions issued by the Soviet General Staff." Like other partisan armies in Soviet-allied states, the Romanian army featured both a party structure and penetration by military counterintelligence. Commissars were introduced in every military unit and were exclusively party members. Like their Soviet counterparts, political commissars were responsible for monitoring the behavior and political reliability of the regular military officers. Also like in other Soviet-built armies, the commissars were not popular with the professional officers. According to the memoirs of one officer, even "making a joke about the authority [of the commissars]" was "enough to have an officer transferred." The officers and political commissars maintained "reciprocal suspicion" and a "lack of appreciation and respect." Political commissars even had power over the intimate lives of commanders: officer marriages had to be approved by political officers.[18]

These infiltration mechanisms were present in every security service. The Ministry of Internal Affairs (Ministerul Afacerilor Interne, MAI) troop directorate featured the same political structure as the army. Counterintelligence officers (*Ofiţeri de contra-informaţie*) served alongside both the political and operational officers. They were recruited on the basis of their perceived alertness to "subversion by their comrades" and "willingness to inform on their friends." Like the political apparatus, these counterintelligence officers had "their own chain of command" and were "not subordinate to their commanding officers." They were also apparently widely feared. In the estimation of US intelligence, "no sensible commander would dare become involved in a dispute with the field security officer in one of his subordinate battalions." Among other responsibilities, these security officers monitored the behavior of soldiers during political lectures and reported regularly to party leadership. Like their KGB counterparts, they also maintained "extensive" networks of informers in MAI units at a typical ratio of one informer to seven or eight personnel.[19]

Finally, the Romanian regime established an expansive secret police force based on the Soviet model, the Department of State Security (Departamentul Securităţii Statului), commonly known simply as "Security" (Securitate). As with its KGB counterpart, party membership was extensive in the Securitate. At the top, the Securitate was led by three Soviet agents. Advisers were attached to each of the national directorates and supervised the training of new recruits. Personnel were selected based on their class background and devotion to the regime. Securitate records suggest the service had some four thousand officers and a registry of some forty-two thousand informers at this time. Like other Soviet-style services, the Securitate had its own militarized security troop section. By 1989, these security troops comprised some twenty-three thousand personnel. Despite its fearsome reputation, the Securitate was, in comparative perspective, a relatively small organization. It was about half the size of its East German counterpart, the Stasi, despite Romania's substantially larger population (twenty-three million versus sixteen million in 1989, respectively). What the Securitate lacked in uniformed personnel it apparently made up for in its network of informers. Internal documents accessed by historians suggested it placed a very high value on this informer network. A typical Securitate officer handled an informer network of fifty or more individuals in the 1980s. While difficult to establish precisely—and subject to post hoc biases and incentives to misrepresent in both directions—according to the director of the postcommunist intelligence service and successor to the organization, the informer network of the Securitate was around four hundred thousand individuals. If taken at face value, this means that by 1989 there was approximately one secret police informant for every fifty-seven citizens. This is a comparably dense informer network: the ratio of informers to population in East Germany was 1:67, and 1:40 in North Korea. Therefore, even when compared to cases of extreme secret police penetration, the Securitate apparently maintained a pervasive presence.[20]

Across Eastern Europe, new state security institutions were built closely on the Soviet model. There were local variations, and the process was more uneven and more gradual than has been commonly thought. Nevertheless, orthodox party states, party security organs, and party armies were constructed to safeguard the pro-Soviet leadership of these new governments. This was achieved through the cooperation of weak local communist allies and thousands of Red Army troops, flush with victory against the German military machine. But it was not just in Eastern Europe and North Korea where the Soviet Union built partner security services in its own image. In regimes as far-flung as Angola, Cuba, and South Yemen, local pro-Soviet regimes hosted Soviet advisers who helped them reshape their security apparatus along Soviet lines.

In areas not under direct military occupation by the Soviet army, security institutions were built with the help of military and intelligence advisers. Advisers performed many roles. These were the party officials, security service personnel, and military officers actually deployed abroad to bring the Soviet vision of political organization to life in an allied country. They helped reform state institutions along the latest practices in their home country, suggested policies, trained military personnel in how to use weapons, organized security institutions, and, in extreme cases, gave orders and commanded military units. The Soviets deployed advisory missions in many different countries in large numbers. In 1983, some nineteen thousand Soviet military personnel acting as advisers were deployed in the Third World, and more than four thousand individuals from the Third World were in the USSR for military training. This was a marked increase from the mid-1970s, when the total number of Soviet advisory personnel was around eight thousand. Advisers were assigned directly to military or state security organizations and academies to provide organizational, tactical, and strategic advice; technicians helped maintain and repair Soviet-bloc military equipment; and instructors and support personnel provided logistical assistance and training. In some cases, Soviet military advisers oversaw the entire reorganization of foreign armies. Most of the Soviet advisers deployed were KGB or military officers. They were often embedded at multiple levels of the host military and were even occasionally assigned to operational combat units (for example, in Syria). Security service (KGB) and military intelligence (GRU) personnel comprised an estimated 10 percent of the total Soviet missions in the early 1980s and focused on building counterpart security and intelligence units, monitoring Western intelligence agencies, and keeping a watchful eye on the behavior of Soviet personnel deployed in the host country. Soviet advisers in both the military and security services devoted considerable attention to cultivating a network of pro-Soviet personnel in the host country.[21]

The Soviet Union also enlisted the help of its own clients in its foreign advisory missions. Eastern Europeans made up around one-tenth of Soviet bloc advisory deployments. East Germany in particular was a major player in helping Soviet allies build new intelligence and security services. According to a US CIA study, the East Germans made up half of the East European advisers deployed abroad in the early 1980s. The Stasi had been a highly successful Soviet creation in Berlin, and the German security agents worked alongside their KGB allies to build counterpart services in the Third World. In the estimation of the CIA, the Stasi agents assigned this task had capabilities that matched if not exceeded those of the Soviet KGB. There was some other functional specialization as well, with Bulgaria tending to provide training for insurgent groups. For the Eastern Europeans, most of the personnel deployed abroad consisted of intelligence and security advisers. Military advisers, especially in the general staffs of client militaries, were typically Soviet personnel. While not all Soviet clients were communist (and indeed some that declared themselves as communist did not receive Soviet attention or assistance), they did tend to grow more *institutionally* Leninist over time. This was not necessarily in economic policy or commitment to socialism, as the appeal of the Soviet Union in these areas had declined significantly since the early 1950s, but in the structure of state security and governing institutions.[22]

The Soviet Union provided support to incumbent regimes in Afghanistan, Albania, Cuba, Egypt, Ethiopia, Somalia, South Yemen, Syria, and Vietnam. These authoritarian governments were already in power when they began to receive large-scale Soviet assistance. In a few cases—Angola, China, and Mozambique—the Soviet Union provided arms and aid before victorious Marxist-Leninist rebel groups succeeded in ousting the incumbent government by the force of arms. While this support was helpful, Soviet support to each insurgent group had dwindled in the years before the actual seizure of power. It was primarily the aid, arms, and advisers that flowed into these nascent governments *after* they had taken power that helped consolidate their rule. As with Eastern Europe, Moscow pushed these clients to adopt orthodox Leninist institutions like vanguard parties, partisan militaries, and internal security organs. In these clients, however, the Soviet presence was advisory rather than backed by the might of the Red Army. These allies therefore had far more room to maneuver vis-à-vis their patron. They could resist Soviet entreaties to strengthen the party and ignore tactical and strategic military advice without the threat, however blunt of an instrument it might be, of Soviet tanks forcing their hand. Clients in existing governments not imposed directly by Moscow were generally happy to receive Soviet support in building new security services and subordinating their armies to party rule. They were less keen on building effective collective leadership institutions that might provide Moscow with a ready replacement for their rule. The limited leverage Moscow enjoyed over these governments rendered it largely impotent in the face of client aberrations from the Soviet model.

The Soviets helped several clients transition from vaguely leftist guerrilla movements to highly institutionalized Leninist regimes. In November 1967, the National Liberation Front (NLF) seized power in Aden, Yemen, after its four-year guerrilla war forced the evacuation of British forces from Britain's only proper colony in the region. The NLF was an obscure group of nationalist activists unknown even to their British enemies through much of their early existence. The NLF included a variety of ideological orientations but maintained a sizable and increasingly influential pro-Soviet flank. As the NLF expanded its base of guerrilla operations, the nervous indigenous colonial army and police struck a deal with the insurgents. In exchange for their not resisting the NLF's final assault on Aden, the NLF would keep the old army in place. This deal deprived the British of their local forces necessary to fight the spreading insurgency and prompted their rapid and ignominious departure. While this deal handed the reins of government to the NLF, it also left the movement saddled with a "largely conservative, tribal-based military" and a British-trained state apparatus.[23]

The NLF had forced the humiliating retreat of Britain, but myriad challenges remained for the obscure liberation movement that sought to lead the newly independent South Yemen. The balance of forces was troubling for the National Front ("Liberation" was dropped after independence). It brought only four thousand guerrillas into Aden and inherited a British-built army of some ten thousand troops. The conventionally structured Liberation Army, guerrilla cells, and People's Guard security service would now serve alongside the colonial-era Federal Regular Army. As a legal matter the NF led the army through the Ministry of Defense, but in effect the former colonial army remained under only limited control. The military even resisted attempts by the NF to communicate directly with troops and forced all communications through the army general staff.

This was an increasingly untenable and even potentially lethal situation for the Front. At its Fourth Congress in March 1968, the left-wing faction led by Abdul Fattah Ismail demanded the "dissolution of the old army." This explicit threat to the army precipitated a coup attempt by the military that nearly succeeded. While the army arrested most of the leftist NF leadership, it did not get the predicted support from more conservative leaders of the movement, and the putsch collapsed. Failing to push ahead proved a fateful error. In response, wartime veterans of the Liberation Army began to arrest regular army officers, and rank-and-file soldiers declared their support for the NF. A party coup within the NF purged its more conservative leadership, and Abdul Fattah Ismail and his comrades were ascendant. In late 1969 and early 1970, the army underwent an "extensive purge and reconstruction," and the British-trained officers were dismissed. The much-diminished former colonial officers planned a final desperate coup attempt, which was discovered and ended with the execution of the insubordinate officers.[24]

This leftward turn brought a significant increase in Soviet support. Soviet advisers arrived to help reform the Yemeni security apparatus. Political commissars were introduced in the army in mid-1970, and the Soviet KGB helped organize the Committee for State Security of the People's Democratic Republic of Yemen (PDRY). So close was the connection that the Yemenis even proudly called themselves "chekists." The operational units of state security were made up largely of party members and were considered "efficient and ruthless." A People's Militia was created in 1972 as an additional "offset" against the reformed army. Soviet military advisers were assigned to "oversee training for each South Yemeni Army brigade." Soviet personnel were "sprinkled throughout all major PDRY military units and security organizations." This extensive Soviet mission built a "strong state security apparatus" and "facilitated the expansion of Soviet sympathizers in the ranks of the bureaucracy, party, and military."[25]

Following the pattern of Soviet policy elsewhere, the PDRY was under pressure to expand its ruling party. The Soviet Union was not particularly optimistic about the prospects for socialism in South Yemen. The PDRY was, in Soviet parlance, "socialist oriented" rather than fully socialist. Soviet leaders were not blind to the challenges of expanding a proletarian constituency in an economic backwater like South Yemen and pushed for gradualism and moderation on the part of their clients in Aden.[26]

Moscow did acknowledge approvingly that South Yemen had won its independence under the leadership of a "revolutionary organization" that had declared its intent to build a socialist society from the very beginning. The NF was an "avant-garde party that proclaimed scientific socialism as its ideology." Moscow pushed the further institutionalization of this party with the formation of the Yemeni Socialist Party in 1978. The YSP was "modeled along Soviet lines," with Soviet advisers assisting in "structuring party organs" and "government ministries" and teaching at party schools. While the YSP was organizationally Leninist, it nevertheless remained "an amalgam of Communists, Ba'thists, and Arab nationalists."[27]

Yemeni leader Abdul Fattah Ismail told Soviet journalist (and KGB agent) Yevgeny Primakov that "since we have chosen the path of scientific socialism" it was "the duty of the Soviet Union to help us." This help extended to building the YSP to "defend the revolution." This was not the only duty that South Yemen felt it was owed by the Soviet Union. Ismail also told Primakov that it was the Soviet Union's "duty" to "put the republican regime in the north on the right path." The Soviet's Yemeni clients attacked their northern neighbors in the Yemen Arab Republic in February 1979. This was unwelcome news for Moscow, which was already embroiled in an escalating conflict in Afghanistan. A prominent South Yemeni official told the horrified Soviet ambassador, "Yes, it's us who've started the war. If we win, we'll create Great Yemen. If we lose, you'll intervene and save us."[28]

The National Liberation Front was not the only liberation movement to receive Soviet help transforming its rebel army into a Leninist party army to defend its revolution. In Mozambique, the Mozambique Liberation Front (Frente de Libertação de Moçambique, or Frelimo), seized power in 1975 after a long war for national liberation from Portugal. The Soviet Union played a key role in transforming Frelimo's disparate and disorganized guerrilla army into a conventional army under party control. Frelimo's armed wing, the Forças Populares de Libertação de Moçambique (FPLM), had emulated Chinese organization and from the early days of the insurgency had featured political commissars. After the 1974 coup in Lisbon, Frelimo negotiated with the new Portuguese government to take power in Maputo. Full independence was achieved in July 1975 when the Portuguese officially handed power to Frelimo. Soviet advisers then began to arrive to help transform the wartime army into a proper state military. The Mozambican armed forces were "largely created, organized, and trained by the Soviets after independence in 1975."[29]

The Soviet Union played a key role in the process of strengthening the Frelimo party apparatus in the military. Soviet advisers helped Frelimo screen recruits and strengthen the party organs in the armed forces. When the regime began to face the South African–backed Renamo insurgency, Soviet military advisers helped plan "operational duties down to the brigade level." By the mid-1980s, there were some two thousand Soviet-bloc advisers in Mozambique. The Soviets also helped establish the National People's Security Service (Serviço Nacional de Segurança Popular, SNASP). KGB officials worked directly in SNASP offices, and the Mozambican service inaugurated a "reign of terror" against real and imagined political opponents. Soviet military intelligence (GRU) advisers also helped establish a counterpart service, the Reconnaissance Directorate.[30]

FROM LIBERATION MOVEMENTS TO SMALL CADRES OF EXILED COMmunists, the Soviet Union helped install and consolidate a wide range of revolutionary governments in Europe, Asia, Africa, and the Americas. This process varied along with the path to power on which each pro-Soviet regime embarked. In each case, however diverse the coalitional composition of the socialist, radical, liberation, or communist parties that took the reins of the state, a fairly orthodox set of Leninist institutions were established as a result of Soviet advice and insistence. In Eastern Europe, the process of building Soviet-style security services involved a very heavy Soviet hand but with the active participation of the local communist party. In places like Ethiopia, Afghanistan, South Yemen, and Mozambique, it was a transformation achieved with the help of Soviet military and security advisers deployed once the regime was already in power, to help it transform its security sector along Soviet lines. Regardless of the path taken, these security institutions were established in remarkably uniform ways. Each regime copied the system of party control over security services from its Soviet patron. Soviet help was critical in establishing these security organs and subordinating the army to partisan rule. In Chapter 5, we will see that these institutions functioned with ruthless efficiency in defending regimes from counterrevolutionary threats emerging from the army.

But first we turn to the efforts of Moscow's superpower rival in building armies and regimes abroad. It was not only the Soviet Union that promoted its vision of modernity abroad to local allies. The United States embarked on a similarly wide-ranging and expansive effort to export its own model of military organization and help friendly governments seize and consolidate power, although with the object being, in this case, to act as bulwarks against communist expansion.

4 | BOLSTERING COUNTERREVOLUTION

ike its wartime Soviet ally, America emerged from the crucible of World War II a fundamentally transformed global power. It began the war as a rising but isolationist industrial power and ended the war having aided immensely the Allied war in Europe and led the defeat of Japan in Asia. At war's end, its military was larger than the combined strength of its Western wartime allies and second only to the Soviet Red Army. Washington was the undisputed leader of the West, the only nuclear-armed state, and sat atop an economy that had exploded in size. After the war, American GDP accounted for over half the world's total, and there were 7.5 million American troops stationed in sixty-four countries. The once dismissed American army had achieved enormous prestige and itself was permanently transformed. Gone were the days where the American army was a tiny peacetime force supplemented by wartime mobilization of volunteers. It was now a permanent standing force organized to meet the host of international responsibilities suddenly thrust upon American policymakers. While the wrecking of British and French power by the war along with consequent decolonization would prove a major catalyst for a huge expansion in political equality, it worried American policy-makers concerned with building a powerful and united democratic West in Europe.[1]

A desire to ensure that Germany and Japan would never again threaten American security committed US forces to long military occupations. Even before the war was over, the ascendant Red Army and Soviet communism loomed. US forces had joined the failed international intervention in 1918 to topple the Bolsheviks during the Russian Civil War, and now America's wartime ally had emerged as a serious postwar rival. Concern over communist subversion of established Western polities long predated the Cold War. Yet the newfound Soviet military power and the rise of movements agitating for decolonization, some of which were led by communist parties, rendered communism a far more formidable strategic threat after the war. Untainted by fascist collaboration, communist parties appeared poised to reap major electoral victories in France and Italy, and communist rebels were on the march in Greece and China. The Red Army commanded the largest military force in the world, and the Soviet Union was rapidly working to close the nuclear gap.

While the Second World War had in part been a battle of two competing versions of political order—fascism versus democracy—it had involved a complicated set of alliances across a variety of political regime types. The United States entered a host of temporary alliances with friendly despots, particularly in the Western Hemisphere. Ever astute observers of changes in the geopolitical winds, several Central American military dictators who had previously expressed admiration for Hitler's Germany were suddenly vocal antifascists willing to join the US-led alliance against the Axis powers. Hemispheric defense priorities trumped US disdain for these despots-turned-democrats, but once the war was over, pressure for liberalization returned. And of course the Allies themselves included the communist Soviet Union and the autocratic

Chinese Nationalist Party. Yet in Germany and Japan the United States was committed to building new democracies and ultimately integrating each state into the US-led alliance system.

American views of how best to interact with friendly foreign tyrants began to change with the onset of the Cold War rivalry with the Soviet Union. This involved considerable whiplash in American views toward certain friendly tyrants. Condemnable autocracies were suddenly viewed as potentially vital partners in countering Soviet power. Even in places like Japan, where the US commitment to purging the scourge of fascism was paramount, the US military administration backtracked from a policy of total exclusion of fascist-era military officers from the new postwar armed forces. This decision was made after the value of Japan as an anticommunist bulwark gained increasing importance with the Chinese Revolution and war in Korea. The influential American diplomat George F. Kennan put evolving American views at the time succinctly when he remarked that "it is better to have a strong regime in power than a liberal government if it is indulgent and penetrated by Communists." Autocrats realized the advantage provided by this new international system almost immediately and sought to burnish their anticommunist credentials to secure American support.[2]

The US proved far more amenable to anticommunist military rule than its genuinely held preference for democracy might suggest. In a meeting of the National Security Council in 1959, Secretary of Defense Neil McElroy remarked that it "had been generally true that military leadership has basically represented a conservative element in societies of the newly developed countries. While in some instances, the military can be troublesome, it remained true that in these backward societies, it was desirable to encourage the military to stabilize a conservative system." For his part, President Eisenhower offered that "the trend toward military take-overs in the underdeveloped countries of Asia and Africa was almost certainly going to continue. Accordingly, we must do our best to orient the potential military leaders of these countries in a pro-Western rather than a pro-Communist direction." US intelligence agencies also thought military rule aligned with US interests in anticommunism, as most militaries were themselves fiercely anticommunist.[3]

After the 1966 coup against Kwame Nkrumah in Ghana, a National Security Council official wrote a memorandum to President Lyndon B. Johnson describing the coup as "a fortuitous windfall" and the new military leaders as "almost pathetically pro-Western." In a memo for CIA director William Colby on March 8, 1974, intelligence officers recommended that the US reaction to a future military coup in Thailand should be governed by the premise that "it is in our interest to continue a close relationship with almost any Thai government that might emerge from a coup" and thus "during any coup attempt the U.S. should maintain a low profile and remain detached from the situation, but should continue all assistance programs and contacts with the government at present levels." Finally, "once a coup has succeeded and the dust has settled, the U.S. should in [a] low key express acceptance of the situation." These suggestions could be taken less seriously as an indicator of official US policy if they had not been so congruous with actual US behavior when a coup occurred in Thailand two years later.[4]

But Washington was not willing to bankroll all friendly autocracies. American policy toward friendly tyrants was the direct consequence of the seriousness with which officials treated the communist threat in any given country. As it turned out, several major developments profoundly changed the perceived threat of communism in Asia, Latin America, Africa, and the Middle East. In Asia three monumental events altered American willingness to bankroll and intervene on behalf of anticommunist dictatorships: the Chinese Communist Revolution in 1949, the North

Korean invasion of the South in 1950, and the collapse of French rule in Indochina and the victory of the communist-led Viet Minh in 1954.

These three developments greatly alarmed American policy-makers and engendered a sense that communism was on the rise. It was in Indochina and Korea where the most extensive American efforts to support friendly autocracies in the Cold War would occur. In Latin America, the Cuban Revolution of 1959 loomed large. Cuban-inspired and supported revolutionaries emerged in many Latin American countries, and anticommunist military juntas proved frequent recipients of American support. By the mid-1950s, the Eisenhower administration "made it clear that Washington would intervene—not so as to aid democratic forces in a Wilsonian manner, but to stop communism even at the price of reinforcing authoritarian regimes." Communism was, in the view of President Eisenhower, an "infection" that threatened the postcolonial world.[5]

The foreign policy framework that underpinned support for friendly autocrats under communist threat emerged gradually in several key postwar policies. One component was promoting economic development. President Harry S. Truman hypothesized that "poverty, misery, and insecurity are the conditions on which Communism thrives." The US sought to export good governance, land reform, and strong economic growth, which would dampen the appeal of communism. But the most important aspect of American assistance for friendly Cold War autocrats was building effective militaries. According to a leading history of American foreign policy, the "most common practice for Americans engaged in countries where a communist threat was perceived was to build up a client military." This served a dual purpose of helping "strengthen an organization capable of both rooting out local communists and, in some instances, of blocking direct Soviet or Chinese expansion." On January 7, 1955, the US National Security Council outlined the central priorities of American national security policy in NSC-5501, a report that highlighted the danger communist "subversion" posed to American interests and identified support for allied governments as central to countering this revolutionary threat. Wherever friendly governments were incapable, the document stated, the US ought to "assist in the development of adequate internal security forces" to prevent the revolutionary seizure of power by communists. Whenever possible, support for building capable internal security forces should be done through assistance and advice, not direct military intervention.[6]

The biggest US aid program, inaugurated under President Truman, the Military Assistance Program (MAP) was intended to "strengthen the mutual defense and collective security of the non-communist world." In exchange for US basing rights, MAP would increase "military self-reliance" of partner nations and "promote tangible evidence of U.S. support." MAP funds were disbursed to a wide range of countries, but half of all MAP aid went to just four countries: South Vietnam, Korea, France, and Turkey. The US also trained hundreds of thousands of foreign military personnel, many through the International Military and Education Training (IMET) program. IMET was intended to both increase the military capacity of the recipient army and increase the exposure of potentially influential military officers to the United States and vice versa. The largest recipients of IMET included South Vietnam, Korea, Turkey, France, Taiwan, Thailand, Iran, Greece, Italy, and Japan. Vietnam, Korea, Turkey, Thailand, and Greece would all experience military rule, and Iran and Taiwan were authoritarian regimes.[7]

Nevertheless, support for friendly autocracies was not something American officials generally found comfortable. The Soviet Union was far less squeamish about supporting regimes that did not hold regular multicandidate elections. American officials sometimes convinced themselves that their autocratic allies weren't really autocrats at all. Under pressure to uphold constitutional rule, maintain theoretically representative institutions, and hold elections with varying degrees of competitiveness, America's autocratic allies often institutionally resembled actual democracies. At least if taken at face value. To take but one example, the US-assisted coup that ousted Prime Minister Mohammad Mossadeq in Iran and returned the shah to power was viewed by American policymakers as saving constitutional rule in that country, not undermining it. In the view of some senior US officials, the shah "represented tradition, continuity, and above all constitutional authority." By ousting the "radical and misguided opportunist" Mossadeq, the United States "merely assisted the shah and the Iranian Army in restoring power to the nation's rightful rulers."[8]

US policymakers, with few exceptions, sought to pressure their authoritarian allies to at least "appear" democratic. After Major General Park Chung-hee seized power in a coup, the United States pushed the Korean dictator to civilianize his rule. Under "strong pressure from Washington," Park pushed through constitutional changes, resigned his military commission, and ran for president as a civilian. While the elections were neither free nor fair, they did render Park a more palatable client for the United States. With Park in a business suit instead of a military uniform, his regime could now claim more plausibly to reflect constitutional civilian rule, if in practice it remained a military regime.[9]

In Laos, Brigadier General Phoumi Nosavan seized power in a military coup in December 1959. The American reaction was permissive, as it appeared Phoumi would have the wherewithal to prevent "the slippage of Laos into the communist camp." Phoumi looked "like the potential anticommunist strongman his country needed." Importantly to Phoumi's American supporters, the coup received a veneer of constitutionality. King Savang Vatthana retroactively blessed the coup, and the new junta pledged elections in the coming months. US officials were confident that the anticommunist candidates would win in a competitive election and sought to persuade their Laotian counterparts to conduct the poll without fraud, which would only sully the likely victory. The royal Lao government was far less sanguine, however, and severely manipulated the vote totals. An implausibly abysmal communist performance in their key areas of support made clear the extent of the malfeasance. When a CIA officer complained about this obvious fraud to a Lao military officer, the latter reportedly asked the American officer for his birth date. He then promptly erased the communist vote total in one district and wrote in 1,927. After these clearly dubious elections, the US insisted that Phoumi and his allies avoid overt military domination of the government, and Phoumi acquiesced, settling for defense minister and de facto ruler.[10]

In short, the Cold War with the Soviet Union brought the US into a position where it sought to entrench the rule of anticommunist strongmen and pro-Western regimes with dubious democratic credentials. Friendly tyrants were nearly everywhere, but only those of geostrategic value or facing a plausible communist threat found real support in Washington. As it set about shoring up the heterogeneous Free World against communist subversion, the United States turned to its own political-military structure as a model for the developing world.

The United States did not have, in comparative perspective, a rich history of foreign interventions to draw on once it became a global superpower. For most of its existence up to the end of World War II, the United States of America was primarily an internal empire. Early US colonization focused on the gradual westward expansion of the American state and the incorporation, expulsion, and sometimes violent elimination of Native American tribes. The United States was a late and relatively minor pursuer of overseas empire compared to its European counterparts. It had nowhere near the experience in building armies in foreign countries of its counterparts in Paris or London. Nevertheless, the US did engage in state building in a handful of foreign countries and colonies in the nineteenth and early twentieth centuries. These efforts featured American methods of state building applied to contexts American advisers often knew little about and paralleled postwar interventions. Building new militaries on the American model was particularly important in these interventions.[11]

In its colony in the Philippines, the United States devoted early attention to building an indigenous military force. The Philippines Scouts were established in 1899 and were led directly by American military officers. The Insular Police, soon renamed the Philippines Constabulary to reflect its blending of law enforcement and military duties, was established two years later. In 1936, personnel from the Scouts were reorganized into a regular army built closely around American organizational and doctrinal patterns as the Armed Forces of the Philippines (AFP). The AFP was also designed as a nonpartisan military under civilian control. It was this military that was inherited by the Philippines upon independence in 1946.[12]

Apart from the Philippines, the US engaged in relatively limited overseas colonialism. However, briefer American imperial interventions in Latin America were commonplace. Several of these interventions involved overseas state building, including the whole-scale US design and creation of militaries in multiple Central American and Caribbean countries. The US built new constabularies after interventions in the Dominican Republic, Haiti, and Nicaragua. The constabulary model of military organization involved training soldiers for internal security and policing duties. These militaries were reflections of US military organization at the time and American views of proper civil-military relations. The Dominican Constabulary Guard was built by an American expeditionary force in 1917. It replaced all preexisting Dominican security forces. American occupation authorities feared that excessive politicization of earlier military forces had been the principal cause of Dominican instability and therefore took great pains to enshrine explicit guarantees the Guard would be "free from politics" and strictly nonpartisan. However, American authorities remained suspicious that Dominican politicians would nevertheless politicize the institution. Their solution only created problems later down the road. Rather than enshrine civilian control over the military, US authorities placed all power of promotions in the hands of the Guard commander rather than civilian politicians. After the US withdrew its occupation forces in 1924, the Guard was renamed the Dominican National Army, and Rafael Leónidas Trujillo became its chief of staff.[13]

An intervention in Haiti brought another new American-built military force. In Port-au-Prince, US Marines fundamentally reshaped the domestic security apparatus during a military occupation from 1915 to 1934. US authorities disbanded existing military forces and created from scratch the Gendarmerie d'Haití in 1916. American officials insisted on a nonpartisan gendarmerie and organized the force along American lines. In Nicaragua, American occupation forces began building a new nonpartisan constabulary in 1927 after an earlier effort had failed. This Guardia Nacional de Nicaragua was led by US Marines and trained a new cadre of indigenous officers and enlisted men. Like in other Central American republics, the US centralized all coercive power in the hands of the Guard and granted the Guard commander power over all promotions. The Guard was declared the "sole military and police force of the Republic," with exclusive control over all security, police, and intelligence functions.

The US State Department viewed the Guard as providing a chance to "transform Nicaragua's armed forces into a nonpolitical force, dedicated to defending constitutional order and guaranteeing free elections." One year before the US occupation authorities departed, Anastasio Somoza García was named commander of the Guard, with the approval of the United States.[14]

These nonpartisan armies would prove to harbor plenty of praetorian impulses. Two of the commanders of US-built constabularies would use their positions to inaugurate decades-long authoritarian regimes. Trujillo and Somoza were both notorious dictators who used their command of US-built armies to dominate political life in their respective countries. In Haiti, the US-built armed forces carried out six coups. While the Philippines Army never seized power directly, it acted as a willing prop to the dictatorship of Ferdinand Marcos and led six coup attempts against President Corazon Aquino in the late 1980s and early 1990s.

As with the Soviet Union, it was the end of World War II that brought the United States into a position where it would be engaged in significant international state building to shore up a network of allies. One early postwar intervention is illustrative of these efforts. The American state-building project in Korea reflected evolving US thinking on how to build and consolidate anticommunist states and regimes in the developing world as a bulwark against communist expansion. The US played an expansive role in Korea, building its military from scratch and providing vital economic and political support to its governments.

The army the United States built was designed to be nonpartisan and the protector rather than the predator of Korean democracy. These efforts ultimately failed. The US-created force became a highly praetorian army that would come to dominate Korean politics for decades. The precarious position of the Republic of Korea (ROK) relative to its northern neighbor meant the army was tasked with the vitally important defense of the nation. Any political interference in army command was therefore viewed with significant alarm by both the United States and Korean officers. Moreover, as the civilian US-supported dictator Syngman Rhee himself flagrantly violated the constitution and democracy, the army could view its insubordination as an extension of its constitutional duties rather than as a violation of them.

American political priorities in Korea after World War II shifted quickly from democracy to political stability. The US first and foremost feared the internal and external communist threats to Korea. These concerns were not baseless and were heightened when pro-communist noncommissioned officers in the American-built constabulary mutinied in October 1948. This concern, and the perceived importance of this clash of governmental systems on the Korean peninsula, ironically considerably blunted US leverage in Seoul and its own preference for democracy. Caught between its democratic ideals and the political stability promised by anticommunist dictators, the US entered a position where it consistently sought to strengthen Korean dictatorships yet also unevenly push liberalization. Korean coup makers were, under American pressure, forced to adopt the formal trappings of democracy: elections, parliaments, courts. Unlimited rule by juntas of uniformed officers was not acceptable to Washington. Yet the US was put in a position where, despite having created the Korean army and deployed a sizable contingent of troops, policymakers felt they had no viable leverage and had to accept a political army in Korea.

When coups occurred in Korea—as they did in 1961 and 1979—they were accepted as faits accomplis. US policymakers did not promote the coups and reacted with alarm when they occurred. Despite the theoretically enormous US leverage stemming from joint command of Korean forces, policymakers felt they had few viable options to reverse the coups. Fearing splits in the army, civil war, and the possibility of an ensuing North Korean attack, American policymakers on the ground reacted quickly to reunify the elite and stabilize the country. It was not until the waning of the Cold War that the US fully embraced democratization in Korea. While the US-Korean relationship was complicated and multifaceted, the military relationship was always at the core. Just as, in North Korea, the party politburo provided a ready pool of reliable pro-Soviet leaders, the ROK army was an institution the US felt was securely pro-American. A strong, autonomous ROK army helped deter North Korean attack and provided a pool of officers amenable to a solid ROK-US relationship.

Like its Soviet counterpart, the United States had initially given little thought and devoted almost no planning for Korea's fate after the war ended. The sudden Japanese surrender in August 1945 pushed Washington to send personnel intended for occupation duty in Japan to an occupation zone in southern Korea. On September 8, 1945, the US Seventh Infantry Division landed in Incheon, marking the beginning of the American occupation. In their hasty assumption of control over southern Korea, US authorities quickly set about building a suitable provisional government. While the US had made clear its intention to grant eventual independence, it also broadcast that this would only occur after a period of direct American administration. Suspicious of the Korean left, the US Army Military Government in Korea (USAMGIK) chose to ally with the conservative Korean Democratic Party (KDP) and reconstitute much of the Japanese colonial structure. There was so much continuity in this transition that in many cases government units were simply renamed "department" from "bureau." In search of a leader for the emerging regime, the US chose to ally with Syngman Rhee, a seventy-year-old anti-Japanese nationalist who had spent many years in exile. Rhee had been imprisoned by the Japanese for political activity in 1899 and had established the Provisional Government in Exile in Shanghai in 1919. He was a lifelong activist for Korean independence and had unimpeachable nationalist credentials. Rhee arrived in Korea on an American military transport to take the helm of the provisional government.[15]

Rhee was considered by many in the US State Department a "nuisance," "unreliable," and overall "irksome." US intelligence officers found him less objectionable, as he was a known entity, and his long-standing anticommunism was likely to prove useful. With the "tacit blessing" of the United States, Rhee emerged as the clear leader of the conservative independence movement. His National Society for the Rapid Realization of Independence was soon the strongest political organization in the area under US occupation. The US had committed itself early to building a democracy in Korea, a goal that was "one of the top priorities" of Lieutenant General John R. Hodge, the commander of US Army Forces in Korea (USAFIK). The perceived stakes in Korea were heightened considerably by the growing rivalry with the Soviet Union. The rivalry was particularly acute in Korea, where a Soviet-backed alternative was active on the northern half of the peninsula. Korea was a place where "democratic and communist principles are being put to the test side by side," and if Seoul were to succeed, it would demonstrate the "practical superiority of democratic principles" to all of Asia.[16]

This perceived clash of governmental systems came with the ironic decline in US pressure for democracy. As the Cold War progressed, "the character of the South Korean regime was less important to the United States. What mattered most for Washington was fighting communism." This trumped support for democracy and led the US to "grudgingly" support the gradual consolidation of authoritarianism under Rhee. While American officials came to disdain Rhee's retrograde and repressive rule, he was viewed as "the only figure capable of blocking the influence of the Korean left."[17]

The institution the United States devoted the most effort to strengthening was the army. General Hodge had decided early to create "an indigenous military force" to "provide stability and hedge against leftist subversion." This force was to be built "from scratch" by US Army personnel as the Korean Constabulary. It would be organized, trained, advised, and equipped by the United States. Of course, no army is really built from scratch. The Korean Constabulary was no exception. When the US first arrived in Korea it quickly took over the Bureau of Police, which had remained largely intact after the war. About 70 percent of the Bureau was made up of Japanese personnel, who were swiftly dismissed. The US also abolished the untenably totalitarian Thought Control section, as well as the Economic and Welfare sections. The rump police force turned out to be woefully inadequate for internal security, and a new constabulary was to be organized. In January 1946 the first recruiting stations opened, and by the end of the month the first battalion of the first regiment of the Korean Constabulary was raised. An American colonel served as the chief of constabulary, and the force recruited primarily from among the paramilitary security organizations that had emerged after the chaos of the Japanese surrender. By the end of April, the Constabulary had around two thousand men. That September the US had planned to convert its role to purely advisory, but in practice American officers continued to command the force. The US pushed for the Constabulary to have operational autonomy within the Korean security apparatus and become relatively self-sufficient.[18]

With the creation of the militarized Constabulary, the National Police were designated a civilian force in March 1946. The two organizations would not forge a harmonious relationship and instead clashed frequently over jurisdictional matters. Despite its status as an American creature, the Constabulary did not immediately grow into a reliable instrument of American influence. The hasty recruitment of the Constabulary had in fact resulted in a considerable infiltration of the force by communist sympathizers. In October 1948, shortly after the formal transfer of sovereignty by the occupational authorities, a rebellion within the Fourteenth Regiment of the Constabulary broke out at Yosu. The mutiny was the result of communist penetration of the noncommissioned officers in the regiment. Loyal constabulary and police units were used to put down the mutiny after it spread to several other towns. After two days of heavy fighting, the remaining mutineers fled to mountains in the north and began a guerrilla struggle against the regime. After the insurrection, a US-supported purge of some fifteen hundred suspected communists from the constabulary was carried out.[19]

Even after the suspected communists were removed, the American advisers had reservations about the reliability of the Korean armed forces. Advisers noted that "political connections rather than ability" had influenced appointments to high command positions. US advisers exerted pressure where they could to eliminate incompetent officers. The US military administration had already come to an end with the formal transfer of sovereignty on August 15, 1948. On August 24, the ROK and the US signed a military agreement that spelled out gradual assumption of full control of the Korean Constabulary by the government in Seoul. In the meantime, operational control of Korean forces remained in the hands of the US armed forces. The formal structure of the US advising mission changed as well, and the Provisional Military Advisory Group (PMAG) was formed. With the change in status came an increase in size, from 100 to 241 advisers. However, the simultaneous expansion of the Korean Constabulary offset the greater adviser-to-native-forces ratio. While theoretically each division, regiment, and battalion had an American adviser embedded alongside a Korean counterpart, in practice the PMAG "never attained such comprehensive coverage of the Korean Army." The PMAG would become the US Military Advisory Group to the Republic of Korea (KMAG) in July 1949. With the shift in the American role to an advisory one, American combat troops began to depart Korea, despite pleas from Rhee for a large force to remain. US combat forces finally withdrew in June 1949.[20]

Soon after independence, Korean officials had already begun to refer to the Constabulary as the "National Defense Army," to the chagrin of their American patrons. In December 1948 the defense forces were reorganized, and the constabulary brigades were transformed into army divisions in the newly christened Republic of Korea Army (ROKA). The ROKA was structured very much like the army of its American patron. The US PMAG also established the Korean Military Academy (KMA), as well as seven other specialized military schools. The KMA explicitly emulated the US Military Academy at West Point. A Command and General Staff College was established in September 1949. By June 1950, these army schools had graduated 9,126 officers and 11,112 enlisted soldiers. While American efforts to build an effective Korean army were therefore extensive, US advising to the Korean police was relatively minimal. In 1950 before the war, there were only four KMAG police advisers.[21]

The American-built army was soon to face a far more challenging test than that posed by the low-grade guerrilla insurgency. On June 25, 1950, North Korean forces attacked and quickly swept across South Korea. The attack had caught the ROKA "in the midst of its building program." This action transformed Korea from a "relatively minor interest for the United States to one that was, front and center, part of the Cold War." The North Korean invasion brought direct US intervention, and the United States "helped build the ROK army into one of the largest in the world." The initial North Korean attack devastated the ROKA. What remained of the force regrouped along the Busan perimeter in August 1950 as American and allied forces intervened to save the beleaguered force and its American advisers. Under the tutelage of another large American combat deployment and in a baptism of fire, the Korean forces were once again rebuilt. In the eyes of American advisers, the Korean army by the end of the war was "radically different from that of 1950 or even 1951." It was an army greatly expanded and now tested by battle. It shed blood alongside the American intervention force, and its postwar strength far exceeded its prewar size.[22]

The US commitment to Korea continued and in some ways was strengthened after the war. A Mutual Defense Treaty was signed on October 1, 1953, massive military and economic aid was granted ($5.8 billion in grants and loans from 1955 to 1967), US combat forces remained, and tactical nuclear weapons were deployed from 1958 to 1991. US aid funded "much of the South Korean state budget." Perhaps most remarkably, the United States retained "operational command of all forces—Korean as well as U.S.—deployed for defense against an attack from the north." But the US relationship with its client dictator grew even more strained after the war. Rhee had "infuriated the US government" when he refused to sign the Korean War armistice in 1953. The US was so concerned with Rhee and the chance he might restart hostilities with the North that the Americans drafted a contingency plan (Operation Everready) to remove Rhee from power. The plan included strategies to maintain the US position in Korea if a variety of contingencies were to occur, including if the government or army proved "unresponsive" to American directives, as well as measures such as relieving "disloyal ROK commanders" and arresting "dissident military and civilian leaders."[23]

The Korean Army emerged from the war not only with a more lethal military organization but also a more pronounced esprit de corps and a profound skepticism toward its civilian leaders. The Korean Army was led after the war by a "nucleus of nationalist officers who were highly trained in technical areas and confident of their superiority to other groups in Korean society. The reformist zeal, ability, and power of these officers had, by the late fifties, paved the way for military government." Moreover, having shed their blood alongside American troops, these Korean officers felt they had a "special friendship with the U.S. military."[24]

The US-organized, -trained, and -advised Korean Army would rule Korea for much of the remaining years of the Cold War. A force designed as a nonpartisan and professional military that would remain outside politics proved durably praetorian. Institutions built by American advisers for one purpose were used for another. This was far from unique to Korea. In Iraq after 2003, US troops that had been deployed to organize a military intelligence section found the Iraqis had a very Soviet understanding of the role of military intelligence. One US adviser recalled that to the Iraqis, "military intelligence is keeping track of what's going on in your unit, not finding and telling the commander how best to kill the enemy." Iraqi officers from the Saddam Hussein era were focused on military *counterintelligence* in the sense common to dictatorships, in effect focused more on the political reliability of troops, in contrast to the US version of military intelligence, which focused on the capabilities and intentions of enemy forces. The United States viewed "authoritarian police systems" as likely to undermine support for governments and exacerbate rather than alleviate the challenge posed by communist subversion. Where Soviet-style partisan structures existed in armies supported by the United States, advisers pushed allies to remove these political controls over the army.[25]

The issues with building a "mirror image" army in the developing world have been long highlighted by scholars and practitioners. Building an army designed to fight a large, conventional neighbor in combined arms warfare has been cited as a critical error in the American efforts to build a viable South Vietnamese army and the Afghan army after 2002. Critics of the perils of mirroring American military institutions abroad have offered many such examples. However, the problems that arose from building a mirror-image force were manifested not just in poor battlefield effectiveness. Such armies also posed civil-military challenges for client governments. Building powerful, autonomous, and professional militaries dramatically upset the balance of power between dictators and their security apparatus. It engendered efforts by nervous autocrats to stymie this process, as well as coups by officers seeking to protect and enhance their autonomy and new professional ethos from political meddling. Autocrats who sought American support were not unaware of this problem. America's friendly tyrants accepted American help in building up their military capacity to contain the threat of communism yet cast a nervous gaze on their strengthening officer corps. To pre-empt any future disloyalty, they promoted political allies to sensitive commands and elevated institutional rivals to the army to guard against coups. These actions angered those officers who were gaining power thanks to American arms and training and who witnessed autocratic behavior that clashed with the ethos promoted by their US trainers. When American-trained armies ousted their authoritarian rulers, the United States accepted these coups d'état as faits accomplis.[26]

Short of a direct military intervention to reverse a coup, the United States had few options other than to accept a successful coup d'état. Coups are often swift, and half of all coups since 1950 have not involved any fatalities. Once the coup makers have removed the current leader and exerted control over key state institutions, options for the United States to reverse the outcome are limited. American policymakers were frequently approached about providing support to countercoups, but such operations were highly risky. It is often difficult to determine the prospects for would-be coup leaders to actually succeed in their proposed plots, and a failed, American-backed countercoup could dramatically sour relations with the new regime. Sanctions against the coup makers were also impractical, as American policymakers had identified a geostrategic interest in maintaining a friendly regime in power in that state. Threats to cut off aid could result in the realignment of that government away from the United States and toward its Soviet rivals. Consider the reaction of the United States to the bloody 1980 coup in Liberia. Master Sergeant Samuel

Doe led a coup against William Tolbert that culminated in the gruesome execution of the deposed president, along with nearly thirty others. This was followed with the mass execution by firing squad of most of Tolbert's cabinet on a beach in Monrovia. These events were met with strong displeasure from the United States. Yet after a brief period of distancing itself from the new regime, the US resumed paying government payrolls and even increased its military and economic aid to the new Doe regime. The stability of a longtime and avowedly anticommunist ally would ultimately trump American disdain for the bloody repression of the nakedly authoritarian military regime.[27]

THE UNITED STATES BUILT MIRROR-IMAGE FORCES ABROAD IN friendly regimes. This may have suited certain American foreign policy priorities, but it also led to unintended consequences for the durability of allied regimes. American-built armies proved highly praetorian and threatened their own governments with their capacity to carry out coups d'état. They were powerful internal political rivals that allied autocrats had a difficult time subverting and undermining. The officer corps was populated by US-trained officers who were confident their American allies would support their coups against repressive and retrograde rulers. Once built, these armies did not behave in the ways their American patrons or ruling regimes expected.

In the next chapters we examine in greater detail how these Soviet- and American-created militaries and security forces behaved toward their own client governments. By tracing how they behaved during periods of intense political crisis, it becomes clear that US allies were highly vulnerable to their own militaries and enjoyed limited US support in countering the threat of coups. Officers were generally correct in their wagers that their American patrons would support their coups if successfully presented as faits accomplis to a superpower ally that was more concerned with anticommunism and stability than democracy. By contrast, Soviet allies enjoyed the support of ruthless internal security services that helped quash incipient coup plots and fought ferociously against coup attempts. These regimes received help subordinating their armies to their rule and found these Soviet-style institutions functioned effectively in protecting their rule from their internal rivals.

5 | COMMISSARS AND COUPS

S oviet military and security service advisers brought with them new institutions designed to secure the rule of friendly regimes. Advisers helped Moscow export orthodox Soviet institutions to friendly regimes in the hopes that such institutions would entrench these revolutionary governments and defend the gains made by such alliances against anticommunist subversion. Parties, politburos, ministries of internal affairs, state security services, and political commissariats were dutifully established. Yet these institutional imports did not just copy the formal organization of Soviet political order. They really worked in some very important ways for the stability of allied regimes.

The USSR was remarkably successful in building internal security services in allied regimes, preventing military insubordination that might threaten the survival of the government. Some of these success stories are particularly surprising, as they occurred in places we would least expect. With Soviet help, regimes were able to extend their control over militaries that predated the regime's seizure of power and had every incentive to resist their own transformation into partisan armies. Without the role played by the

Soviet Union, these armies would have had the power to resist such encroachments. Two case studies provide particularly stark illustrations of the critical role played by Soviet assistance in consolidating the rule of pro-Soviet regimes under extremely challenging circumstances.

In Afghanistan, the Soviet Union's radical Marxist-Leninist allies faced the daunting prospect of exerting party control over the army they inherited after their surprise coup d'état. The People's Democratic Party of Afghanistan (PDPA) offers a very improbable instance of party control of the armed forces and regime durability more generally. The PDPA came to power extremely weak, with little organized popular support and a tenuous grip over the armed forces. While the Soviet Union would eventually intervene in Afghanistan directly with its own combat forces, for two critical periods the Soviet role was limited to aid, arms, and advisers. From May 1978 until December 1979, Kabul received Soviet assistance but was not occupied by the Soviet army. After the withdrawal of Soviet troops in February 1989 until the collapse of the regime in April 1992, the Soviet presence was again relegated to the provision of assistance and advice.

THE PEOPLE'S DEMOCRATIC PARTY OF AFGHANISTAN SEIZED power in a military coup on April 27, 1978, in what was later termed the "Saur Revolution" after the Dari name for the month of the putsch. The party had been founded in January 1965 and, like many clandestine socialist parties, was riven by factions. These factional differences led to a split two years later. One faction, Khalq ("the people" or "the masses"), was led by Nur Muhammad Taraki. The other, Parcham ("the banner") was led by Babrak Karmal. Both men would eventually lead Afghanistan. The small size of Afghanistan's industrial class led the PDPA to recruit among the armed forces. Soldiers had beat the party to the job of organizing a clandestine network in the armed forces, forming the Army Revolutionary Organization several months before the PDPA. Many members of this secret military organization joined the party. Not long after the PDPA began to recruit among the army, a military coup would elevate the political importance of the army considerably. On July 17, 1973, the Afghan military overthrew King Mohammed Zahir Shah. The bloodless coup was organized by the king's cousin, the former defense minister Mohammed Daoud Khan. Daoud had been relegated to the political wilderness nearly a decade earlier, and his coup succeeded only after securing the participation of the increasingly powerful communist networks in the army. In exchange for their cooperation, PDPA-aligned officers were granted prominent positions in the new regime. Perhaps unsurprisingly, this alliance proved short-lived. Fearful of the political ambitions of the communist officers, Daoud began to purge the two factions of the party from the army and banned the PDPA entirely after 1974.[1]

Leaders of a hunted and illegal party, Parcham and Khalq reunited in 1977 after resolving their factional differences at the insistence of Soviet officials who had taken an interest in the emerging communist party of their neighbor. The party continued to recruit among soldiers and officers. After the reunification, Taraki was made general secretary of the party; his Khalq faction members had achieved the greatest success in recruiting among the soldiers. The recruitment drive was aided by the passive attitude of many noncommunist officers, who did little to hinder the party's efforts. At this time, the party was in regular contact with Soviet intelligence services. KGB officers in Kabul had been approached by the PDPA with the news that the party was ready to seize power from Daoud in a coup. Soviet officials, however, sought to dissuade the party from any coup attempt, viewing the action as premature and likely to fail and destroy the party. KGB officers informed Taraki at a meeting in Kabul that they had information suggesting "irresponsible elements" within his faction were planning an armed uprising against Daoud. They conveyed that it was "the opinion of the CPSU Central Committee that this is dangerous for the party and all left-wing forces." They also warned Taraki that, if aware of these "extremists," he should "influence them and not allow any oversights that could harm the world communist movement."[2]

KGB fears turned out to be partially misplaced: it was Daoud's actions, not the Afghan communists, that precipitated their coup d'état. On April 17, 1978, after a secret PDPA meeting in Kabul, a prominent party member, Mir Akbar Khaibar, was assassinated. While his slaying has remained something of a mystery, it was likely carried out by anticommunist Islamist groups who feared an eventual PDPA takeover. Nevertheless, the party blamed Daoud. A large street demonstration accompanied Khaibar's funeral, and the illegal communist party brought as many as fifteen thousand to the streets in a considerable show of strength. Knowing full well the party had been earnestly recruiting in the army and fearing a PDPA coup, Daoud preemptively struck against the party. At first, it appeared he may have succeeded. Most of the top leadership of the party, including Taraki and Karmal, were arrested on the evening of April 26. The next day, however, the PDPA struck back. Two party members who were mid-ranking officers in the Afghan army that led critical troop commands—Lieutenant Colonel Abdul Qadir and Captain Aslam Watanjar—led a coup against Daoud.

Unlike the swift and bloodless 1973 coup, this putsch was extremely bloody. Daoud's Republican Guard and loyal troops in the Seventh Division fought viciously against Qadir and Watanjar. As many as fifteen hundred soldiers were killed in a single day. Resistance began to falter when rank-and-file communists in the Seventh Division learned it was the PDPA behind the coup. While noncommunists still dominated the army, much of the force remained uninvolved in the heavy fighting near the palace.

After the dust settled and as destroyed tanks and dead soldiers littered the streets, it was Lieutenant Colonel Abdul Qadir
who stood at the center. President Daoud was unceremoni-
ously shot in the palace and buried in a mass grave. Declaring
a military-revolutionary committee led by himself, Qadir set
about freeing the imprisoned party leadership. Two days later, he
stepped down and handed power to a newly formed Revolutionary Council led by the Khalqi leader Taraki. Taraki then declared
the formation of the Democratic Republic of Afghanistan.[3]

The coup took foreign governments, including the Soviet
Union, by surprise. American intelligence did not know about the
coup beforehand and reported the next day that "Afghan President
Daoud may have been overthrown and replaced by a leftist military government, although the situation remains highly fluid and
confused." Moreover, "while the Soviets are no doubt watching
events in Kabul with great interest, we have no indication that they
were directly involved in or aware in advance of the coup attempt."
Soviet sources support this assessment. Despite its long-standing
ties to the PDPA, the Soviet Union was not aware of the coup plot
before it began and was surprised by its success. As mentioned
above, Soviet intelligence had in fact sought to dissuade the PDPA
from any coup planning shortly before the coup. Using Russian
sources, Vasilii Stepanovich Khristoforov writes that the Afghan
revolution occurred "without any initiative and support from the
Soviet Union." The head of KGB foreign intelligence, Vladimir
Aleksandrovich Kryuchkov, remarked that "few expected a revolution in Afghanistan, especially a revolution that from the very
beginning proclaimed socialist goals." While the Soviets approvingly referred to the coup as a revolution, they knew this had been a
coup and not a popular revolution (*narodnaya revolyutsiya*).[4]

While the PDPA had defeated Daoud and triumphantly
declared their people's republic, they faced formidable challenges
in consolidating power in the face of a bitter intraparty rivalry and

an army with a wide array of political sympathies. Luckily for the new Afghan leaders, help was on the way. Despite the Soviets' surprise and reservations, their assistance began soon after the coup. By May, advisers had arrived to help the PDPA reorganize its security services. When the Soviet general Vasily Zaplatin arrived in Kabul, Taraki's deputy (and future leader) Hafizullah Amin told him that "we need political organs [*politorgani*] like you have. No need to change anything. Exactly as you have it." Throughout the summer, more advisers began to arrive, along with a flurry of aid agreements. Two areas saw critical Soviet institutional assistance: a political apparatus for the army and new internal security services.[5]

An early priority for the regime and its Soviet patrons was to create an expansive new intelligence and security service modeled on the KGB. The first security service, established just days after the Saur Revolution, was the Department for Safeguarding the Interests of Afghanistan (AGSA). AGSA was reorganized in September 1979 as the Workers' Intelligence Department (KAM), and as the State Information Service (Khadamat-e Aetla'at-e Dawlati, KhAD) after the Soviet intervention. While it would later be renamed the more orthodox Ministry of State Security (WAD), KhAD was the name that stuck with the soon-to-be feared organization. Like their KGB counterparts, KhAD operated counterintelligence agents in all branches and levels of the armed forces. Also like the organization after which it was designed, KhAD was a sizable military force in its own right. It maintained combat units with a total personnel strength of twenty thousand to twenty-seven thousand in May 1988 (compared to forty thousand in the army). KhAD would ultimately be viewed by the Soviets as the crowning jewel of their institution building in Afghanistan. It was, in Moscow's view, the most functional part of the Afghan state. It was the revolution's "sharp sword" and "flourished" under KGB guidance. With the aid of advisers from the Soviet Ministry of Internal Affairs (MVD), the new regime also received help establishing the Sarandoy (Pashto for "Defenders"), a paramilitary security service in the interior ministry. The Soviet MVD deployed some five thousand advisers in the Sarandoy, which, like the KhAD, grew into a formidable force, with as many as twenty thousand members by May 1988.[6]

In addition to these new security services, the Soviet Union helped the PDPA establish party control over the army. Political commissars were introduced shortly after the Saur Revolution. It was an early priority for the Soviet mission to build a political department and a network of political officers to "bring the army units under political control." Political commissars were embedded in each unit, and party cells joined the commissars to recruit soldiers into the party and help the commissars monitor the units. The efforts to penetrate the army were ultimately successful: by the mid-1980s around 80 percent of military officers were members of the party or the party's youth wing. In addition to solidifying party control, the Soviet Union devoted considerable energy to unifying the Khalq and Parcham factions at higher levels. Party unity was a consistent but often futile priority of Soviet advisers. While many Soviet advisers were in fact skeptical of the prospects for socialism in Afghanistan, they nevertheless set about establishing the institutions of Marxist-Leninist rule.[7]

The PDPA faced tremendous challenges to its rule both inside and outside the regime. With party leadership explicitly modeling their revolution on the Bolshevik example, the PDPA sought the "total reshaping of Afghan society and politics" after coming to power and pursued "sweeping, radical changes." A program of "radical socioeconomic reforms" was announced in early May 1978. The new rulers sought to "eliminate or neutralize" the "tribal aristocracy." While the new regime trod somewhat lightly around Islam, isolated acts of violence against mullahs and mosques were carried out with increasing regularity by PDPA cadres. In private conversations with Soviet officials, PDPA leaders were more explicit about their goals. The new regime sought to build "social-ism on the Soviet model." When the head of KGB foreign intelli-gence met with General Secretary Taraki in July 1978, he was told that "what the Soviet Union had done in sixty years [in its own land] in Afghanistan would be done in five." A bewildered Vlad-imir Kryuchkov was told that if he were to come back in a year, he would see that "the mosques will be empty." Contrary to popu-lar belief, at this point Soviet foreign policy was largely focused on reining in overly radical clients. The radicalism of the Lenin years had long since dissipated in the Soviet Union itself, and Khrush-chev's adventurism and brinksmanship was replaced by stagnation and stability under Brezhnev (1964–1982). Soviet advisers therefore looked at such statements with alarm and tried in vain to moderate their ambitious and increasingly beleaguered Afghan clients.[8]

The radical social and economic policies and the coercion that accompanied even potentially popular changes like land reform cratered whatever popular support the regime had upon coming to power. Contemporaneous US intelligence reports assessed that the regime had "no widespread popular support" and a particular lack of approval among religious conservatives. This view was vin-dicated by the onset of what would ultimately prove to be a power-ful (and soon US-aided) Islamist insurgency as early as June. Based as it was in a predominately rural and largely conservative society, this insurgency posed a serious challenge to Kabul's increasingly isolated communist rulers.[9]

Rather than moderate in the face of resistance, however, the regime doubled down. In February 1979, the PDPA "destroyed" the "most influential national religious leadership" by executing seventy male members of a prominent religious family (the Mujad-didi). At the same time, the PDPA security services executed the members of Islamist movements they inherited in Daoud's pris-ons. Things continued to spiral out of control. That same month, a mass uprising involving as many as two hundred thousand people took over the key western city of Herat, hunting down party members and killing as many as fifty Soviet advisers. The local garrison proved incapable and unwilling to put down the uprising, and forces had to be brought in from elsewhere to crush the insurrection.[10]

The other challenges to consolidating the revolution were internal. Rhetoric notwithstanding, the PDPA came to power through a coup rather than a popular revolution. As a result, the party "inherited the state institutions of the old regime more or less intact." In part because the party used the army to come to power, the military was the most pressing political problem for the new regime. As the army was the "main pillar of the regime," the removal of its support could bring the entire edifice crumbling down. One immediate concern was the noncommunist senior officers. Some had resisted the coup, but many others had reacted passively, waiting to see who would come out on top. The bulk of the army, in fact, did not participate in the coup at all. The coup leaders—Qadir and Watanjar—were of relatively junior ranks.[11]

Despite these challenges, the PDPA did have several strengths coming into power. Given the dangerous and clandestine nature of its recruitment efforts, it was extremely successful in enlisting military officers and men into the party. By the time of the coup, one expert estimated that approximately 30 percent of the officer corps were party members. While this was an enormous achievement, it still left the majority of Afghan army officers outside the party. The army was also rife with other political factions: while many of the royalists had been purged after Daoud's coup five years earlier, the army still had plenty of Daoud sympathizers, Islamists, and Maoists hostile to the Soviet Union–aligned PDPA. The first priority for the party was the republican officers close to Daoud. Some had been killed alongside their leader during the actual coup, and soon after all but two of the sixty-two serving generals were arrested, forced to retire, or shot. Their replacements were PDPA members of much more junior rank. This amounted to a considerable shift in the army hierarchy.[12]

Such turmoil in the army was unsurprisingly not devoid of controversy. US intelligence at the time viewed changes in the military as the single most pressing problem for the PDPA. An August 1978 assessment noted that "disillusionment within the military could eventually prove more dangerous to President Taraki's regime than the dissatisfaction of either rightwing opposition groups or tribal dissidents." This disaffection was more likely "if Taraki's policies appeared to be anti-Muslim or if the regime allied itself too closely with the Soviet Union. Continued actions against the tribesmen—some of whom are relatives of military officers— could also provoke a military coup." Further, the attempts to introduce a Soviet-style political apparatus in the army were generating more grievances. The CIA noted that Taraki had purged the army of suspected opponents, introduced mandatory indoctrination, and began "close civilian supervision of officer assignments down to the brigade level." Moreover, despite (or because of) the army's role in bringing the party to power, the PDPA had publicly sought to "downgrade the military's contribution to the April revolution." This "pillar" of the regime was increasingly viewed as a threat to the political leadership, who wished to subordinate the army to the party.[13]

The purges of the army did not stop with non-PDPA officers associated with the ancien régime. Fear of counterrevolution soon came for the most sensitive officers in the army: those who had made the revolution possible. Qadir, who had been made minister of defense after the coup, was accused of coup plotting against the regime and was arrested along with two hundred other officers in August 1978. This plot was corroborated by "confessions" procured after torture, and several of the alleged plotters were killed by their interrogators. Soviet advisers tried in vain to stop the purge. The arrest of Qadir further aggrieved the military officers, who were "already unhappy about the influx of Soviet advisers and fighting against the Pathan [Pashtun] tribes." As the survival of the regime depended "almost entirely on the military," such actions were highly risky. At this early and fragile period, the loyalties of the officer corps were "uncertain." US intelligence even believed "one or more attempted countercoups" were "probable." Yet counteracting this serious threat of a military reaction to attempts to reshape the army was the increased Soviet presence. The CIA viewed the "expanded" Soviet presence as providing Moscow with "an increased capability to intervene militarily on short notice, if it should decide to do so in the future to protect a pro-Soviet government in Kabul."[14]

The purges and personnel turnover in the army affected the intra-PDPA factional balance. With Khalqis dominating the top leadership positions after the coup, Parchami officers were passed over for promotions. Within days of the Saur Revolution, Parchami officers had begun to organize a coup that was ultimately never attempted. Turmoil within the ruling Khalq faction accelerated the purges. President Taraki had grown increasingly disaffected from his protégé and key regime leader, Hafizullah Amin. Tensions culminated in a plot to have Amin captured or possibly killed. However, Amin outmaneuvered the plot and instead had Taraki arrested and smothered to death with a pillow. Soviet officials were alarmed by the infighting and very displeased with the ascent of Amin, an individual they had come to distrust. Pro-Taraki army officers attempted to remove Amin from power, but their putsch failed. Amin responded with a ruthless campaign to rid the army and security services of rivals. In addition to and in part because of these bloody party factional battles, the Afghan armed forces were performing poorly in the escalating counterinsurgency. To add to Moscow's growing list of grievances, Amin was feeling out the United States and attempting to normalize relations. The Soviet Union finally answered Amin's repeated entreaties for Soviet intervention, but it was not the outcome he might have expected. On December 27, 1979, Soviet special forces stormed the Tajbeg Palace, killed Amin, and whisked Babrak Karmal from exile into power. By the time Amin was ousted from power by Moscow, however, the officer corps "might have experienced a 90 per cent turnover," and the army was less than half the size it had been before the revolution. This was a remarkable self-immolation, which greatly alarmed Kabul's patrons in Moscow.[15]

The Soviet intervention marked the beginning of the Soviet war in Afghanistan, but at the time it was not clear that this would be the outcome. The Soviet intervention was not intended to herald the deployment of Soviet combat forces for direct fighting on behalf of the beleaguered PDPA regime. Instead, the goal was simply to remove a troublesome client ruler and shift the balance of power within the party toward the hopefully more reliable Karmal and the Parcham faction. Shortly after the intervention, the Soviet ambassador to the United States, Anatoly Dobrynin, asked the foreign minister Andrei Gromyko, "Why did they bring troops into Afghanistan, since we will have a big fight with the Americans?" Gromyko reassured his subordinate that "it's only for a month. We'll do everything and leave quickly." This was of course shown to be exceptionally wishful thinking. Soviet policymakers found their clients in Kabul to be far weaker than anticipated and in need of much more prolonged Soviet assistance to rebuild their security organs and fight the expanding insurgency.[16]

Like all advisory missions, the Soviet mission was plagued by issues stemming from insufficient preparation. Many Soviet officers had only a "vague idea" about the "country, its customs, traditions, way of life, religion" and about "the work of an advisor in a foreign army." Officers in the Soviet Union deployed as advisers came with their own educational backgrounds and sought to transform Afghanistan "on the basis of Marxism-Leninism, which often did not coincide with Afghan realities." As Elizabeth Leake points out, "Even while many officials throughout the Soviet communist party remained skeptical as to whether the Soviet socialist model offered the best fit for Afghanistan, most nevertheless worked to replicate it, bereft of alternatives." In addition to insufficient training and their communist orthodoxy, Soviet advisers from different security organs—the KGB, GRU, MVD, and Ministry of Defense—sometimes found themselves on opposite sides of PDPA factional disputes as the two factions were unevenly represented in the different Afghan security forces that each Soviet service advised. Like the American intervention in South Vietnam, the intervention in Afghanistan would gradually come to drag in more and more Soviet personnel. It would soon become Moscow's largest military campaign since the Second World War. The Afghan war would ultimately cost 13,000 Soviet lives (with 40,000 wounded), and 800,000 to 1.2 million dead Afghans. This death toll would be the highest faced by Russian troops after World War II until the 2022 invasion of Ukraine.[17]

While Soviet advisers had quietly assumed some operational command over Afghan military forces as early as August 1979, the Soviet intervention brought a marked increase in Moscow's direct organization of the military campaign against the multiple groups of Pakistan- and US-backed Islamist insurgents. Soviet advisers "attached to Afghan units" controlled the "administrative and operational activities" and even made "all decisions concerning operations, organization, promotions, and transfers of officers." Soviet efforts to build up the effectiveness of Afghan security forces during the war were uneven. Despite years of effort, Moscow could not build a politically reliable Afghan air force capable of surviving on its own. Desertions continued to plague the army, and the Afghan state was an archipelago of cities loosely projecting power into the surrounding countryside. This patchwork state nevertheless continued to hold the major cities as Soviet aid poured into government coffers. Recognizing the quagmire in which they found themselves, Soviet policymakers sought a viable exit from Afghanistan. These plans accelerated with the ascent of Mikhail Gorbachev. Soviet troops ultimately left Afghanistan on February 15, 1989, almost a decade after the nearly two thousand tanks and almost one hundred thousand soldiers under the Fortieth Army had rumbled across the Soviet border.[18]

The Soviet withdrawal was widely viewed as heralding the imminent collapse of the regime. Before the withdrawal, US intelligence had assessed that the "Afghan regime will probably collapse within six to twelve months following the departure of Soviet forces from Afghanistan." This prediction eerily presaged the analysis of US intelligence agencies several decades later about the predicted longevity of America's own client state in Afghanistan. However, both predictions were off by considerable margins. The Soviet client government long outlasted expectations, surviving until April 1992, nearly four more years. This remarkable longevity even outlasted its patron: by the end of December 1991, the Soviet Union itself did not exist. By contrast, the American client government in Kabul did not even last until the withdrawal of American troops.[19]

The survival of the Soviet-assisted government in Kabul after the withdrawal of Soviet troops can be attributed to multiple factors, including the simultaneous decline in American, Saudi, and Pakistani aid to its opponents and continued Soviet economic and military aid. But in part the regime's resilience reflected the successful construction of internal security institutions capable of preventing its disgruntled military from carrying out a coup. While this is in some ways a story of political instability, it is also one of surprising resilience. Thanks to a Soviet-assisted internal security apparatus, the PDPA regime survived far longer than we might have expected, given its monumental challenges and brutal behavior. Some might argue that repression alone can help explain the survival of the Afghan communist regime. But repression is as much a puzzle as an explanation. Repression requires establishing control over a security apparatus reliably enough to use violence to stave off challengers. For the PDPA, this control came thanks to Soviet help.[20]

The Soviet withdrawal prompted several changes in the Afghan security apparatus. Mohammed Najibullah, a longtime PDPA member who had led the Afghan secret police, was tapped by Moscow to replace Karmal in 1986. Ever the chekist, Najibullah feared a military coup after the departure of Soviet troops. He strengthened his Special Guard, an institution meant to protect the party leader. Changes to the Special Guard constituted a dramatic transformation, as it had previously not been a major institution. It formed the "embryo of a second army" after 1989 and was renamed the National Guard. In addition to this strengthened palace guard, the regime channeled Soviet assistance into the Sarandoy and the Ministry of State Security (WAD), the renamed KhAD secret police organization.[21]

The strengthening of the paramilitary force, praetorian guard, and security service came at the expense of the beleaguered army. Throughout the summer of 1989, rumors circulated that there was a planned coup against Najibullah. Najibullah's former agency, WAD, successfully uncovered this plot. In August, 127 officers were arrested by WAD agents. This successful raid did not stop the coup, however. On March 6, 1990, ahead of the trial of the plotters, Defense Minister Shahnawaz Tanai launched a coup. The rebellion very nearly succeeded. Airstrikes from planes loyal to Tanai pounded government installations in Kabul in an attempt to kill Najibullah. As Najibullah huddled with other members of the politburo, a bomb landed on top of the palace, dropped by a pilot loyal to Tanai from a Soviet-built MiG-21. Interior Minister Watanjar, one of the leaders of the Saur Revolution, arrived at the bunker where Najibullah and the other politburo members had survived the bombing. Along with the WAD chief, Watanjar began to organize the defense of the regime. Watanjar mobilized troops from a motorized Sarandoy battalion and security troops from WAD to intercept the tank brigade Tanai had deployed to reach the presidential palace. After heavy fighting, the internal security services, created and armed for this very purpose, defeated the Fifteenth Tank Brigade. The coup collapsed, and Tanai fled to Pakistan.[22]

The security institutions established with Soviet help proved ultimately effective in preventing acts of military disloyalty from overthrowing the regime even under extremely challenging conditions. These institutions functioned even when we might expect them to be least successful: after the departure of Soviet troops and in a period of declining Soviet investment in supporting the communist regime. We might have expected the communist regime in Kabul to be highly vulnerable to a coup. It was unpopular, repressive, economically unsuccessful, and attacked entrenched social norms and hierarchies. It also was engaged in a failing war against multiple insurgent groups with powerful external supporters. Yet the regime was protected by a formidable Soviet-built security apparatus.

Najibullah and his fellow PDPA party members were not the only dictators who found Soviet support critical in establishing control over their armed forces. Ethiopia under its own Marxist-Leninist military government offers another clear illustration of the role played by Soviet military aid in establishing durable authoritarianism.

FEW MODERN DICTATORS HAVE DESERVED A COUP AS BADLY AS Mengistu Haile Mariam. The tyrannical Marxist-Leninist strongman of Ethiopia currently resides in Zimbabwe, safe from those who might enforce the ruling that he had committed genocide and other atrocities while in power. Mengistu oversaw military and economic disasters of unimaginable scale. His coercive land reform policies killed hundreds of thousands in famines. When his military campaigns against the much less formidable insurgent groups failed, he frequently executed his commanders on the spot. It was not popularity that kept Mengistu in power. Instead, he survived so long in such inhospitable conditions thanks to the formidable internal security apparatus and partisan military structure his Soviet advisers helped him build.

A career soldier with an obscure childhood that he rarely discussed, Mengistu rose through the Imperial Ethiopian Army despite a reputation for insubordination. He had attended three training programs in the United States, and by the time President Richard Nixon resigned from office, Mengistu had reached the rank of major. The year 1974 was to prove monumental for Major Mengistu. After an army mutiny that had begun that year in southern Ethiopia spread across the military, mass demonstrations protesting the government of Emperor Haile Selassie rocked Ethiopian cities. Mengistu joined other junior officers to coordinate the growing movement in the armed forces, helping found the Coordination Committee of the Armed Forces, the Police, and the Territorial Army, or the *Derg* ("Committee"), and forced the abdication of Haile Selassie in September.[23]

While a lieutenant general led the new regime, it was Major Mengistu who gradually emerged as the power behind the throne. With a key network of loyalists in the army, Mengistu would use his troop command to outmuscle his fellow coup makers. A man invariably described as determined, intelligent, well-spoken, and "quasi-messianic" about his responsibilities, Mengistu was a ruthless political operator who skillfully maneuvered against his opponents, real and imagined. A Soviet diplomat recalled his impression upon meeting the young officer that he was a "very resolute person," and Fidel Castro described him as "calm, intelligent, bold, and brave." On November 23, Mengistu ordered the arrest and summary execution of over sixty officials, including the chairman of the Derg, twenty-nine senior civilian officials, and twenty-three senior military officers. Just over two years later, Mengistu put a capstone on his power. On February 3, 1977, two weeks after Jimmy Carter was sworn in as president of the United States, residents of Addis Ababa, the capital of Ethiopia, could hear heavy gunfire from the headquarters of the Derg. After calling his ruling coalition to a meeting, Mengistu personally executed seven members of his top command on the spot. He was now the "undisputed leader of Ethiopia," and he had achieved his position under very challenging conditions. Not only did he face the more senior members of the military he had outflanked in his succession of bloody purges, but he faced powerful elites from the deposed imperial regime, a variety of highly mobilized revolutionary civilian opposition parties, multiple serious insurgencies, and a potent conventional military threat from his well-armed and irredentist Somali neighbors.[24]

The gradual accumulation of power by Mengistu was mirrored by the realignment of Ethiopia away from its former American patrons to the Soviet Union. Moscow played no role in the coup that brought the Derg to power, and the US-trained Ethiopian officers initially sought to keep American support. Unfortunately for the ambitious new leaders, their coup had come at an inopportune time. The US military communications facility in Kagnew had been rendered obsolete only a year prior. This considerably reduced the geostrategic value of a continued US-Ethiopian alliance. With a less critical stake in maintaining alignment, the US soured on the repressive new regime. American coolness was keenly felt in Addis Ababa, and Derg leadership instead turned to Moscow for support. The Soviet response was not immediately warm. In the recollection of a diplomat in the Soviet embassy, the "revolutionary potential" of Ethiopia was not considered particularly promising. The Soviets had expected the Selassie regime to retain the support of the armed forces and viewed the political backwardness of the population as a major hindrance to any revolution. US intelligence reported in October 1974 that they were aware of requests from the new rulers in Addis Ababa for Soviet aid. The US assessed that the Soviet response was "cautious," as Moscow was not yet convinced that supporting Ethiopia was worth jeopardizing its considerable investment in neighboring Somalia, an important client for the past several years.[25]

While initially skeptical over his communist bona fides, the Soviet mission began to warm to Mengistu and his self-proclaimed Marxism-Leninism. The Soviet diplomatic mission had come to see the seizure of power as something more "profound" than a mere military coup d'état. Yet as late as May 1976, Moscow was continuing to reject requests for military aid, as it was unsure of the Derg's stability and continued to harbor concerns about its own relationship with Somalia. The opportunity provided by an avowedly Marxist-Leninist regime in a large and strategically important African country soon proved too good to pass up. The day after Mengistu personally executed several key members of the Derg in February 1977, the Soviet and Cuban ambassadors held meetings with the new Derg chairman and expressed their support for him and his regime.[26]

This meeting was followed by a military aid agreement. Weapons began to arrive on Soviet transports in September. The first aid agreement was significant, worth around $507 million at the time, or over $2.3 billion in current US dollars. This was the largest Soviet military aid agreement with an African country, and more than twice what had been offered to Somalia in the previous decade. The alignment to Addis Ababa over Mogadishu was made very explicit, with advisers departing Somalia and heading straight for Ethiopia. Within months, nearly two thousand Soviet military and security advisers had arrived, and twelve to eighteen thousand Cuban combat troops accompanied them. US sources place the Soviet advisory mission below the figure given by Fantahun Ayele (using Ethiopian archival sources), but there is broad agreement that the USSR went from a nonexistent military

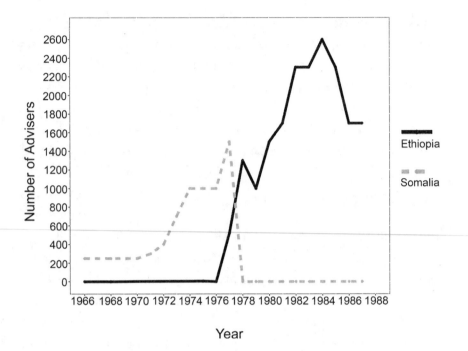

Figure 5. Soviet military advisers in Somalia and Ethiopia
(*Source:* Declassified CIA documents)

mission to the largest advisory deployment in sub-Saharan Africa thereafter. Moreover, the Cuban deployment was comparatively large: only Angola had a larger Cuban combat presence (thirty-five thousand in 1984). According to US sources, the Cuban force in Ethiopia reached its peak at over eleven thousand in 1982 and declined to three thousand three years later.[27]

The large Soviet advisory mission was not just to train Ethiopian soldiers on how to use specialized weaponry or service Soviet military deliveries. Instead, Soviet military advisers were "integrated into all elements of the Ethiopian army down through [the] brigade level."[28] A further indication of the importance given to aid to Ethiopia was the deployment of the Soviet ground forces commander general Vasily Ivanovich Petrov to oversee major operations against insurgent groups. Soviet advisers like Petrov planned operations directly and were "attached to Ethiopian military units in the field." The Soviet Union would ultimately provide enough material assistance to make the Ethiopian army the largest in sub-Saharan Africa, doling out over $9.5 billion in military aid to the regime.[29]

Mengistu's position as a key officer in the 1974 coup provided both great advantages and considerable risks. On the one hand, he commanded enough coercive power as an officer with an actual troop command to successfully outmaneuver civilian rivals for the post-Selassie political order. Yet his rivals and even his allies in the military posed a formidable challenge. They alone had the means to thwart his ascent. Luckily for Mengistu, he had the aid of the Soviet Union. With a patron willing and able to provide the expertise, resources, and cover for the creation of new internal security institutions, Mengistu set about building a Soviet-style security apparatus in earnest. The Soviet Union and its Eastern Bloc allies "extensively reshaped the Ethiopian intelligence apparatus." The key security service established with Soviet help was the Public Security Organization (PSO), the "primary intelligence gathering, counter-intelligence, and surveillance service." The PSO was established in August 1978 as the Ministry for Public Safety and Security until it was renamed the PSO in 1980. It was built in part on the old imperial intelligence service, but only after a thorough purge of the high-ranking officials from the old organization. Rank-and-file members were allowed to apply to join the PSO, and many did. Soviet KGB and East German Stasi personnel provided organizational assistance to the PSO immediately after its creation. Mengistu took a keen interest in the activities of the PSO. While it theoretically reported to the Ministry of Internal Affairs, in practice it was directly responsible to Mengistu and was led by Colonel Tesfaye Wolde Selassie, who was apparently the best man at Mengistu's wedding. The Derg chairman even personally approved all major operations.[30]

Within the PSO was the Military Security Organization (Wata-darawi Dehninet Tibaqa Dirijit, MSO), which was later renamed the Military Security Main Department (Watadarawi Dehninet Tibaqa Wana Mamria, MSMD). The MSO/MSMD was also cre-ated in 1980 with Soviet help. It was tasked with military counter-intelligence and monitoring the political reliability of the army. The security organ penetrated all branches of the military down to the squad. It was organized especially to "prevent coup attempts" and acted "as a kind of secret police within the armed forces." The MSO/MSMD was "very much disliked by the professionally ori-ented officers" and collected "information on the private lives and activities of the armed forces' personnel," claiming that "no detail was too minor to be noted." MSO/MSMD officers were attached directly to army units as military security personnel. They were "expected to protect the army from infiltration by insurgents, recruitment by foreign secret services" and to "control plots and mutinies" and stop desertions. Mengistu also was intensely inter-ested in this department of the PSO, and it was led until 1991 by a close longtime ally. Another military counterintelligence organiza-tion, the Military Intelligence Department (MID), was assisted by Soviet military intelligence. A military intelligence service under the army general staff had operated since the 1950s under the Selassie regime. After the Soviet Union began to support Mengistu, the MID underwent a reorganization. Like its Soviet counterpart, it remained under the military chain of command and reported to the chief of staff of the armed forces.[31]

In addition to these security services, the Soviet Union pres-sured the regime to create a vanguard party. This reflected Soviet beliefs that a party would provide the basis for a broader and more stable regime that would also provide a cadre of pro-Soviet elites and reduce Moscow's reliance on Mengistu alone. Mengistu resisted Soviet pressure for party building for the same reason the Soviets pressed him to build one. While he held out as long as he could, Moscow's willingness to bankroll his multiple wars and failing economy meant he couldn't ignore the Soviet entreaties forever. In September 1984, he finally established the Workers' Party of Ethiopia (WPE). The WPE was modeled closely on the Communist Party of the Soviet Union, and Moscow played a key role in designing its structures and policies as well as funding the training of some eighteen thousand cadres for the new party. Mengistu wasn't the only member of the regime who feared a powerful WPE, however. US intelligence reported that senior military officers viewed the party as "a threat to their power." Ultimately, however, Mengistu had little to fear from the WPE. Contrary to Soviet hopes, the party proved to ultimately serve as a highly personalized appendage to Mengistu's rule. It did not grow into an autonomous source of regime strength at either mass or elite levels, and instead amounted to the "personal tool of Mengistu." The party itself was dominated by senior military officers, and the upper echelons were all Mengistu allies. It was, in short, a closely controlled organization to ensure it "would pose little threat to the regime."[32]

While the party may not have constrained Mengistu, military officers at the more junior ranks were right to dread its establishment. The party accompanied Soviet-supported efforts to build an orthodox partisan army. Moves toward the establishment of a party army had predated Soviet support but accelerated considerably with the arrival of Soviet experts. Commissars were introduced early in the Ethiopian revolution, but the system was institutionalized with Soviet help in 1983 with the establishment of the Main Political Administration of the Revolutionary Armed Forces. Alongside the military counterintelligence officers of the MSO/MSMD, commissars played a key role in monitoring the armed forces. Like in other party armies, the commissars were intensely disliked by the professional officers. Commissars and their security service counterparts did not answer to the military commander and exacerbated the acrimony by frequently interfering in commander-issued decisions and reporting officer misbehaviors up the party chain of command.[33]

The Ethiopian armed forces were organized along an extreme form of the typical Soviet system, locally known as "triangular command." Ethiopian military units were led by the simultaneous command of three separate institutions: the MSO/MSMD military counterintelligence officers, the political commissars, and the regular military commanders. In theory, these three officers all had separate responsibilities and "were supposed to forge a harmonious working relationship." In practice, "the triangular command structure bred mistrust, mutual recrimination, and conflict." It is difficult to establish whether these intrusive security institutions and mechanisms of regime control could have been established without Soviet help. However, US intelligence did assess that it was the presence of Cuban combat troops that discouraged coup plotters while these institutions were first established. US intelligence further assessed that Ethiopian officers did indeed view these measures—commissar creation, embedded secret police, and the creation of a ruling party—as direct threats to their personal and collective interests.[34]

These security services played a key role in Mengistu's improbably long tenure. Mengistu survived in office for years against seemingly insurmountable odds. In large part this reflected the success of his Soviet patrons. Aided by a "pervasive" web of agents embedded in the army, Mengistu was able to monitor and remove disgruntled officers in his military. While it helped stave off elite challengers, Mengistu's meddling in the army severely undermined military performance. With their orders evaluated by political and security officers, his military commanders proved highly risk-averse and tactically inflexible. Mengistu's penchant for personally issuing orders and bypassing the chain of command meant officers often sat immobile waiting for instruction while insurgents laid waste to the much better-equipped Ethiopian army. For each failed offensive, Mengistu had more commanders executed for their alleged ineptitude or "counterrevolutionary" disloyalty. That a coup plot emerged against his regime was unsurprising. If anything, the surprise was how long it took to happen.[35]

The coup itself came at a bad time for Mengistu. Mikhail Gorbachev was growing tired of the drain on the Soviet economy that military and economic support for Ethiopia had created, particularly given the dismal returns. As a result, Mengistu would find his patron condemnably aloof when his military rose against him in May 1989. While protesters gathered in Tiananmen Square in Beijing, senior commanders in the Ethiopian army began an operation they hoped would result in the overthrow of Mengistu's regime. But Mengistu had the aid of the security services the Soviet Union had helped him build to forestall this very event. His military counterintelligence service uncovered the conspiracy and warned Mengistu of the coup plot. Mengistu's chief political commissar urged him to travel abroad during the planned strike and prepared a counterattack. When the senior military commanders gathered at the Ministry of Defense to begin the coup, they were met by the Soviet-built security services. While the plotters successfully killed the minister of defense, the capital was secured within hours. When Mengistu triumphantly returned home, he announced on the radio that his "revolutionary forces" would "liquidate" his enemies. Rebel forces continued to mutiny in northern garrisons until, after four days of heavy fighting, the security services and loyal troops subdued the rebel forces, killed their commander, and arrested hundreds of officers. After the coup collapsed, Mengistu had twelve generals executed for their participation. US intelligence noted after the coup that Mengistu's "East German–trained security forces" had "proved their effectiveness— the coup leaders are all dead, under detention, or in hiding."[36]

The durability of the Mengistu regime is surprising given the abysmal state of the economy, the devastation of multifront wars, and the extremely unpopular changes in the army he and his Soviet advisers pushed through. A ubiquitous security service ensured that Soviet military aid helped strengthen regime control over the armed forces rather than elevate a rival to his increasingly personalized regime. Safe from the threat of a coup, Mengistu was able to survive in office far longer than his abhorrent record as ruler should have allowed.

In both Afghanistan and Ethiopia, however, the system of political control that ensured the invulnerability of each dictatorship to a military coup d'état also played a role in weakening the battlefield effectiveness of the army. Both the PDPA regime in Afghanistan and the WPE in Ethiopia ultimately fell to the insurgent armies they battled for years. In Ethiopia, the complicated system of triangular command and the fear of purges had immobilized field commanders, who struggled to counter an increasingly sophisticated rebellion in the north. In Afghanistan, while the KhAD and the Sarandoy proved fairly effective organizations, the regular army was never able to gain the requisite military strength to defeat the insurgents. Struggles to build military effectiveness in client governments was not limited to the Soviet Union. Later, we turn to this problem in considerable length, considering the repeated failures of American advisers to build an effective military in Cambodia thanks to the interaction between military aid and the domestic politics of dictatorship.

6 | NONPARTISAN PRAETORIANS

The American effort to build a viable noncommunist regime in South Vietnam is perhaps the most studied intervention to prop up a friendly dictator in the entire Cold War. Though it isn't always thought of that way. The corpus of academic studies and archival sources on US support for Saigon is enormous and provides a wealth of information useful for the present study. In addition to the informational advantages, South Vietnam offers several analytical advantages. The regime under Ngo Dinh Diem (1954–1963) had American support from its very first days in office. American support did not arrive too late to make a difference in Saigon, but instead was a major factor in the trajectory of the regime throughout its tenure. Moreover, not only did the US directly fund government payrolls and provide military matériel, but American advisers played an extensive role in organizing South Vietnamese security forces. Despite the creeping American involvement under Diem's tenure, the deployment of combat troops did not occur until approximately two years after he was out of power. Therefore, South Vietnam under Diem was a classic client regime. As such, it provides us the ability to assess how the nature of support offered by the United States shaped South Vietnamese civil-military relations and regime survival.

The scale of US support to the Diem regime was staggering. By one "modest" measure, US economic aid to Saigon over the republic's entire existence amounted to $23.2 billion in current USD, with an additional $45.9 billion in military aid. Economic aid alone constituted, on average, about one-fourth of South Vietnam's entire gross national product. By the late 1950s, the US was supplying around 60 percent of government revenue. In 1955, there were already some seven hundred military advisers training South Vietnamese. By 1962, there were over ten thousand military advisers and two hundred intelligence officers advising their Vietnamese counterparts. After the full Americanization of the war in 1965 until the removal of US troops in 1973, some fifty-eight thousand US soldiers died and over three hundred thousand were wounded trying to support the American client government in Saigon. The total number of Vietnamese dead was over fifty times higher, with some three million killed, nearly two-thirds of whom were civilians. The US Air Force detonated more explosives in the war than in all of human history up to that point: equivalent to 450 of the atomic bombs dropped on Hiroshima during World War II.[1]

The Republic of Vietnam emerged out of France's failed war against the communist-led Vietnamese Independence League (Viet Nam Doc Lap Dong Minh, or Viet Minh) in an attempt to reclaim and hold on to its colonial possessions in Indochina. The United States had been largely indifferent to Indochina in the period immediately after the Second World War. While unsympathetic to French recolonization efforts after the Japanese defeat, American anticolonialism was tempered by a desire to see French power in Europe rebuilt, and the United States took a position of neutrality toward the conflict. The US position changed abruptly after the victory of Mao's communists in the Chinese Civil War in 1949 and the beginning of Chinese aid to Ho Chi Minh's Democratic Republic of Vietnam. Resolve to aid the French war effort hardened further after Kim Il Sung's forces poured over the thirty-eighth parallel into South Korea in June 1950. In an attempt to build a more legitimate protectorate and reduce popular support for decolonization and the Viet Minh, France declared the formation of an "independent" State of Vietnam on March 8, 1949, with the colonial-era monarch, Emperor Bao Dai, as its head.

However, this largely cosmetic decolonization fooled few: Paris retained control over foreign policy, security, and government finance. American officials were hardly enamored of Bao Dai or convinced by this sham sovereignty but nevertheless reluctantly extended US recognition of Vietnamese independence on February 7, 1950. US aid to Bao Dai and his French protectors began that year, with the establishment of a United States Military Assistance Advisory Group (MAAG) to the nominally independent state. US support grew as the French counterinsurgency efforts floundered. While ultimately deciding against a direct US intervention, Washington began to pour resources into French coffers. By 1954, the US was subsidizing nearly 80 percent of the cost of the war.[2]

Few US-backed autocrats have fallen from such high esteem to such disdain as Ngo Dinh Diem. Diem was born in 1901 as the son of a Catholic civil servant in French Indochina. Under Bao Dai, he rose to the position of interior minister in 1933. Diem's nationalist credentials were burnished when he resigned over French refusals to grant more autonomy to the indigenous administration. However, Diem stayed out of the French war to retain control over its colony in Indochina, leaving the country in 1950 for a self-imposed exile largely lived out in the United States. His American sojourn introduced him to American officials, who came to view him as a strong nationalist alternative to Bao Dai and one who could win real popular support. He also benefited from the low American opinion of the emperor. Never particularly enamored with foreign monarchs, American policymakers looked with reproach on the royals in much of Southeast Asia. It was at American insistence that Diem returned to his native Vietnam in June 1954 to take the reins of government as prime minister.[3]

When Ngo Dinh Diem arrived in Saigon on an American transport, he came as the anointed head of a government over which he exercised the most nominal of control. The leader of the Saigon station of the US Central Intelligence Agency reported to Washington that Diem had undisputed control over only his palace grounds. That was probably an exaggeration. Outside the walls, Diem had to contend with myriad serious challengers to his regime: armed politico-religious organizations ("the sects"), a French-built army led by disloyal officers, and the communists to the north.[4]

The so-called sects were an enormous early problem for Diem. These three groups—the Cao Dai and Hoa Hao politico-religious groups and the Binh Xuyen criminal syndicate—were holdovers from the French colonial period. The cash-strapped and over-burdened French authorities had sponsored the three groups as cost-effective solutions to building colonial state capacity. The Binh Xuyen had been given control over the Saigon police and controlled some ten thousand men under arms. The Cao Dai and Hoa Hao were less proximate to the center of political power but nevertheless maintained armies of thirty thousand and fifty thousand, and claimed adherents numbering around six hundred thousand and one million, respectively.[5]

The sects would have been less of a nuisance if Diem had an armed force of his own to rely on. Instead, the Vietnamese army was a second thorn in Diem's side. Diem's government inherited the French-built state and military intact. Some twenty thousand French troops remained in Vietnam, and Paris was "openly committed to the replacement of Diem at the earliest opportunity." Bao Dai was not a fan of his former protégé, and also sought his ouster. Diem did have some breathing room as Bao Dai, never one for hardship, had decided to reside in Paris despite remaining the head of state. Of more proximate concern was General Nguyen Van Hinh, the Francophile general in charge of the army who wished to remove Diem from office. While Van Hinh's true control over the army was also somewhat suspect, it was clear that the army was far more Van Hinh's than it was Diem's. The final challenge was posed by a communist-led insurgency or even an invasion by North Vietnam. While the US viewed the latter as unlikely, and a domestic communist insurgency was not yet simmering, American officials assessed the former as the most pressing long-term challenge to Diem's regime.[6]

Diem was able to overcome these formidable challenges through a combination of luck, skillful maneuvering, and US support. Of particular importance was an early and consistent American conviction in the first years of the regime that no other politician in South Vietnam offered a viable nationalist alternative to Diem. American officials did not look favorably on the colonial lackeys like Bao Dai or General Van Hinh. The sects were considered too "backward, irrational, and incapable of providing effective national leadership" and a major drag on the development of an effective national army. American policymakers feared that the communists provided the only strong nationalist group other than Diem and his brother Ngo Dinh Nhu. In the view of President Eisenhower, South Vietnam was an "outpost" the United States had to sufficiently strengthen so that the Pacific would not become a "Communist lake." While harboring reservations about the "House of Ngo," the weakness of alternatives stiffened American backing for Diem. All the aforementioned alternatives sought American support to remove the weak prime minister. Bao Dai was warned by US officials not to move against his prime minister, and General Van Hinh was similarly denied American support for his planned coup d'état. Van Hinh was seen as a holdover from inefficient French military policies, devoid of a base of local support, and overly close to Paris. His entreaties for support were repeatedly rebuffed.[7]

Even though he did not get the hoped-for American support, General Van Hinh felt Diem was sufficiently weak that he could oust the prime minister anyway and present the coup as a fait accompli to Washington. Tensions came to a head on September 19, 1954. Van Hinh held a press conference where he condemned Diem, who in turn accused his military commander of insubordination. Assuming Diem was doomed, the majority of his cabinet resigned. However, the expected coup never materialized. Once it became clear Van Hinh would not move the army in a coup, several coconspirators rejoined the cabinet in exchange for amnesty. Despite lacking the resolve to actually attempt a coup, Van Hinh continued to brashly voice his supposed coup-making abilities publicly until he finally resigned, defeated, in November. He rushed off to Paris to join his patron, Bao Dai. Van Hinh's ignominious departure granted Diem a long-sought opportunity to remake the officer corps. He purged officers close to Van Hinh and promoted allies to key commands. This infusion of new blood into the upper ranks gave Diem increased confidence he could use the army to go after his other domestic rivals.[8]

In the meantime, Diem had some luck co-opting members of the three sects into his regime. However, on March 3, 1955, leaders of the three movements formed a "United Front of Nationalist Forces" that demanded Diem's removal from office. Like Van Hinh's failed pronunciamento, this too was followed by little real action. The sect leaders sought US help in removing Diem but were immediately denied. The Binh Xuyen proved the tougher problem. On the evening of March 28, as Diem had begun to mass troops from the army for a strike against the criminal enterprise, the mobsters attacked. The fighting would be known as the "Battle of Saigon," and after pitched battles and heavy shelling, the army beat the police, and Binh Xuyen fled the city. This climactic battle marked the death knell for the sects.[9]

US support for Diem during these challenges was predicated on the unattractiveness of the alternatives. American policymakers were increasingly uneasy with the repressiveness of Diem's rule but continued to hold out hope that his government was the best available noncommunist option. US officials hoped to see more order and more democracy, but securing a noncommunist government in office continued to trump these other concerns. Diem proved adept at using democratic rhetoric and adopting formal democratic institutions while effectively ignoring all legal constraints on this rule. The Van Hinh coup d'état that never was had been consistently rejected by American officials in Saigon, but privately the United States was not so resolved against a military coup. Had General Van Hinh acted on his threats and removed Diem, it is not clear that American threats to sever ties would have been carried through. However, Diem's victory over these myriad challengers reduced American reservations about his leadership. Diem put a capstone on his new power by presiding over a managed plebiscite on October 23, 1955, which deposed emperor Bao Dai once and for all and declared the formation of the Republic of Vietnam. Diem now stood in supreme control of the South Vietnamese state. Or so it seemed.[10]

As Diem was focusing on removing rivals to his rule, the United States had set about a mammoth mission to remake the Vietnamese security apparatus to defend this anticommunist government from insurgents and North Vietnam. At its core, the American effort was to "transform the South Vietnamese state in accordance with American values and principles." While the American aid program to Saigon was extensive and multifaceted, the most important aid was military in nature. President Eisenhower "believed that a strong army was the key prerequisite for a strong government, rather than the other way around." Secretary of State John Foster Dulles echoed these sentiments in the summer of 1954, remarking that "one of the most efficient means of enabling the Vietnamese Government to become strong is to assist in reorganizing the National Army and in training that army." The Army of the Republic of Vietnam (ARVN) was reformed and rebuilt in the US Army's own image: its organization and training followed the American model closely.[11]

While the American Military Assistance Advisory Group in Vietnam had been working to reform the Vietnamese armed forces since 1950, the US was not building a new army ex nihilo. After the reintroduction of French colonial rule over Saigon, Paris had begun "a few faltering steps" toward building a Vietnamese army in 1948. By May 1950, there were some sixteen thousand regular Vietnamese forces under French command. On December 8, 1950, Paris signed an agreement with Bao Dai that established the Vietnamese National Army. This army was still led by French officers but formally reported to the emperor, and it was given new uniforms to mark a break from the colonial force. This was the army inherited by the Vietnamese state upon full independence in 1954. Recruitment into the colonial-era force was difficult. By May 1951, the army had fewer than forty thousand soldiers and a tiny indigenous officer corps. Much to the chagrin of the American assistance mission, French officers proved "extremely reluctant to listen to American counsel." It was not until Diem arrived in Saigon to take over a more effectively sovereign Vietnamese state that American advice rather than only material assistance started to really transform the army.[12]

The American military mission in 1950–1954 was very pessimistic about the state of the Vietnamese National Army and its French training. In an eerie presaging of their own troubles four years later, US advisers noted that military units often existed on paper only, with little resemblance to reality. They also cabled home that the French were far behind their stated progress in building the army. As French defeat loomed, the Bao Dai government authorized a draft of all males from twenty to twenty-five years old. However, only 9,000 of the expected 150,000 conscripts came forward to join the national army. After besieged French troops at the garrison in Dien Bien Phu were decimated by the communist People's Army of Vietnam, the French began their exit from Indochina. This also heralded the handover of training and advising responsibilities to the United States. By July 1955 US military advisers outnumbered the French, whose presence dwindled steadily until their total removal in March 1956. It was now America's responsibility to build up the Vietnamese army.[13]

When US advisers took over the mantle from the French, their assessments of the state of the army remained bleak. As part of the Geneva talks that led to decolonization of the four states to emerge out of French Indochina—North Vietnam, South Vietnam, Cambodia, and Laos—US support to the army had temporarily paused. In what should have been a stark warning, this relatively brief end to material supplies led to a "complete breakdown of combat capabilities." The army had a theoretical strength of 150,000, supplemented by 35,000 auxiliaries, but US advisers assessed that many of the battalions were "considerably understrength" from desertions and defections. After the formation of the republic in 1955, the renamed Army of the Republic of Vietnam grew rapidly, reaching an actual strength of some 147,000 soldiers by October 1955. This ballooning in size was actually contrary to American advice. Initially, American defense planners believed the force should be between fifty thousand and eighty thousand strong and focused solely on internal security as a large constabulary, in line with earlier US military missions abroad. External defense should be left to the new regional security organization, the Southeast Asia Treaty Organization (SEATO), an organization that would never live up to early expectations that it could operate as an Asian NATO. This clashed with Diem's vision for the ARVN. Aided by changes in the military advising mission's leadership and facing Diem's obstinacy, American planners reluctantly acquiesced to the building of a large conventional army in Vietnam.[14]

The US training mission focused on organizing the army on US lines and increasing military efficiency. From the beginning, advisers "felt they were working against a desperately short timetable." US advisers found little to like in the army they were trying to reform. They complained that South Vietnamese soldiers engaged in regular abuses against the civilian population and that political considerations seemed to regularly enter into Diem's staffing decisions. In the view of the State Department, the US MAAG personnel had "consistently aimed at inculcating in Vietnamese officers the U.S. concept of a responsible, dedicated, non-political corps." American officials viewed the army as suffering from "an acute shortage of officers" qualified for higher command. This was exacerbated by Diem's valuing of "political reliability in senior officers far more than military expertise." In the view of US military advisers, the "officer corps was riddled with favoritism and corruption. Officers who had failed to manifest personal loyalty to the president often fell victim to secret denunciations by jealous or ambitious rivals." Officers were given little effective autonomy under Diem, who instead insisted on closely controlling the army. A US Army study found that the Vietnamese Department of National Defense was characterized by "conflicting, duplicating chains of command" and agencies "installed in widely separated areas so as to hamper coordination, rapid staff action and decision making." A major US mission under General Maxwell D. Taylor to assess the state of the ARVN in 1961 found that Diem often "exercises arbitrary control of military operations and by-passes command channels of the joint general staff, corps, and divisions." Policymakers were frustrated by these attempts to retain personal control over the army and ensure its political loyalty, which the US viewed as contributing to poor battlefield outcomes. Nevertheless, American officials believed in this period that "exposure to American training schools and methods would solve many of the problems of the South Vietnamese Army."[15]

In addition to his meddling in the regular army, Diem channeled considerable energy and resources into building up counterweights he might rely on in the event of a military coup. Some of these other internal security organizations received American help, but US advisers did not seek to build these organizations to fight a coup. Instead, US aid to paramilitary organizations and intelligence agencies in South Vietnam pushed for depoliticization and centralization, not fragmentation. Yet the US advisers could rarely compel Diem to do their bidding outright. Pushed and prodded, he acquiesced to some changes but generally subverted all reforms to suit his political purposes against the wishes of his American patrons. The most important counterweight to the army was the Civil Guard. Organized in 1955 by merging a hodgepodge of militia forces and provincial guards, the Civil Guard was quickly built up by Diem as a "kind of second-line army" equipped with helicopters and armored vehicles. It was led by individuals Diem viewed to be particularly loyal. But Diem remained suspicious even of the Civil Guard and balanced this force with a fairly pitiful and "notoriously ineffective" Self-Defense Corps of rural militia.[16]

Diem consistently chose fragmentation over centralization in his security apparatus. This was very clear in the intelligence apparatus. With three separate formal agencies as well as at least six smaller informal networks, the Vietnamese intelligence apparatus was particularly fractionalized. Intelligence agencies devoted a considerable amount of their time and attention to spying on each other rather than gathering critical information on the communist insurgents or North Vietnamese military capabilities. Frustrated by this fragmentation, the US continually insisted on centralization of the internal security and intelligence apparatus. Diem finally acquiesced in the creation of the Central Intelligence Organization in May 1961, but rather than consolidate all intelligence operations in one agency as the US desired, he simply built the CIO as yet another rival agency.[17]

Developing adequate internal security forces alongside the ARVN was a key priority for the US in its effort to strengthen the Vietnamese state. However, in the view of one expert on American internal security assistance, US advisers "approached the reform of South Vietnam's internal security apparatus as though the country were a democracy at peace." The advisers saw the Civil Guard as "a civilian police force similar to the Pennsylvania State Police or the Texas Rangers," and an advising group from the Michigan State Police was sent to help organize the force. By contrast, Diem wanted a politically pliable and militarized force willing and able to fight a coup attempt. The steady proliferation of police and paramilitary agencies consistently troubled Diem's American advisers. US advisers preached depoliticization, even of the political police, which they viewed as ideally a nonpartisan organization dedicated to identifying threats to the state like communists, not noncommunist political opposition to Diem's personal rule. US training for the Civil Guard was focused on helping alleviate the rural security burden on the ARVN, not to build a Saigon-based counterweight to balance the army.[18]

Diem's American patrons consistently pushed for centralization, professionalization, and autonomy for military and security forces in Vietnam. But these efforts posed a potent political risk to Diem, who instead engaged in politicization, personalization, and fragmentation. Diem was no puppet. He ignored and subverted American reforms to centralize the security apparatus and to grant more autonomy to military commanders. In Diem's security state, commands were to flow down and information up, with no lateral communication between the various security organs. This would help prevent any interservice collusion that might endanger Diem's rule by forming the basis for a coup d'état. Redundancies in the security apparatus were not the result of errors but design. While these behaviors frustrated his American patrons greatly, they were the rational actions of a dictator nervous about the loyalty of his own coercive apparatus. Events would soon show this fear was not misplaced.[19]

On November 11, 1960, two days after Vice President Richard Nixon conceded he lost the presidential election to Senator John F. Kennedy, a group of Diem's elite American-trained paratroopers began a violent coup to unseat his regime, citing the politicization of the army and Diem's autocratic rule. An American adviser awoke early in the morning to the sky "streaked with tracers" as paratroopers fired on Diem's presidential compound, stormed army headquarters, and seized control of the airport. Diem was defended by forces from his paramilitary Civil Guard, the organization he had strengthened for this very occasion. "Badly outgunned," they fought back desperately against the elite army force. US intelligence had no advance warning of the coup and got its first indication something was afoot when armored vehicles lumbered through the predawn Saigon darkness, followed by heavy gunfire at the Presidential Palace. Given the size of its investment, Washington was primarily concerned about limiting intramural fighting, which weakened the Vietnamese armed forces. When Diem phoned US ambassador Elbridge Durbrow as the paratroopers laid siege to his palace, the American representative declined to give him unequivocal support and urged Diem to negotiate. US personnel in contact with the paratroopers somewhat reluctantly implored them not to storm the palace. Unable to decide whether to carry through with a final assault on Diem's beleaguered position, the rebel leaders equivocated until Colonel Tran Thien Khiem, a

Diem loyalist, arrived with a contingent of loyal army troops. The mutinous paratroopers then fled.[20]

Diem was understandably furious about the tepid American reaction to the coup and doubled down on his strategies to weaken and divide the army so it could not strike again. The fact that his paratroopers had been considered the most loyal force in his army was particularly troubling. Diem rapidly accelerated his manipulation of promotions in the army to install loyalists in more key commands, further reducing its combat effectiveness in the expanding insurgency and exacerbating unrest in the army command.[21]

The United States had finally had enough. Confident the South Vietnamese army would produce a reliably pro-American and hopefully more effective alternative ruler, the United States now began to actively encourage coup plotting against Diem. For obvious reasons such machinations had to remain covert, lest they drive Diem into a long-shot reconciliation with the communists. After the US administration gave up hope that a coup would ever materialize, on November 1, 1963, three weeks before President Kennedy would be assassinated in Dallas, Diem's army finally struck against him in what would prove to be a fatal blow. At 1:30 in the afternoon after an abnormally quiet day in the capital, US Embassy personnel suddenly noticed troops "pouring into Saigon." An aide to a South Vietnamese general informed the Americans that the long anticipated coup was underway. From a vantage point overlooking the Presidential Palace, CIA personnel could see hundreds of rebel troops and several dozen armored vehicles heading toward the compound as gunfire rang out.[22]

Hunkered down in his palace bunker, Diem phoned the American ambassador to plead for assistance and ask for the American reaction to the rebellion. The US ambassador replied coldly that "it is four-thirty A.M. in Washington, and the U.S. government cannot possibly have a view." This was hardly the answer Diem had hoped for. After failing to get through to Diem by phone, coup leader General Duong Van Minh finally got in contact with the besieged president and implored him to resign and threatened to "blast him off the face of the earth." Around eight that evening, Diem and his brother escaped from the palace into a waiting car. At daybreak the next day, Diem called his army headquarters and offered to surrender in exchange for safe passage out of Vietnam. To the dismay of the United States, Diem was instead captured, bound, and executed in the back of a military vehicle.[23]

Diem—a man once viewed as critical to the survival of a non-communist Vietnam—had been violently removed from office by the army his American patrons had built. Yet this would hardly prove the stabilizing event American policymakers had hoped for. Instead, it unleashed a flurry of subsequent coups d'état. Half a dozen regime changes in the next two years alone led to a further deterioration of the South Vietnamese position against the insurgents. The generals were apparently more concerned with securing their political power than their battlefield positions. They were, after all, backed by the superpower United States. The flow of American weapons and advisers engendered a sense of invulnerability among South Vietnamese elites, which sharpened the proximate threats of internal political rivals and dulled the distant threat of the communist guerrillas. With disaster looming, President Lyndon B. Johnson made the fateful decision to deploy American combat forces to Vietnam. What began as an attempt to prop up an anticommunist regime under Ngo Dinh Diem and build an effective American-style army had led to a succession of coups and the direct participation of American forces in a war that would cost the lives of fifty-eight thousand American soldiers and three million Vietnamese. Large-scale American aid had not stabilized Diem's regime. Instead, by building up a powerful counterweight to the regime leader, arms for Vietnam destabilized the distribution of power within Diem's regime.[24]

NGO DINH DIEM WAS NOT THE ONLY AMERICAN-BACKED AUTO-crat who would find that the army strengthened by his American patrons would prove lethal to his rule. The United States armed, advised, and organized the Thai military beginning in 1950. This army was organized along American lines, with emphasis put on a nonpartisan orientation and a cohesive, autonomous organization. However, the army built by the United States proved remarkably praetorian. Thailand experienced a dizzying number of coups and coup plots in the twentieth century, many while advised and assisted by the United States. The army strengthened and organized with American aid would come to dominate Thai political life long after American policymakers tired of bankrolling military despots in Bangkok. The Thai army rules to this very day and has again come to enjoy increasingly close American ties. While not yet experiencing a rapprochement reminiscent of Cold War–era closeness, US-Thai defense ties are likely to continue to strengthen as the Sino-American rivalry heats up.

Initial interest in Thailand by the new postwar superpower was minimal. The seizure of power in a military coup d'état by Field Marshal Plaek Phibunsongkhram (usually referred to as "Phibun" or "Pibul") in November 1947 "could not have more exasperated the United States." Phibun had allied himself with fascist Japan in the Second World War and was strongly disliked by the United States and other Western allies. His return to power was "actively opposed" by London and Washington. At the same time, US pressure against his government was limited by the marginality of Thailand to the newly US-led global order. Linkages to be exploited for leverage against the Thai junta were sparse. Instead, the United States adopted a cool posture and did not officially recognize the government until March the following year.[25]

The US government refused to hold its nose and support Phibun's avowedly anticommunist regime because it was not yet convinced Thailand faced a serious communist threat. While the Communist Party of Thailand (CPT) had been founded in 1926, it was a small party almost completely dominated by its Chinese Communist Party (CCP) sponsors. It was also limited by its almost exclusive recruitment among ethnic Chinese in Thailand, which, while a sizable minority, limited its appeal among ethnic Thais. In 1947, the situation in neighboring Indochina was not yet dire, although American concerns about the Viet Minh and the prospects of the French counterinsurgency were mounting. Within Thailand the picture was more optimistic—the small CPT was still marginal, Thailand's economy was relatively strong, and the lack of a history of colonization had dampened support for communist mobilization against the existing regime.[26]

However, by the spring of 1948, American concern for the region more generally and Thailand specifically grew rapidly. The victory of the CCP in the Chinese Civil War in 1949 and Viet Minh gains rendered an anticommunist government in Bangkok suddenly much more attractive. Washington made good on this growing rapprochement with the Thai military leadership by extending $10 million in military aid in January 1950 and economic aid shortly thereafter. The true watershed moment for the US-Thai relationship, however, was the outbreak of war in Korea in June 1950. With the Thai decision to send a small contingent of combat troops to aid the US-led effort came a quid pro quo of vastly accelerated American assistance. This assistance took the form of a Military Assistance Advisory Group that began the task of reorganizing the Thai military along American lines into a force "capable of defending the country from outside attack or subversion." The MAAG in Thailand had, by October 1951, engaged in "intensive training" for the Thai army and air force. After the MAAG infantry training courses, Thai officers were in a position to train nine US-equipped battalions. The US Military Advisory Group became the Joint US Military Advisory Group, Thailand, or JUSMAGTHAI, on January 21, 1954.[27]

While the US was bolstering the Thai military, it also encouraged the Phibun regime to engage in a managed liberalization of its politics. Starting in 1955 Phibun had introduced "a number of democratic reforms," including submitting to elections for the first time in February 1957. The weak political organization of the ruling military regime and its minimal civilian infrastructure spelled disaster in the elections. Though the Thai junta had no intention of allowing their slate of candidates to face defeat, they lacked the infrastructural capacity to forestall such an outcome without resorting to naked fraud, which is what they did. By two in the morning on February 28, all but thirteen polling units in Bangkok had reported their results. At this point, returns suggested the military-organized Seri Manangkhasila Party (SMP) would win only five seats in Bangkok. Panicked interior ministry officials delayed releasing the final votes for the remaining thirteen units for eight hours, after which they announced that the SMP had suddenly surged ahead thanks to the final polling units and had now won seven seats with a sharply increased margin for Prime Minister Phibun. The US Embassy noted the obvious—that there was "good evidence that the returns" were "manipulated" and that "this was the general belief of the public." That this eleventh-hour manipulation was even necessary despite the "massive ballot box stuffing operation" in favor of the SMP spoke to the considerable weakness of the regime.[28]

The blatant fraud spurred mass protests against the regime. At this time, the upper echelons of the regime were a triumvirate of two field marshals from the army and a police general: Field Marshal (and prime minister) Phibun, Field Marshal Sarit Thanarat, and General Phao Siyanon. General Phao, the minister of the interior, was blamed for the poor performance in the elections, and his stature within the triumvirate further declined after he suggested using force against the protesters. Phibun instead turned to Field

Marshal Sarit Thanarat, minister of defense and commander of the army, to take over as overall commander in a state of emergency. This placed Sarit "in effective control of the government." His power was curtailed on March 12, but he retained control over the army. The rise of Sarit's relative power in the triumvirate, coupled with his disdain for Phao, spelled trouble for the stability of the Phibun-led junta. The US was pleased with the avoidance of violence, but the US ambassador had actually reassured Sarit that he could use US-supplied military equipment for the "maintenance [of] law and order," as this was "one purpose [of] US assistance [to] Thailand."[29]

More broadly, however, this political instability displeased the US government. The relative political stability of Thailand was a key source of Bangkok's appeal as an ally and, in the view of the American mission, a vital factor in preventing the growth of communism. Nevertheless, officials continued to voice confidence in Phibun. That summer, top officials in the State Department noted that "we continue to believe that he [Phibun] is the most reliable and constructive of the triumvirate and hope that he can preserve the balance of power and retain his leadership." The US ambassador wrote to Washington in May that the "assumption of power [by] Sarit would have repercussions not consistent [with the] best interest[s of the] US." The US was of course not wholly satisfied with Phibun's leadership and cast a jaundiced eye on the "marginal accommodation to Communist China," a development the US wished to "stop, or at the very least retard."[30]

In the meantime, the shaky ruling coalition continued to unravel. On September 10, 1957, Sarit asked Phibun to dismiss Phao as minister of the interior and director general of the Thai National Police. Phao refused to resign, and Phibun refused to force his resignation. On September 12, Sarit distributed live ammunition to his troops in Bangkok and now demanded Phibun himself resign and form a new cabinet. This pronunciamento coup soon turned into a full military coup d'état when Phibun refused. At around 11:30 p.m. on September 16, in a "well-prepared," "well-organized," and "excellently executed" operation, army units surrounded the principal installations of Phao's police and other major buildings in Bangkok. The coup was swift and bloodless. In the early hours of September 17, army headquarters announced that "due to present troubles" the army had "taken control for the good of the country" and that the Thai king had declared Field Marshal Sarit the military governor of Bangkok.[31]

While it was certainly a military coup d'état, it was unsurprisingly not referred to as such by the conspirators. Sarit declared publicly after the coup that it was just a "small irregularity" and that there would be "no arrests. It isn't a coup and it isn't a rebellion." Sarit's archrival and former drinking buddy General Phao was, according to Sarit, given the option of "living abroad or becoming a Buddhist priest." In a curious statement for a man who had just used military force to overthrow the prime minister and take power himself, Sarit declared after the coup that "I have nothing to do with politics."[32]

While the coup took the US mission by surprise, the shock was very limited. Embassy telegrams had noted the possibility of a coup for months, and in the days and hours leading up to the coup the embassy was well aware things might come to a head. The embassy had been approached by a British representative in May with news that Sarit planned a coup, a warning it viewed skeptically. Messages from the US Embassy in late August continued to reinforce that a coup was still unlikely. As late as September 14, the US ambassador wrote to Washington that a coup, "while possible [is] not probable." Just hours before the coup the US ambassador asked for authority to meet with the king and urge his reconciliation of the Sarit, Phibun, and Phao factions and the use of "legal means" to resolve "current political differences."[33]

While Field Marshal Sarit had given the US Embassy no advanced warning of his coup or asked for any American permission in his move against Phibun, he had, in the view of the American ambassador, "made [a] point of keeping contact with [the] Embassy through emissaries to keep us informed [of] major developments." The morning after the coup, he dispatched a representative to the embassy informing the ambassador he wished to meet with him later that day. Three years after the coup, a member of the embassy staff reported a meeting with a "Capt. Somwang Sarasas," who claimed he had been dispatched on the day of the coup to give a "most urgent message to the American Ambassador" around 4:00 p.m. However, he had been apparently unable to locate the ambassador. The American official who recounted this conversation with Sarasas in 1960 noted that he had "no basis for giving credence to any statement" from the captain.[34]

Thai ministers not part of the coup also frantically reached out to the embassy, presumably to see if the US was either behind the coup or had information they did not. An embassy staff member sent a telegram to Washington that morning remarking that an unnamed Thai minister had called to ask "urgently for any details we might have" on the disturbances in Bangkok. "He expressed particular interest in learning whether all Thai armed forces [were] involved or whether [the] army [was] opposed by [a] combination of navy and air force." The day after the coup, Sarit sent a statement to the US Embassy outlining why the action had been necessary. In this statement, Sarit explicitly stated that there would be "no changes whatever in the general field of foreign policy." Several days after the coup, Sarit met with Ambassador Max Waldo Bishop and reassured him further of the desire for close continued ties with the United States and that the change in government would lead to absolutely no changes in Thai foreign policy.[35]

The US first learned of the coup about fifteen minutes after it had begun, when the acting foreign minister appeared at the ambassador's residence and "said that a coup had just started and that the government was being taken over by Sarit and 'his army.'" By midday on September 17, it was clear the coup had succeeded. Ambassador Bishop wrote to Washington that "Field Marshal Sarit has now taken over control [of] Thailand." The US Embassy reaction to the coup was hardly enthusiastic. Bishop, in a telegram to the State Department the afternoon of September 20, wrote that "it would be a grave mistake to view this development as anything but a major setback for [the] interests of [the] United States and [the] Free World in SEA [Southeast Asia]." He viewed the involvement of the royal family, previously marginal to Thai politics after the 1932 coup had ended the monarchy, as the harbinger of future deterioration in Thai political stability. Bishop noted that in his many interactions with the royals they had demonstrated that they were "dilettantes" who have never "had to deal with practical problems" and they "fail to understand or appreciate the menace of communism and of communist China." Field Marshal Sarit was also maligned by Bishop, who wrote that he has "always felt [the] rise to power of Sarit will and does require careful evaluation of our programs and even our objectives here in Thailand."[36]

The reaction at higher levels of the State Department was more ambivalent. Indeed, a telegram sent from Secretary of State John Foster Dulles on September 3, two weeks before the coup, was remarkably frank about what US views toward a possible coup in Thailand would be. Referencing a July 5 telegram from the embassy in Thailand that there was a possibility Sarit might seize power and that this "development would force the United States" to make "major adjustments" to its military aid program, Dulles noted this was far from automatically the case. Instead, Dulles reminded his subordinates,

As the Embassy is aware[,] it is United States policy to support and promote the stability of the legal government of Thailand.

Premier Pibul Songgram, the head of that Government, is regarded as the most reliable, constructive and statesman-like leader capable of holding power in Thailand, and it is hoped that he can preserve the balance of power and retain his leadership. At the same time there is reason to believe that neither of the Prime Minister's principal colleagues would desire that Thailand withdraw from the Southeast Asia Treaty Organization, thus leaving Thailand at the mercy of its expansionist, hostile Chinese neighbor.[37]

MOREOVER, DULLES SENT ALONG A COPY OF NATIONAL INTELLIgence Estimate (NIE) No. 62-57, which stated that the most likely outcome of any leadership change in Thailand was Sarit's ascent. The NIE noted it was unlikely that Sarit's taking power would lead to major changes in either Thai domestic or foreign policies. Dulles stated that the department "considers that this is the best estimate which can be developed" and therefore "under these circumstances and in view of the highly fluid state of domestic Thai politics, the Department considers that the most constructive policy is to maintain the best possible rapport with those Thai leaders who have given general support to their Government's policy of defending Thailand against Communism, while at the same time continuing United States support for Premier Pibul Songgram." Finally, in light of all of this, "it cannot be said with certainty at this time that if Sarit should become Prime Minister it would automatically mean that the U.S. would have to make major adjustments in its programs in Thailand."[38]

In a telegram to the ambassador a day after the coup, the under secretary of state for political affairs, Robert D. Murphy, wrote that it "appears [the] coup [is] now [a] successful fait accompli. Provided [there are] no new major developments such as [the] establishment [of a] government unfavorable to our interest take[s] place, we intend [to] take [the] public position" that this was an "essentially internal political development" and is not "expected [to] alter US-Thai cooperation." In light of the still unfolding situation, the State Department viewed it as prudent to "say as little as possible and take only such actions" as "absolutely required vis-à-vis [the] new authorities." Murphy also suggested that Ambassador Bishop approach the Thai king and emphasize that the US hopes a "new government will be formed under established Thai institutions" and that the new government "will foster continued close Thai-US relations." Murphy noted the US must walk a thin line between not offending Sarit or prejudicing "US relations with those who apparently are in firm control [of] Thailand or who may yet emerge." This also would be beneficial in that if Sarit were "left somewhat uncertain [of] our attitude towards him" he would "be under some pressure [to] adopt positions favorable [to] US interests." Nevertheless, to identify the US government publicly with Sarit and his coup this early "would appear both unwise politically and dishonest [in] view [of] US past public support [to] Phibun."[39]

The question of whether the coup was "constitutional" was something the American foreign policy establishment devoted considerable energy to finding out. The US ambassador wrote a telegram to Washington early in the morning on September 19, three days after the coup, noting that Sarit and his allies had been making "every attempt" to "maintain law and order" and to "justify their actions as being constitutional (which, of course, they are not)." Later that day, he wrote a second telegram to Washington asking that the phrase "which, of course, they are not" be removed from the text. In Washington, State Department lawyers noted two days after the coup that "since Thailand was a constitutional monarchy and there had been no change in the reigning head, the question of recognition did not arise in connection with the recent change in government." In a message sent to the US Embassy in Thailand a little over a week later, Secretary of State

Dulles wrote that the State Department ultimately had insufficient information to determine whether the coup was constitutional or not, but that in any case while the US "generally favors peaceful processes in changing governments, US policy regarding coups is pragmatic rather than inflexible." In the Thai case, the department viewed the coup as a "fait accompli," and the US government desired means to develop "constructive influence in [the] new situation." One of the priorities the State Department outlined for American policy toward the new regime was the "need [to] persuade Thai authorities [to] take [a] strong stand against leftists and pro-Communists." Dulles further noted that unless the "political and economic factors which dictated existing programs no longer exist," there was no reason to alter American aid because of the coup.[40]

After the coup, the US Embassy noted that the "present political uncertainties" make it difficult to justify increased aid for Thailand, but "it should not be forgotten that despite current internal political turmoil, Thailand's posture re[garding] collective security, Communism and Free World has in no way deteriorated and if anything is somewhat stronger." A joint JUSMAGTHAI-Embassy estimation of the consequences of the coup for Thai internal security noted that "on balance, change has been for the better in terms of internal security, since Phao had been actively dealing with the Chinese Communists and the government as a whole had followed an extremely timorous policy in its opposition to pro-communist activities," and there were now signs of "a genuine intention to take firm action" against communism in Thailand. In May 1958, with Sarit firmly in control of Thailand, US officials continued to view Thailand as "the hub of our security efforts in Southeast Asia." The State Department also held out hope that "provided the [coup] group maintains its stability and balance, it may preside over measured, orderly progress toward the free, representative government which will best serve the interests of the Thai and the Free World."[41]

An analysis of Thai politics in 1959 noted that while "political power in Thailand continues to be based on a military group which controls the armed forces," this military junta "does not constitute a dictatorship based on ideological or pseudo-ideological grounds. There is a high degree of individual liberties which are much valued. In exercising its power the military group is very responsive to its estimate of public opinion and tends to govern in the paternalistic tradition of Thailand." In a review of US military aid to Thailand to date prepared ahead of a royal visit to the United States, the State Department had a "goal" for 1965 in Thailand that envisioned a "smooth transition from government by military oligarchy operating under martial law to one following orderly democratic procedures within the framework of the constitutional monarchy," where Thai "domestic political institutions are administratively stable and responsive to the ideals of the Thai people" and the "monopoly of political power by military leaders" is "gradually" eliminated.[42]

This would amount to extremely wishful thinking. A subsequent coup in November 1971 was also accepted passively by the United States. While a brief period of democratization arrived in Thailand in 1973, it was followed by a bloody military coup and a return to military rule three years later. Coup plotters continued to sound out American attitudes and try to glean a likely response. The most common reaction, however, was ambivalence. US-backed autocrats in Thailand continued to be remarkably vulnerable to military coups and enjoyed no US support in any measures to coup-proof the military that would run contrary to US efforts to promote autonomy and professionalization.[43]

The military continued to rule Thailand to the detriment of other noncommunist political parties, such that by 1985 the US CIA would quip that "Thailand's military has often been called the nation's largest and best-organized political party." Thailand's praetorians continued their interventions despite increased professionalization. Training in some cases increased the prae-torian impulses of military officers. In the view of US Army personnel, as the "level of competence" of the junior officers had risen "markedly in recent years," they were increasingly "unwilling to abide the ineptitude of many star wearers." The view that coups were not a violation of military professionalism if they promoted the corporate autonomy and purported professionalism of the military led the "Young Turk" faction of the army (graduates of the 1960 class of the Royal Thai Military Academy) to "ironically" attempt to overthrow Prem Tinsulanonda under the argument that "military involvement in politics detracted from the professionalism of the armed forces." Thailand would be persistently saddled with a highly praetorian army that has been one of the most coup-prone forces in the world.[44]

Both Diem and Phibun had to contend with armies strengthened with American aid that sought to translate their new military power into political power. Unfortunately for both dictators, the United States proved unwilling to aid their efforts to reduce the coup threat posed by these armies. Instead, the US consistently pushed its allied dictators to leave the army alone.

In neither case was this advice followed, and the political ambitions of military officers manifested in coups d'état. America's allies in Saigon and Bangkok found the United States a fickle friend during these coups. US officials chose not to intervene during coups and accepted the results as faits accomplis.

This vulnerability to military coups meant that despite the massive influx of American military aid, these regimes remained highly vulnerable to internal challengers. Unlike their Soviet counterparts, they did not have American support in building internal security agencies to monitor and crush acts of military disloyalty. Instead, American military aid strengthened a political rival and rendered client dictators vulnerable to overthrow by their own state armies. These dictatorships survived in office for a shorter time than the average autocracy despite support from their superpower patron. American aid did not lead to regime durability but instead notable political fragility. While military aid did strengthen the armies of client regimes, it proved a mixed political blessing that did not guarantee the survival of those regimes.

7 | HOLLOW ARMIES

When black-clad Khmer Rouge soldiers entered Phnom Penh, the capital of Cambodia, on April 17, 1975, they arrived as the harbingers of one of the most notoriously brutal regimes in the twentieth century. These "Red Cambodians," the moniker given to the Communist Party of Kampuchea (Cambodia), were also known ominously simply as the "Organization." In the recollection of a defector from the group before it seized power, party cadres were told that the Organization "has as many eyes as a pineapple and cannot make mistakes." As the Cambodian communist army descended on Phnom Penh that chaotic April, government troops laid down their arms and shed their uniforms, the war finally lost. Their officers and many enlisted men were summarily executed by the Khmer Rouge soldiers. By the time the Khmer Rouge were ousted from power a little less than four years later, the Organization caused the deaths of around one quarter of the Cambodian population.[1]

The Khmer Rouge launched their millenarian revolution by defeating on the battlefield a government that was financed, armed, and advised by the United States. The United States provided some

$1.6 billion in economic and military assistance to the Khmer Republic that fell to the communist guerrillas after five years of war. In its bombing campaign on behalf of the government in Phnom Penh, the United States dropped 257,465 tons of explosives in 1973 alone, a staggering total equal to half as many tons as were dropped on Japan during all the Second World War.[2]

The US effort to build a durable noncommunist regime in Phnom Penh is worth sustained attention, as the intervention in Cambodia offers considerable insights into not only how US aid shaped the coup prevention strategies of allied autocrats, but also the consequences of these dynamics for military effectiveness and even state collapse. The US effort to support the Khmer Republic has received relatively scant attention relative to similar US efforts in South Vietnam and, to a lesser extent, in Laos. Despite its relative neglect, Cambodia nevertheless demonstrates the pitfalls of security assistance for authoritarian client regimes at war. The US funneled aid to a military dictatorship that systematically destroyed its own already limited military capacity. Its dictator, Marshal Lon Nol, chose his officers for their political loyalty and not their battlefield effectiveness. His most effective forces were intentionally fractured and distributed among his corrupt commanders so they could not challenge his regime in a coup d'état. Convinced until the very end of his tenure that the United States would save his government, Lon Nol focused on internal rivals over the growing communist insurgency.

The consolidation of power by Lon Nol in Cambodia also demonstrates that organizational power often trumps charisma or ability in authoritarian contexts. Just as Stalin used his position as head of the party apparatus to outmuscle and ultimately cast aside his formidable opponents, Lon Nol used his position as head of the Cambodian army to dominate his regime. While the Cambodian army was in poor fighting shape, it was a powerful political resource for Lon Nol and was the key power player in Cambodian politics. The assumption of unrivaled power by Lon Nol is surprising, as he was a man who had risen through the ranks *because of* his perceived incompetence. In the esteem of US Ambassador John G. Dean, he was a man "no one would pick" to "lead a modern state."[3]

Cambodia achieved its independence in 1953 when France transferred control to the colonial-era monarch, Norodom Sihanouk, whose family had ruled the Kingdom of Cambodia since 1860. The eccentric but politically astute monarch dominated Cambodian political life. A keen political operator, Sihanouk balanced demands from militant nationalists and Francophile conservatives to navigate independence during the widening Indochina War.[4]

After independence, Cambodia joined its Laotian and South Vietnamese neighbors in welcoming a US military training mission to reform its small army inherited from French rule. The aid was substantial: 15 percent of the national budget and 30 percent of the military budget came from American coffers. While this military aid was helpful in building Cambodian military power, Sihanouk also feared it might be the source of his undoing. Sihanouk saw an American and Thai hand in several coup plots his growing army may or may not have actually incubated, and the prince reacted by abrogating the US economic and military assistance programs in 1963 and severing diplomatic relations the following year. While Sihanouk had viewed this as necessary to stave off the threat of a coup, the end of American assistance brought demoralization and decline to the Royal Cambodian Armed Forces. French aid to the army continued at a "trickle" and did little to compensate for the loss of American matériel.[5]

To offset this military weakness, Sihanouk sought to pursue neutralism and remain out of the raging war in his neighboring states. By 1970, the army was a largely "ceremonial" body whose soldiers were used as extras in Sihanouk's many films, which surprised no one when they invariably won first prize at Phnom Penh film festivals. Nevertheless, the war was coming for Cambodia. By the end of the 1960s, US troops were fighting Viet Cong and North Vietnamese forces in huge numbers as royalists, neutralists, and communists fought a three-way war in Laos. Cambodia's location along the famed "Ho Chi Minh Trail" that brought communist supplies and troops to South Vietnam resulted in gradually greater incursions on Cambodian territory by Vietnamese forces. Sihanouk struck clandestine agreements with Hanoi to allow the use of Cambodian territory as well as the port of Sihanoukville to smuggle supplies to aid the National Liberation Front (Viet Cong). The creeping involvement in the war was partly out of Sihanouk's control. Cambodia's location, less than forty miles from Saigon, would render it all but destined to participate in the widening war.[6]

With the communist presence in Cambodia growing, the Royal Cambodian Army engaged in sporadic fighting against communist forces on Cambodian territory. These pressures would soon see Cambodia emerge as a full-fledged front in the Indochina War, with its own indigenous communist movement. The Vietnam-based Indochinese Communist Party (ICP), founded by Ho Chi Minh in 1930, had intended to create a branch in Cambodia, as it had in Laos in March 1931. However, the ICP had largely failed to recruit ethnic Cambodians into the party before the Second World War. When the war began, the ICP dutifully expanded its coalition in line with Stalin's favored global communist doctrine. In May 1941, the ICP led the creation of a nationalist front, the Vietnamese Independence League, or Viet Minh. This national front strategy extended to ICP collaboration with noncommunist Cambodian resistance groups.[7]

After the end of the Second World War and the beginning of the first Indochina War (1945–1954) against France, the ICP continued its wartime policy of collaboration with the indigenous noncommunist Cambodian armed movements. At this time, the loosely organized and Thai-sponsored Khmer Issarak nationalist front joined the Viet Minh. In April 1950, the Viet Minh tried again to create a Vietnamese-sponsored Cambodian communist group, the First National Congress of Khmer Resistance. However, indigenous uptake was still minimal, and only 20 percent of the leadership was ethnically Khmer. Another effort a year later by Khmer communists led to the creation of the Khmer People's Revolutionary Party. The KPRP was still under heavy Vietnamese influence, and its armed units comprised a mix of Khmer and Vietnamese cadres. After the Geneva Conventions in 1954 ended the first war, about half the party withdrew to Vietnamese territory, and the other half moved into a semiclandestine existence in Phnom Penh.

Future leadership of the Communist Party of Kampuchea (CPK) emerged out of the Phnom Penh–based branch of the KPRP and student groups. Saloth Sar had been studying in France until he returned in 1953 to join the Viet Minh guerrillas and took the nom de guerre Pol Pot. After one of the senior communist leaders in the Phnom Penh faction of the KPRP defected to Sihanouk, the party was almost destroyed, with purges eliminating around 90 percent of the party cadres. The surviving party membership regrouped and reformed as the first truly autonomous Cambodian communist party, the Workers Party of Kampuchea, in 1960 (the party was renamed the Communist Party of Kampuchea in 1971). Saloth Sar was named third in command and would take over as party secretary in 1962 after the death of party leader Tou Samouth.[8]

It was Sihanouk who would coin the popular name for the communist movement, calling them Red Cambodians, or Khmer Rouge. While their power would eventually reach epic and horrific proportions, the Khmer Rouge did not emerge as a formidable movement. After the formation of the autonomous party in 1960, the cadres had so few weapons it took them a year to arm enough individuals to simply guard their leaders. With the Vietnam-based faction receiving the bulk of the military aid, the indigenous communist party had a hard time getting weapons. This weakness delayed their fight against Sihanouk's government for years.

The Khmer Rouge (KR) had a lucky break when government missteps provided them an opening. In April 1967, peasants around Samlaut began a disorganized uprising to resist the requisition of rice crops. The insurrection was brutally repressed. Sihanouk would years later callously remark that he "read somewhere" that ten thousand peasants had been killed. The KR leadership sensed an opportunity to organize this violent discontent and begin their armed revolutionary struggle. The first offensive was an important if profoundly limited success: a January 1968 raid resulted in the seizure of ten guns.[9]

While the Khmer Rouge would ultimately prove the most threatening group to the royal government in Phnom Penh, it certainly did not seem that way in the 1960s. The opposition figure that Sihanouk feared most was his cousin, Prince Sisowath Sirik Matak. Sirik Matak's branch of the royal family had been passed over by the French back in the nineteenth century when they chose Sihanouk's Norodom lineage for the crown over his Sisowath branch. Sirik Matak was a competent, energetic prince with a powerful network of supporters in the Sino-Khmer commercial elite. Sihanouk's fears were not misplaced. Sirik Matak would ultimately prove to be the main instigator of the coup that would transform Cambodia forever.[10]

The main benefactor of the coup was also a prominent figure in Cambodian politics under Sihanouk. Lon Nol was born on November 13, 1913, the son of a minor government official in Prey Veng Province. A "quiet," "unpretentious," and deeply religious (and superstitious) man, he entered the colonial police force and became Phnom Penh police chief in 1950 before joining the French-led army two years later. In one of his first post-independence combat forays, he displayed a keen knack for flattering Sihanouk for his superior's supposed tactical brilliance, despite the French direction of the operation. From then on, he rose through the ranks of the Royal Khmer Armed Forces (Forces armées royales khmères, FARK) as Sihanouk's "loyal hatchet man." By 1955 he was made commander-in-chief of the army and, in 1960, chief of the general staff. He also began to accumulate political offices, chosen as deputy premier in 1960 and prime minister in 1966. Lon Nol had attained this meteoric rise thanks to the patronage of Sihanouk and the perception he was a "staunch royalist." Yet he was more politically ambitious than he let on. He carefully cultivated a network of support in FARK and even reportedly kept "extensive dossiers" on his friends and foes alike.[11]

In early 1970, Sihanouk left Cambodia for a prolonged trip abroad, which included travel in France, the Soviet Union, and China. With his cousin out of the country, Sirik Matak began to plan his removal from office. Lon Nol was a formidable barrier to coup plotting. As army commander and a longtime Sihanouk loyalist, he could probably stop any coup. Sirik Matak feared Lon Nol might go along with the conspiracy only to betray the plotters to Sihanouk. The planning had not been terribly discreet, as Sihanouk's brother-in-law and head of the police Oum Mannarine got wind of the conspiracy and attempted to arrest Sirik Matak and, assuming he was part of the plot, Lon Nol. While not yet sure about whether to support Sirik Matak's planned coup, Lon Nol was not keen on being arrested and had his troops disarm the policemen sent to capture him.[12]

Despite staving off his pending arrest, Lon Nol was still uncommitted to the plot to oust his longtime patron. Later that same day, Sirik Matak and three army officers visited him at home and implored him to sign a declaration supporting a vote in the assembly the next day to depose the prince. According to some accounts, Lon Nol supported this action only after one of the officers leveled a pistol at him. He was, at a minimum, a very reluctant participant in the putsch. Despite this hesitation, he took steps to assure that any

coup would succeed, including apparently securing the support of
the exiled giant of Cambodian nationalism, Son Ngoc Thanh, and
gaining his pledge to send his American-trained Khmer troops
from South Vietnam to aid the new regime.[13]

The following day, on March 18, 1970, with soldiers closing
the airport and arrayed in strategic points across Phnom Penh,
the National Assembly voted to remove Sihanouk as head of
state. The "relatively colorless" assembly president Cheng Heng
was named as his replacement and Sirik Matak as deputy prime
minister. In an indication of his power if not his enthusiasm for
the coup, Lon Nol was named prime minister. A bemused American reporter for *Time* wrote that the coup had "a distinctive Cambodian flavor," as "scores of soldiers were seen snoozing on the
grass, many without shoes."[14]

The sleepy soldiers underscored that few realized at the time
how monumental the coup had been. Like in many coups, few of
the conspirators "gave any thought to the postcoup period." For
his part, Sihanouk learned of the coup from Soviet premier Alexei
Kosygin, who informed him with no apparent sympathy, while in
a car on the way to the airport, that his government had been overthrown. Whatever residual hesitation Lon Nol felt toward the coup
dissipated after he learned Sihanouk pledged to kill all the partici-
pants when he returned.[15]

Scholars disagree about the exact role of the United States in
the coup. Given the extensive presence of the US in neighboring
South Vietnam and Laos and its dislike of Sihanouk's dealings
with the communists, it is not difficult to understand why some
saw an American hand in the overthrow of the prince. In his excel-
lent study of the war, Wilfred P. Deac writes that "the most probable scenario is that individual U.S. military mid-operating levels,
including an air force general, did encourage Khmer counterparts
to depose the prince in the interest of the Vietnam War effort" but
did so without higher-level approval. Nevertheless, "it is clear that

Lon Nol carried out the coup with at least a legitimate expectation of significant US support." As Deac concludes, "It would not be the first time Americans said they would not support a coup but would recognize the successor government if it succeeded."[16]

For an entity as large as the United States government, it isn't always terribly meaningful to ask whether the US "knew" about the coup. Sometimes plots or planned attacks were known by nearly all major parts of the American foreign policy apparatus: the Defense and State Departments, the National Security Council, the CIA, and other intelligence agencies. As we saw in Chapter 6, coup plotting in South Vietnam in 1963 was widely known about, discussed, and encouraged in Washington. In other cases, like the al-Qaeda terrorist attacks on September 11, 2001, parts of the government knew parts of the plot. In the case of Cambodia, the coup wasn't terribly *surprising* to anyone in the US government, but there is limited evidence that any knowledge of it had reached the top levels of the American foreign policy apparatus. It's also not clear that would have made a difference. The same uncertainty that characterized the American response to the coup after it occurred would likely have characterized any response to credible reports of a planned putsch.[17]

In any case, the US response to the coup once it did occur was cautious. That same day, Secretary of State William P. Rogers told the assistant to the president for national security affairs, Henry Kissinger, that "I think we should be very careful not to say anything until we know more about it." Uncertainty over the prospects for the putschists lingered. Five days after the coup, CIA director Richard Helms stated that "our current information on the exact balance of forces in Cambodia—information which would be essential to formulating realistic plans—is thin." The hesitant American response in part reflected apprehensions about Lon Nol. US assessments of the new Cambodian strongman before the coup were not very enthusiastic. In September

1968, Secretary of State Dean Rusk offered that if Lon Nol were in charge he would "follow a pro-American line and crack down on leftists." However, "we doubt that any real and permanent shift of power to Lon Nol would be advantageous to U.S. long-run interests." The State Department feared that the "political elite might quickly break up into quarreling cliques," and the US was skeptical of Lon Nol's anticommunist credentials, as there was evidence, though equivocal, "that he has been deeply involved in munitions deliveries to the VC [Viet Cong], perhaps more for financial than ideological reasons." Overall, the State Department's assessment was that "we see little permanent value in moving this way with a government lacking in popular support, likely to fall at any time to pressure by leftists or by Sihanouk who could then reverse policy and which might have wholly unrealistic expectations about USG [US government] economic or military aid."[18]

To those in high positions in Washington outside of the intelligence agencies and Departments of State and Defense, Lon Nol was mostly an unknown entity. It was commonly asserted that the White House knew only that his name was a palindrome, though this analysis overstates official ignorance of Cambodian politics. Nevertheless, according to William Shawcross, "almost nothing was known of him in the White House at the time of the coup."[19] Misgivings and missing information aside, most officials viewed Lon Nol as offering "a more pro-U.S. and pro-Thai policy." Until the situation was clarified, the National Security Council staff recommended to Henry Kissinger that the US should not "publicly commit ourselves to the existence of the Lon Nol regime," finding that the objective of "a Cambodian Government under Lon Nol or anyone else which is anti-Communist and in control of the whole territory" to be "unrealistic."[20]

Those advocating restraint did not find a friend in President Richard Nixon. The day after the coup, Nixon demanded a plan for "maximum assistance to pro-U.S. elements in Cambodia." Five days after the coup, CIA director Helms provided the president a series of proposals to "support and sustain the present Cambodian Government" through "the provision of covert economic and political support." On April 24, 1970, Lon Nol wrote to President Nixon that he requested that the United States "help the Khmer people to defend its liberty and to save its fatherland from the terrible grasp of Asiatic communism."[21]

One immediate step the United States took was to facilitate the dispatching of the American-trained Khmer Krom (ethnic Cambodians living in southern Vietnam) units Lon Nol had requested from Son Ngoc Thanh before the coup. The absence of existing aid programs meant other US support would begin to arrive slowly, however, and would soon be complicated substantially by congressional opposition to an intervention to prop up yet another anticommunist dictatorship in Indochina. The actions of the new regime also hardly helped its cause. Anticoup protests were brutally repressed, and horrific pogroms against Vietnamese residents were carried out by Lon Nol's troops.[22]

On April 27, US Senator Jacob Javits (R-NY) delivered a speech at the University of Richmond in which he summed up his opposition to providing aid to a government that came to power "through a military coup d'état" and had whipped up "racial chauvinistic emotions" that culminated in the "repugnant" "mass slaughter among local Vietnamese civilians." The US should not, in Senator Javits's view, provide "any arms until the Cambodian government has demonstrated its viability. We cannot get into the business of propping up incompetent or unpopular governments." His colleague Senator Stephen M. Young (D-OH) put it this way three days later: "The truth is that the underdeveloped countries of Laos and Cambodia are not worth the life of one American youngster. This jungle and mountainous area more than 10,000 miles distant from the United States is of no importance whatever to the defense of our country."[23]

While it is difficult to say what US aid might have looked like had Nixon not made the fateful decision to launch an invasion of a small area of southeastern Cambodia that April, the unauthorized expansion of the Vietnam War met a vociferous response from Congress. On April 28, 1970, Nixon authorized the incursion into Cambodia to attack Viet Cong and North Vietnamese positions. This decision was made despite knowing the Senate was opposed to an expansion of the war and to any considerable aid for Lon Nol. When asked by White House staffers if this invasion did not breach the "Nixon Doctrine," which had pledged a reduction in direct US intervention in favor of bolstering friendly governments to do the fighting themselves, Kissinger replied, "We wrote the goddamn doctrine, we can change it."[24]

A "grim" Nixon delivered a television address to the nation on April 30 in which he situated the invasion as necessary to attack "the headquarters for the entire Communist military operation in South Vietnam" and worth risking a one-term presidency. The congressional and public reactions were swift. A day after Nixon had green-lighted the operation but before it was public, Congressman Jerome R. Waldie (D-CA) had introduced a resolution to prohibit "the introduction into Cambodia of troops, advisors, [and] arms supplies from the United States without the specific consent of Congress, and further prohibiting the use of U.S. airmen or aircraft in Cambodia without congressional consent." On April 30, Senator Joseph M. Montoya (D-NM) described Lon Nol's government as "repugnant to anyone who respects democracy and values the individual" and Cambodia's army as a "comic opera farce" lacking the "will, training, and ability to even contain the Communists, much less throw them back from positions they have recently reached." The day before the invasion was made public, Senators Frank Church (D-ID) and John Sherman Cooper (R-KY) had begun drafting legislation prohibiting any military assistance or operations in Cambodia from funds appropriated by Congress.[25]

The invasion also sparked a popular backlash in the United States. At Kent State University in Ohio, fifteen students protesting the invasion were gunned down by the National Guard, and four were killed. As one hundred thousand protesters gathered in Washington, DC, Nixon announced US troops would only penetrate twenty-one miles into Cambodia and would be withdrawn to South Vietnam by June 30. A revised "Cooper-Church amendment" was passed by both houses of Congress on December 22, 1970, and enacted on January 5, 1971. It forbade "the provision of American advisers to Cambodian forces" and "air operations in direct support of Cambodian forces" and explicitly stated American support "did not constitute a commitment to the defense of Cambodia." As a military operation, the invasion was unsuccessful. The purported Viet Cong base of operations was never found, and the intervention pushed North Vietnamese and Viet Cong troops deeper into Cambodian territory, where they began to clash with Lon Nol's poorly equipped troops.[26]

The strength of the domestic reaction to Nixon's intervention forced the US administration to pursue creative solutions to aid the Cambodians. Prohibitions on in-country training meant the US military advisers would train their Cambodian counterparts from bases in Thailand and South Vietnam. Limits to the amount of American personnel did not prevent an advisory presence in Phnom Penh in the form of the Military Equipment Delivery Team, Cambodia (MEDTC). While the US was able to provide substantial military aid to Cambodia, congressional restrictions meant it would not meet Lon Nol's apparent expectations of unlimited American support. This was an inauspicious start to what would ultimately amount to a five-year American effort to aid the Khmer Republic in its war against North Vietnam and the Communist Party of Kampuchea.[27]

The consolidation of power by Lon Nol over his coconspirators is a testament to the power of organizational resources over charisma in authoritarian politics. Lon Nol—the man a US diplomat remarked had been "appointed *because of* his incompetence"—had within a few months of the coup "usurped most of the power." Sirik Matak might have seemed the obvious choice for regime leader. He was the favored choice of the US Embassy and the Kampuchean commercial elite, and he had even organized the coup itself. But these bases of support offered Sirik Matak few organizational tools with any real bite. His supporters were wealthy but commanded no troops. On the other hand, Lon Nol had led the army for years. Its officers owed their position to his patronage, and norms surrounding the chain of command made him a clear focal point for support.[28]

Lon Nol's accumulation of power after the coup was gradual, but within two years he had consolidated effective personal control over the regime. He also gained a suitably lofty military rank after his promotion to marshal in April 1971. Lon Nol gained the support of his military officers by tolerating the pilfering of American aid and sheltering his incompetent subordinates from punishment. He also redirected US military aid to help his political prospects in more direct ways. Rather than rain bombs over Khmer Rouge or North Vietnamese positions, his US-supplied DC-3 aircraft dropped thousands of pictures of him over Phnom Penh.[29]

After Lon Nol's reelection with 55 percent of the vote in June 1972, US intelligence summarized for President Nixon the results of the voting by stating that although "this week's presidential election results fell short of Lon Nol's expectations, the outcome appears to augur well for Cambodia's short-term political stability." This optimistic read was because "the government engaged in just enough skullduggery to ensure Lon Nol's election, but it stopped short of manipulating the lopsided victory Lon Nol wanted but could not win honestly." Since the results were not pure fantasy, "the opposition elements cannot make a strong case for foul play" and "Lon Nol's claim to legitimacy is enhanced." Nevertheless, "the narrowness of his victory exposes the fragility of Lon Nol's hold on the Cambodian people." His election had been won with the open backing of senior military leaders, and absent the votes of military personnel, he might have lost.[30]

Lon Nol's government gradually came to rely more and more on the military for its support, as the loose coalition that had come together to oust Sihanouk began to unravel. By October 1971, with the exception of Sirik Matak, Lon Nol surrounded himself exclusively with advisers from the military. In the coming spring, Sirik Matak too would be purged from the inner circle, leaving Lon Nol surrounded exclusively by a coterie of generals. Nevertheless, even as Lon Nol's autocratic government became increasingly composed only of the military brass, it received some eyebrow-raising endorsements by US officials for its supposed liberalism. Senator Gale William McGee (D-WY) declared on June 21, 1972, that the "Cambodian people have chosen to stand up and defend their country," and while they have engaged in "a full-scale military struggle," they have "voted overwhelmingly in favor of a new democratic constitution" indicating "the determination of the Cambodians to develop their country in a democratic fashion." This was a curious statement, given that in October the previous year Lon Nol had declared openly he would no longer play the "sterile game of outmoded liberal democracy" and would be ruling by decree.[31]

After the 1970 coup, the Cambodian army dropped "royal" in favor of "national" in its official name, the Forces armées nationales khmères, or FANK. In March 1970, when it overthrew Sihanouk, the army was understrength of its allotted thirty-five thousand troops. Intent on bringing the fight to the communist forces, Lon Nol called for a popular mobilization en masse. The army was also reorganized. Like other regimes where the military seizes power, other internal security services saw their portfolios diminished relative to FANK. The Provincial Guard, a force under the National Police, saw their units dissolved and personnel spread across FANK. Soon the National Police itself was absorbed into the army. Despite its newfound political power, the army was in poor shape. A US National Security Council memo in April 1970 described the Cambodian army as "extremely weak both in competence and spirit." The following month, the Cambodian army was described in the American press as a force more accustomed to "mak[ing] roads, not war." FANK troops rode requisitioned PepsiCola trucks into battle, and soldiers were forced to procure their own uniforms.[32]

It is difficult to tell how strong or weak an army is before it has to fight a war. Yet the FANK soon laid bare its considerable weakness. A mere three months after the coup, the army swelled to some 110,000 troops. Despite this influx of often eager recruits, FANK was repeatedly routed by the far more formidable North Vietnamese forces, widely viewed as the best fighting force in Asia. Soon after the coup, the communists controlled around one-fifth of Cambodian territory and menaced the remaining government positions. Many of FANK's most highly regarded units were destroyed in these first forays into the war. These units were replaced by so-called twenty-four-hour soldiers—a grim homage to their sharply curtailed training regimen. In the view of a former senior Cambodian officer who was then deputy chief of the general staff, the massive expansion of the army reflected a "fairyland ambition to see the FANK transformed overnight into a grand armed force made in the image of the RVNAF [South Vietnamese army] or even the US forces."[33]

By the end of the year, US assessments of the Cambodian military remained pessimistic. A review led by the deputy national security adviser General Alexander Haig concluded on December 17, 1970, that the Cambodian military forces "are very weak, lack leadership, and do not seem to comprehend the nature of the enemy they are engaging." Yet only a week prior, President Nixon remarked superlatively that "the quarter-billion dollar aid program for Cambodia is, in my opinion, probably the best investment in foreign assistance that the United States has made in my lifetime." The Cambodian army had tripled in size over the course of only several months but clearly had only limited capacity to absorb the new poorly trained and poorly armed troops. The FANK officer corps was composed of loyalists who were unaccustomed to combat operations. The only truly elite troops available to the regime were the Khmer Krom forces dispatched from South Vietnam to aid the new government. The US considered these to be the "most effective combat forces on the government side." However, elite troops also constituted "a political threat" to Lon Nol. As a result they were "thrust into all the worst meat-grinder battles, and few survived."[34]

While covert aid was dispatched as quickly as possible, and US forces had invaded a small section of Cambodia in April 1970, more substantial aid was slow to arrive. Official military assistance began on April 22 but was still limited. This changed in August 1970 with the signing of a "U.S.-Cambodian military aid agreement providing for $185 million during the fiscal year beginning in mid-1970. The next fiscal year's assistance pledge would increase to about $200 million." A US Defense Department analysis noted that despite the "austere" beginnings of US military assistance to Cambodia, it grew into the "second largest U.S. assistance program" within a year.[35]

The most direct support to FANK was provided through a massive US bombing campaign against real and alleged communist positions. The aerial bombardment was a mixed blessing for the regime, however. The air raids killed a staggering number of innocent civilians, with as many as half a million killed over the course of the war. The frequently indiscriminate bombings generated enormous grievances against the government. According to its own records, the US Air Force dropped some 2.7 million tons of explosives over Cambodian territory from 1965 to 1973—more ordnance than was dropped in all of World War II. In the first half of 1973, the US "brutally postponed a Communist victory" with an intensified bombing campaign before Congress prohibited any further bombardment.[36]

As the US was forbidden by Congress from giving tactical military advice, American advisers focused on organizing government forces along American lines. Considering the prohibitions on a large in-country mission, US training of FANK proceeded remarkably rapidly. Around a year after the beginning of US military assistance, the US Defense Department estimated it would train 39,000 FANK personnel, the bulk of the 35 percent of the 180,000 or so troops it considered "trained." "By [the] time it formally closed down in February 1973, the Special Forces program had trained eighty-five Khmer infantry battalions and a marine fusilier battalion. The basic training of FANK soldiers by then had shifted into Cambodia, where existing centers were improved and new ones built."[37]

While pessimism colored many American analyses of FANK, there was a sense of relative gains among certain observers. Fred Ladd, a political-military counselor in the US Embassy, wrote a cable to General Haig of the NSC on May 10, 1971, in which he sought to dampen criticism of military aid for FANK. Ladd wrote that most of the American military representatives sent to observe the Cambodian army came away with the impression that the "operation may seem almost hopeless." However, these advisers "did not see FANK a year ago" and "do not recognize the rather dynamic changes for the better that have taken place in that time frame." He further bemoaned a tendency among the US Army representatives to "make FANK like us as quickly as possible," an unrealistic goal given the previously dire state of the Cambodian armed forces. However, he also warned that more extensive American organizational assistance might engender a "let them do it" attitude by the Cambodian officers, which would create "even greater requirements for involvement on our part."[38]

Other observers were less sanguine. Senator Stuart Symington (D-MO) bemoaned that "an army we pay for" in Cambodia was "increasingly reluctant to fight" and was led by a government that was "taking on the economic and political characteristics of another South Vietnam." While the US exerted considerable effort in building up FANK, it did not engage in any attempts to build a Cambodian intelligence agency. Cambodia essentially lacked a dedicated intelligence agency throughout the war, which forced the CIA to establish a liaison with the military's largely inept operational intelligence staffs at regional and provincial levels. Lon Nol's brother Lon Non did operate an intelligence network, the Comité de Coordination Spéciale, which boasted thousands of informants, but its performance was almost uniformly inept and its size almost certainly exaggerated.[39]

FANK was not the only armed force to experience a significant expansion. The Khmer Rouge had grown considerably in the two years before the coup. By the time Lon Nol ousted Sihanouk, they held around one-fifth of Cambodian territory. At this point, the KR had some five thousand fighters and was receiving much more significant assistance from the North Vietnamese. Within two years, the Khmer Rouge would grow to some forty thousand fighters. Their armed wing, the People's Liberation Armed Forces (PLAF), had an increasingly sophisticated structure, with village guerrilla units (Kang Chhlop), a regional army (Kang Damban), and the regular army (Kang Sruoch). The PLAF was under strict party control. Political commissars were present in all levels of the army down to the company. According to Ith Sarin, a KR candidate member who defected in 1973, the political commissar's "authority over combatants is indisputable." A secret police force under party control—the Santebal—was created in 1971 and led by Kaing Khek Iev (nom de guerre "Deuch"), a close ally of Pol Pot. In only four months after Sihanouk fell from power, the KR had overrun half of Cambodian territory, "taken or threatened 16 of its 19 provincial capitals," and harassed all road and rail links to Phnom Penh.[40]

Two major counteroffensives by the FANK in 1970 and 1971 were disasters. While the first "Chenla" operation in 1970 was not a total rout, the second campaign the following year resulted in the ignominious collapse of the government forces assigned to clear the route to the besieged garrison in Kompong Thom. While the exact cost of the failed operations is unknown, a senior Cambodian officer estimated they cost ten battalions' worth of personnel and twenty battalions' worth of equipment. The military performance of the Cambodian army frequently frustrated its American patrons. The problems were multifaceted, but authoritarian politics lay at the center of it all. Lon Nol was surrounded by a coterie of sycophantic generals who validated his increasingly erratic behavior. It was frequently observed that the marshal and his inner circle were wildly out of touch with reality. On December 7, 1971, General Haig of the National Security Council sent a cable to the US Embassy in Phnom Penh in which he noted that, based on the messages he was receiving, "it seems clear that Lon Nol himself is living in a dream world." This "dream world" accusation was leveled against Lon Nol repeatedly. A bewildered US Embassy cable from 1972 reported that Lon Nol was convinced that "the Khmer Communist Movement does not pose a serious threat to his government."[41]

One of the most pressing problems was rampant corruption in the armed forces. With the US footing the military bill, Cambodian officers found ample opportunities for graft. One of the most militarily costly forms of corruption was the practice of paying "phantom soldiers." These phantoms were creations of corrupt commanders who received funds to equip fictive soldiers and pocketed the pay. The US General Accounting Office found in 1973 that around $1 million was being paid to phantoms every month. In 1971, American auditors reported that only 6 to 8 per-cent of FANK's salaries were actually being dispensed to troops. In a meeting in Washington, Kissinger asked the CIA director if he understood correctly that "Cambodian commanders are now pocketing the pay of actual troops, not just that of the phantoms?" to which Director Colby answered "yes." By the end of 1972, a Cambodian military spokesperson admitted that every month commanding officers pocketed the pay of some one hundred thousand phantom soldiers. When confronted with this admis-sion from someone in his own government, Lon Nol was unper-turbed. "Calm down," Lon Nol admonished. "The Americans are killing a thousand of our enemies every week. Victory is ours."[42]

Focused on their political fortunes and their bank accounts, commanders were frequently absent from the front. Battalion and brigade commanders were often in Phnom Penh villas they pur-chased with the salaries of their phantom soldiers while their real soldiers fought. This had a predictably negative effect on the morale of American-trained junior and field-grade officers. FANK officers even sold US military supplies to the enemy. The rot permeated all branches of the armed forces. "Pilots were keener to fly for con-traband than for combat, and then often demanded bribes from ground units before providing air support."[43]

Lon Nol also turned out to be a poor tactician. The dictator "reordered battle plans according to the predictions of his personal astrologer" and "restructured military campaigns in order to cap-ture holy monuments rather than an enemy position." Lon Nol "insisted on maintaining personal control over the war effort." He would even call unit commanders directly by telephone, bypass-ing the general staff. This was made even more damaging to FANK as his tactical suggestions were "often absurd." Lon Nol subverted American aid to focus on internal rivals to his regime rather than his formidable external foes. According to a leading study of the war, "units equipped by the Military Equipment Delivery Team would be dissolved overnight, their materiel shifted elsewhere or sold. Despite the objections of the embassy, Lon Nol created the 9th Infantry Division as his Palace Guard. He placed it under one of the most ineffective and corrupt commanders in the entire country."[44]

Deac writes that "incredibly, even as the battle for Phnom Penh raged around them, a lion's share of the government's military and civilian leaders refused to discard the corrupt practices that were weakening the very forces they needed for survival." "Even in the final weeks of the war, some Cambodians in Phnom Penh expected that the United States would rescue their cause." Even if Cambodian elites weren't convinced the US would save the republic, they were certain it would save them personally. "The highest-ranking officials were certain that the Americans would whisk them away in helicopters if things did not work out."[45]

Lon Nol's poor health, ineffective leadership, and cultivation of loyal cronies over competent commanders gradually alienated his superpower patron. In a scathing telegram in August 1974, Ambassador Dean wrote to Secretary of State Kissinger that "no one would pick Lon Nol to lead a modern state." He was "not particularly intelligent or well-organized" and grew ever more "dependent on a coterie of 'yes-man' advisors and ill-equipped cronies devoted more to their personal aggrandizement than to the national interest." The marshal "lavishly rewards loyal subordinates and permits them to carry on well past the point where their incompetence becomes manifest."

As the United States prepared to draw down its wars in Indochina in 1973, officials began to urgently consider alternatives to Lon Nol in order to save a noncommunist Cambodia. In high-level deliberations, US officials repeatedly remarked how "expendable" Lon Nol was and how willing they were to see him replaced by anyone more competent. President Nixon remarked in March 1973 that "they've got to get Lon Nol the hell out of there, some way or another, but you can't overthrow him."[46]

Two US government analyses from this period provide valuable insights into American thinking about the viability of alternatives to Lon Nol. One study by the CIA on March 26, "The Cambodian Political Situation," was described by William Stearman of the NSC as a "useful but somewhat alarmist document" that he and his colleagues had found disturbing. The second analysis was produced by the embassy in Phnom Penh on September 10. Both studies considered the prospects for a coup against Lon Nol.[47]

In both the CIA and State Department estimations, there were only four figures with both the motive and capacity to remove Lon Nol from office. Two of these officers were some of the only competent generals in the entire Cambodian army. Brigadier Generals Dien Del and Un Kauv were each division commanders (Second and Seventh Divisions, respectively). Dien Del was viewed by the CIA as "one of FANK's best field commanders," and Un Kauv as "probably the best in FANK." Both Dien Del and Un Kauv commanded the loyalty of their sizable forces, and both apparently had grown estranged from Lon Nol. Dien Del had complained to personal friends about FANK deficiencies and the "drift" of the government and, according to the State Department report, spoke "openly and bitterly against Lon Nol." Un Kauv was thought to share his views and favor eliminating phantom troops, and the men were close friends.

However, both men were Khmer Krom, which posed a political liability in Phnom Penh's often xenophobic politics. As mentioned above, the Khmer Krom had earlier posed a potent potential threat to Lon Nol, and he had done his best to disperse these better-trained soldiers throughout the army to diminish their power. They had borne "the brunt of combat to the point where their morale, efficiency, and loyalty has been seriously affected."[48]

The third field commander, Brigadier General Norodom Changtaraingsey, was important for any prospective coup largely because his fiefdom was close to the capital, and he was thought to harbor views sympathetic to a regime change. A prince in the deposed royal family, he ruled his area "in the manner of a warlord" and refused to deploy his thirteen thousand troops outside his zone of control.

The most important man in any speculative coup, however, was the chief of the army staff, Major General Sosthene Fernandez. In the view of the CIA, he was "the key figure to any successful military coup," and it was unlikely that Un Kauv, Dien Del, or Norodom Changtaraingsey would move without his support. Fernandez was a longtime colleague of Lon Nol. Short of physical stature, he "pampered his vanity by having a set of miniature furniture and platforms constructed for his office so as to appear taller and larger." He was considered a Sihanouk loyalist, and his Filipino and Portuguese descent was not a political asset. Fernandez was elevated to commander-in-chief of the armed forces in June 1973 in a long-overdue promotion. He was something of a reformer and had tried to carry out "badly needed military reforms," but many of his actions were stymied by Lon Non.[49]

Lon Nol, however, had long been suspicious of General Fernandez. The distrust was apparently mutual. While Fernandez's authority may have been sufficient to muster loyal commanders into a coup, Lon Nol had explicitly prohibited him from moving any forces without the approval of the army's assistant chief of staff for operations, a Lon Nol lackey. This arrangement was set up by Lon Nol "as an additional control mechanism for himself over troop units tasked with defending Phnom Penh" that would be key in any coup. A further limitation was that Fernandez had "many friends but few true admirers" among the officers who would be important if there was a coup and was viewed as having been ineffective in saving the army's interests from Lon Nol's clique.[50]

Other figures were more appealing to American officials but less plausible options. Major General Sak Sutsakhan, for example, was highly regarded by the United States as an officer who had "managed the singular feat of staying honest and close to Lon Nol." However, he was a staff officer without a troop command and thus had considerable barriers to carrying out a coup. Son Ngoc Thanh was esteemed highly by the United States (even once referred to as "Cambodia's George Washington"), but his advanced age and perceived closeness with Saigon was a serious impediment to his accumulation of power. As his power base lay with the Khmer Krom, he had the same impediments to a coup as Dien Del and Un Kauv. The CIA ultimately concluded that "Son Thanh is politically dead" as "his power base among the Khmer Krom units in the army has largely dissipated."[51]

Lon Nol had undertaken multiple measures to prevent any coup from threatening his government beyond the peculiar command arrangement noted above. The brigadier general in charge of the critically located First Division, Ith Suong, had a fate "tightly linked with Lon Nol's" and was viewed as likely to "fight for the president against a coup effort," and his division would "form the nucleus of any counter-coup preemptive bid Lon Nol might make." The loyalties of other officers—such as the Third Division's Brigadier General Nguon Ly Khea and the Phnom Penh Special Region commander Brigadier General Deng Layom—were more difficult to ascertain.[52]

The most important countercoup maneuver was to elevate Lon Nol's brother to important commands in the army. Lon Non was born in 1930 and studied in France as well as at the Cambodian Military Academy. Lon Non had entered military intelligence and was made head of army counterintelligence in 1960. At the time of the 1970 coup he had been the commander of Phnom Penh's military police for two years. The US was generally very opposed to any seizure of power by Lon Non. In the estimation of the Central Intelligence Agency, Lon Non was "intensely disliked by key military commanders and does not have a particularly solid military power base of his own." What "political entourage" he had consisted of "young opportunists" whose support "would quickly evaporate at the sign of a serious threat to Lon Nol's authority." In the event he seized power, he would "meet strong opposition" and would only survive with "direct and unqualified support from the US." Lon Non's behavior also undermined military effectiveness. In March 1973, George Carver of the CIA noted in a meeting with other top officials that "Lon Non has the military commanders in a state of apprehension. The Cambodian generals are all nervous, each thinking he may be next on Lon Non's list. It's having a very serious effect on military effectiveness. None of the commanders want to stick their necks out or take any initiatives." Nevertheless, despite the very low opinion of Lon Non, top officials in the US did consider prodding him to overthrow his brother and take power.[53]

American officials were ultimately unsure how to approach these coup prospects. On the one hand, US intelligence suggested that a successor regime of almost any of Lon Nol's opponents other than his brother would be no worse, and might be better, for American goals in Cambodia. On the other hand, the US did not feel that it should directly encourage plotting. After reviewing the recent CIA recommendations and intelligence on the potential for a coup, William Stearman of the NSC informed Kissinger on August 6, 1973, that he shared Kissinger's "apparent view that we not support Lon Nol if any independent, unified attempt is made by the High Council to remove him. However, this does not mean that we should encourage coup plotting in any way, but only that we accept a fait accompli, if and when it occurs." Stearman felt it would be unwise to directly promote a coup, as "the political risks are high and the negotiating dividend minimal."[54]

This basic orientation shaped the American response to coup plotting. The CIA reported that Fernandez and Brigadier General Dien Del had both considered a coup in the summer of 1973. The NSC responded to the CIA report saying they were "in basic agreement with this appraisal." According to the NSC,

It has been our impression that selected Cambodian military leaders, in particular Major General Sosthene Fernandez, have been taking soundings as to the U.S. Government's willingness to back a coup. However, General Sosthene and the others have been repeatedly told in categorical terms that the U.S. does not and would not foster any coup efforts, and that FANK must address itself to the military situation which requires its full and undivided attention. Although General Sosthene and the others are very much aware of the U.S. position, this does not preclude the possibility that, if the Cambodian military leaders are faced with significant deterioration on the military, political or economic front, they might undertake a coup without the U.S. Government's blessing.[55]

In September 1973, the US Embassy in Phnom Penh concluded that while "several" key officers "have decided that Lon Nol's administration should go, few if any have any firm concept of what and who should replace it nor how to go about the operation." Barring any "ill-timed pre-emptive move from Lon Nol," a coup attempt "is not in the immediate offing." Several more active interventions were considered but ultimately not acted upon. In a meeting of the Washington Special Action Group (WSAG) on July 10, 1973, Kissinger asked Admiral Thomas Moorer of the Joint Chiefs of Staff whether the Cambodians were willing to fight. Moorer replied, "If Lon Nol were out, Fernandez in, and the troops were paid, they will fight." When asked how exactly this was to be done, CIA director Colby suggested "we should just go up and say 'go'!"[56]

The operations side of the CIA suggested the US effect the removal of Lon Nol and Lon Non from Cambodia, which would render it possible to "persuade the remaining members of the GKR High Council that their first priority efforts must be devoted to improving the effectiveness of the FANK." One key step in reforming FANK to be more effective would be to give Sosthene

Fernandez "supreme military authority" and to carry out a purge of corrupt and ineffective officers. As the issue was not insufficient funds but corruption, it was theoretically possible to actually pay the troops fighting the rebels. It was even suggested that US personnel pay the troops directly to prevent commanders from stealing the funds.[57]

On the other hand, some senior officials in the US government felt this discussion was distracting from the more pressing issues. Kissinger remarked in March 1973 that "our behavior has been like that of a maiden aunt. We've been giving the Cambodians advice on how to constitute the basic political structure of their government when they have a knife at their throat." Ultimately, no coup would remove Lon Nol. Sosthene Fernandez would never try to oust his boss and would instead stay on the slowly sinking ship. In March 1975 he was demoted. His fate came "to symbolize the inadequacies of the government's military performance."[58]

THE KHMER REPUBLIC ULTIMATELY OUTLASTED EXPECTATIONS. CIA director Colby suggested as a "personal statement" and not necessarily a reflection of agency thinking that Phnom Penh would last "up to three months" without American air support. The government instead hung on nearly another two years.[59]

On March 5, 1975, aware that the government could collapse at any time, Kissinger lamented that "we never put enough in Cambodia to win a military victory. We never did enough to bring it to a conclusion." Yet this analysis leaves much to be desired. Not only did a much larger investment in South Vietnam similarly fail to build an effective anticommunist regime, but the collapse of the Cambodian military was in some ways a product of large-scale American support. With American aid paying for the war, Cambodian commanders oversaw monumental corruption that destroyed the Cambodian state.[60]

In her book on the period, scholar Marie Martin ponders why the US "maintained in power an individual who combined such incompetence and eccentricity," suggesting that "perhaps the White House did not wish to deal with someone capable of defying it." The historical record does not support such a conclusion. Lon Nol was no lackey and in fact repeatedly defied and frustrated his American patrons. Moreover, US officials frequently considered and sometimes even endorsed plans to support the removal of Lon Nol. Ultimately, the US did not itself instigate a coup and did reject attempts by Cambodian officers to involve the embassy directly in their coup plots. But the US had desperately wanted strong leadership in Phnom Penh, not a weak lackey. Instead, American military assistance insulated Lon Nol from the debilitating consequences of his political survival strategies. Trading the prospects of eventual defeat for immediate protection from his internal rivals, Lon Nol misused American aid to personalize his regime and prolong his tenure. These actions cannibalized the coercive capacity of the Cambodian army and ultimately led to the collapse of the government and the victory of one of the most brutal revolutionary dictatorships of the twentieth century.[61]

Many of Cambodia's corrupt military commanders were whisked out of Phnom Penh on American transports as Khmer Rouge forces approached. Some would go on to live in the United States, and Lon Nol would die in Fullerton, California, in 1985 at the age of seventy-two. Others, like Dien Del, watched their corrupt commanders flee as they readied themselves to trade places with the Khmer Rouge, heading to the jungle to begin an insurgency against their victorious adversaries. Perhaps the most tragic twist in the saga of American intervention in Cambodia was the volte-face in 1979 after the Khmer Rouge were themselves ousted by a Vietnamese invasion. The Khmer Rouge, a group the United States had opposed tenaciously with arms, aid, and bombs, was now the recipient of a clandestine US program to help it fight the occupying Vietnamese army.

The five-year effort to shore up Lon Nol's regime and build an effective Cambodian military ultimately ended in failure. The causes of this outcome were myriad, and it cannot be reduced solely to the dynamics elucidated here. Yet the politics of authoritarian survival interacted with American aid at nearly every point in the American effort to support the anticommunist regime. American advisers were frustrated at the repeated subversion of their aid by an autocrat more concerned about preventing a coup from his internal rivals than with the communist guerillas who lurked ever closer to the capital.

As the Cold War wound down in the late 1980s, interventions like Cambodia also came to a gradual halt. The decline of proxy warfare did not reduce the misery of civil war in the postcolonial world, and many of these conflicts continued to drag on after Soviet and American interest in supporting the opposing sides dissipated. In the end, interventions like Cambodia, Vietnam, Afghanistan, and Laos were the bloody hallmarks of superpower interventions to support beleaguered client regimes. With the end of the Cold War came publics and policymakers in both Washington and Moscow who sought to forget and move on from these often disastrous interventions. But the shadows of these wars were long.

8 | AFTER THE COLD WAR

Despite the failures to build an effective Cambodian, Laotian, or South Vietnamese army or keep friendly dictatorships in power for long, the United States won the Cold War. Conversely, Moscow's remarkable success in consolidating resilient dictatorships in the Third World did not prevent the Soviet Union's own collapse. The failures and successes of both superpowers' policies toward their allied autocrats would soon fade in importance with the end of their rivalry. The end of the Cold War would transform the triumphant United States and its foreign policy toward friendly tyrants.

The United States emerged from the Cold War in a position of unparalleled and unprecedented global power. Its economic power was greater than "any other state in history," and its defense budget was as large as those of the rest of the world combined. This budget supported a large global military footprint. The US maintained deployments of over one hundred troops in dozens of countries, and from 1999 until 2016 alone the United States trained nearly 2.4 million foreign military personnel. As the US became the singular global hegemon, Russia rose from the ashes of the Soviet

Union as a much-diminished power. Soviet troops began to leave even their closest Cold War allies, and the subsequent Russian presence was much reduced. Some 650,000 Soviet troops and tens of thousands of tanks departed Eastern Europe. The Soviet armed forces hemorrhaged troops, falling from some 5.3 million in 1985 to 2.7 million under the new Russian Federation. The Soviet-era overseas military facilities that remained were almost all shuttered shortly after the turn of the century. Moscow's former Warsaw Pact allies gradually joined NATO, along with the former Soviet Baltic republics.[1]

The end of the Cold War brought several important transformations in great power policies toward friendly dictatorships. First, the collapse of the Soviet Union and the large-scale global retrenchment of its primary successor state virtually eliminated one major source of foreign support for dictatorships. It also radically changed the attitude of the remaining superpower toward friendly tyrants. With the US increasingly freed from the need to cultivate unsavory allies against the Soviet threat, the rationale behind American support for autocrats quickly unraveled. Some dictatorships—particularly those important to the US alliance with Israel—found continued geopolitical relevance, ensuring largely uninterrupted or renewed American support. But other dictatorships found the attitude in Washington to their unreformed rule had shifted considerably. With the Soviet threat gone, the United States and its Western allies began to apply "unprecedented political conditionality" on military and economic aid, insisting on democratization in much of the world.[2]

In practice, of course, support for friendly tyrants ended in different places at different times. Some US-backed dictatorships found their support wane quickly as the US-Soviet rivalry cooled, while others found continued US assistance until the Soviet Union itself collapsed. In Asia and Latin America, the US supported democratization in many of its client regimes beginning in the late

1980s. In Africa, the US stood aside when its unruly Liberian ally Samuel Doe was killed after insurgents toppled his regime the year before. Mobutu Sese Seko in Zaire held on for a bit longer, but he too found himself cut off from American assistance once the Soviet Union disintegrated. Other Cold War–era clients continued to receive American support. These regimes—including Egypt, Jordan, Pakistan, and Saudi Arabia—were concentrated in the Middle East and South Asia, and their waning American commitments were resuscitated by the global "War on Terror" that followed the September 11, 2001, terrorist attacks on the United States.[3]

The Soviet withdrawal from its network of alliances also varied across time and space. The most dramatic events took place in Eastern Europe. There, beleaguered client regimes looked in vain to Moscow for guidance as they faced mass protests calling for an end to party rule. With a reformist and distracted Soviet regime led by Mikhail Gorbachev in Moscow unwilling to crush the protests, Soviet clients fell one by one. Only Romania, the most estranged Soviet ally in Eastern Europe, carried out a bloody crackdown on its protest movement. As with elsewhere, the Soviet response to events in Romania was remarkably passive. At the height of the unrest, Soviet officials told their Romanian counterparts that the "dramatic events taking place in Romania are your own internal problem." The Romanian regime tried to use violence anyway. Repression ultimately failed to quell the protests, and General Secretary Nicolae Ceaușescu was executed just ten days after the unrest began.[4]

For other allies, support continued until the Soviet Union itself collapsed. Regimes in Angola, Cuba, Syria, and Vietnam continued to receive Soviet military and economic aid through 1991. Soviet aid continued to flow to Mengistu's Ethiopia until it was defeated by insurgents in May 1991. In other places aid began to wane earlier. When South Yemeni party leadership approached their Soviet patrons in December 1989, they were told that the People's

Democratic Republic of Yemen "should stand on its own feet" and were reminded that "its debt to the Soviet Union was $6 billion." Military advisers were removed from Mozambique in 1989, and Soviet personnel left Mongolia in 1990. The years 1989 to 1991 were difficult for communist regimes. Many could not withstand the ballooning protests and the collapse of the superpower at the core of the communist world system. Some just barely outlasted their own patron: governments in Afghanistan (April 1992) and Mongolia (June 1993) lasted a bit longer than the Soviet Union (December 1991). Yet others have proven remarkably resilient: Angola, China, Cuba, Mozambique, North Korea, and Vietnam are still ruled by former Soviet client regimes.[5]

The ascent of the United States to unrivaled global superpower status led to several important changes in its foreign policy behavior. Most importantly, the United States began to promote democracy more actively and consistently. In 1989, President George H. W. Bush declared that "the day of the dictator is over." The seemingly temporary exigencies that had in fact led to decades of support for friendly tyrants were largely gone. The communist regimes that remained were either themselves engaged in market liberalization or were increasingly isolated outposts of retrograde Stalinism that did not pose the threat they had as allies of a now defunct superpower rival. Dictators could no longer find a sympathetic audience in Washington for military aid to fight a communist menace that largely disappeared along with the Soviet Union. Unless they could leverage another pressing geopolitical concern, autocrats faced pariah status if they did not liberalize to accommodate the new global system. Of course, adjusting to the new international system through liberalization did not always lead to sustained or successful democratization. Autocrats proved skillful in embracing the more visible aspects of democracy while nevertheless manipulating elections, jailing opponents through ostensibly legal means, and otherwise maintaining an uneven playing field. Nevertheless, open military rule and highly visible repression brought costly international isolation. While regimes in Myanmar and Eritrea chose isolation over liberalization, many others could or would not withstand the external pressure.[6]

UNITED STATES MILITARY AID DID NOT END WITH THE END OF THE Cold War, though it did change, undergoing two major transformations. The first is that the US began to provide military assistance to a far wider range of countries than before. As the pre-eminent military power with no rival and only a disparate set of enemies, the United States was the most popular source of military assistance. The second is that US military aid has placed a relatively greater emphasis on respect for human rights and civilian control of the military. In 1990, Congress expanded the objectives of the International Military Education and Training (IMET) program to focus on "fostering greater understanding of and respect for civilian control of the military." Prior to this, US military training had included an emphasis on human rights, but the primary focus remained increasing military capacity and forging connections with potentially influential foreign military personnel. While IMET comprises a relatively small share of the overall US military and economic aid budget, it has a wide reach: 121 non-NATO countries received training in fiscal year 2020 at the cost of $90.3 million. Despite relatively greater emphasis by the US on civilian control of the military and human rights, US government reports suggest uneven emphasis on human rights and civil-military relations in IMET programs. At the Western Hemisphere Institute for Security Cooperation, formerly known as the School of the Americas, all trainees must go through a mandatory ten hours of training on human rights, which includes emphasis on civilian control of the military and the role of the military in a democratic society. Despite this new emphasis, academic research has found that even in the post–Cold War period, US military aid is not associated with either civilian control of the military or respect for human rights. US military assistance is in fact associated with increased coup risk and more abuses of human rights.[7]

Especially since 9/11, US military aid has also come to embrace the creation of so-called enclave units—elite counterterrorism units that are often closely tied to state leadership or even part of the praetorian guard. In Burkina Faso, the United States trained the Presidential Security Regiment (Régiment de sécurité présidentielle, RSP) of dictator Blaise Compaoré (r. 1987–2014) in counterterrorism operations. The RSP was an elite unit separate from the army with superior weaponry, training, and uniforms. As we will see, it also led a subsequent coup d'état. In Cameroon, efforts by Western countries to train the Rapid Intervention Battalions (Bataillons d'intervention rapide, BIR) for counterterrorism operations against Boko Haram have also proved a mixed blessing. While security force assistance may have increased the military capacity of the BIR, these battalions report directly to longtime dictator Paul Biya (r. 1982–present) and have played an active role in domestic repression against mass protests. The BIR added another layer to a highly fragmented coercive apparatus that balances against the regular army, the gendarmerie, and the presidential guard to prevent a coup d'état.[8]

In another ostensible counterterrorism success story, the Danab ("Lightning") Brigade in Somalia has proven a political as well as a military resource. The Danab Brigade has been considered a military success by its American sponsors. It was the "only unit within the overall Somali National Army fully capable of lethal, offensive operations" and the "only effective, apolitical fighting unit in the country's war against al-Qaeda-affiliated al-Shabab." To maintain this efficiency, US advisers kept the Danab Brigade "largely separate from the rest of the army." Yet Danab's strength relative to other forces made it a potentially decisive player in internal politics. In December 2020, a regional Danab commander was killed in an al-Shabab attack in Galkayo when he was attending a campaign rally for the prime minister. Involvement by the elite unit in fighting against militia allied against al-Shabab in Guriel in 2021 prompted the US to "review" but not end its support for the commandos. Just as efforts to build apolitical and nonpartisan armies failed to graft onto domestic political realities in the Cold War, contemporary US counterterrorism security assistance helps build security forces that either act as a force for government repression or destabilize regime politics.[9]

In spite of these problems, military coups declined rapidly after the end of the Cold War. The 1990s saw fewer than half the number of coups as the preceding decade, and that number fell by half again each subsequent decade. But it was not curricular changes in US military aid that led to a decline in military coups after the Cold War. Instead, coups fell so dramatically because coup makers were much more consistently punished after seizing power. The United States and other members of the international community did not prevent coups by fixing the praetorian impulses of armies through training but by lowering the value for military officers of carrying out a successful coup.[10]

Consider the 2015 coup d'état in Burkina Faso. In September, members of the elite US- and French-trained presidential guard led by General Gilbert Diendéré staged a successful coup against an interim government. Yet the victorious putschists were "surprised by the vehemence of the continental response." The African Union, the United Nations, France, and the United States immediately condemned the coup, and the West African economic bloc began to organize a response. The Russian diplomat that led the UN Security Council at the time even condemned the coup "in the strongest terms." The coup leaders had their assets frozen and were immediately banned from international travel. Utterly isolated externally, Diendéré stepped down a week later.[11]

This kind of swift and unified international response also characterized other coups in post–Cold War states. The March 2012 coup in Mali was also rapidly condemned and greeted with sanctions. It was particularly unwelcome, as Mali had offered a hopeful case for democratic development. France called for elections "as soon as possible," and the US demanded an "immediate restoration of constitutional rule" and refused to recognize the junta. Isolated and unable to reverse the battlefield losses that had motivated their coup, the coup leaders agreed to hand power to a civilian government and step down.[12]

While such cases were typical in the post–Cold War period, there were of course coups that were ultimately tolerated by the international community. The Obama administration took great pains to avoid calling the 2013 military coup against the Muslim Brotherhood government in Egypt a coup, as this would have made the large American aid package very difficult to legally disburse.[13]

Nevertheless, for much of the past thirty years, coups have been met with a far harsher reaction than during the Cold War. In turn, they fell to very low rates after the superpower rivalry between the Soviet Union and United States ceased. Coups are highly visible acts that openly violate democracy and civilian control of the military. As a result, they provide a clear focal point for international condemnation, more than the gradual subversion of democracy by elected incumbents that characterizes the other primary mode of democratic breakdown.

In the past several years, however, there is some evidence that we are seeing a return of the military coup. From 2020 to 2022, there were coups in Burkina Faso (January and September 2022), Mali (August 2020 and May 2021), Guinea (September 2021), Myanmar (February 2021), and Sudan (October 2021). In 2023, Niger saw a coup (July) as did Gabon (August). While more a case of authoritarian succession than a coup, the transition of power to General Mahamat Déby, son of the longtime strongman Idriss Déby, after the elder Déby's death battling insurgents in April 2021, directly involved the Chadian military. A military junta declared Mahamat Déby chairman of the Transitional Military Council, and he continues to rule Chad. In addition to these coups, there were failed coups in Niger, Sudan, Guinea-Bissau, and Russia. Coup plots were apparently foiled in Mali, the Gambia, Madagascar, and Sierra Leone, and military insubordination nearly escalated to a coup plot in Armenia.[14]

The rate of coups is indeed increasing. With over seven attempts per year for the 2020–2022 period, coups have been attempted at three times the rate of previous years. World leaders have taken notice. In November 2021, United Nations Secretary-General António Guterres described this as "an epidemic of coups." Analysts have been quick to notice that the leaders of recent coups in Mali (2020 and 2021) and Burkina Faso (January 2022) were trained by the US military. In a particularly embarrassing moment for the United States government, the Guinean special forces that ousted their government in September 2021 had been trained by American Special Forces that very morning. There is no evidence that any of these coups were supported by the United States, and all were condemned. But what is clear is that coup leaders increasingly hope to leverage cracks in the international response to hold on to power.[15]

In some cases, the international response has indeed been split. The African Union, regional blocs like ECOWAS, and the UN have overall been mostly consistent in condemning or sanctioning coups. The reactions of France and the United States, however, have exhibited more subtle variation. When General Mahamat Déby took over in Chad, the African Union called for a swift end to military rule. Paris, on the other hand, chose to support the takeover.[16]

In Burkina Faso's first coup of 2022, the US- and French-trained Lieutenant Colonel Paul-Henri Sandaogo Damiba declared himself president as the head of the Patriotic Movement for

Safeguard and Restoration. The coup was motivated by the deteriorating government position against Islamist militants. While France has no military bases in Burkina Faso, French troops operated there as part of Operation Barkhane (2013–2023). Unsurprisingly, the new junta sought to assuage international opinion and promised that Burkina Faso would return to constitutional rule "when the conditions are right." The response from regional bodies was swift. The African Union and ECOWAS both condemned the coup and suspended Burkina Faso. France condemned the coup but also stated there was no reason France would end its security operations in the Sahel as a result. The US response was somewhat equivocal. While condemning the takeover and urging a swift return to civilian-led government, the US State Department acknowledged "the tremendous stress on Burkinabe society and security forces posed by ISIS and JNIM [the two major militant groups] but urge military officers to step back" and "return to their barracks."[17]

The Russian response was different. Putin ally Yevgeny Prigozhin publicly praised the coup and offered instructors for the Burkinabe army. Although he had a complicated relationship with the Russian state, the late Prigozhin was closely connected to the Russian government. Later that year, Prigozhin finally acknowledged he had founded the notorious Wagner Group. The US Defense Department publicly acknowledged rumors of Russian involvement in the Burkina Faso coup but declined to confirm whether there was an actual Russian role. China's reaction to the coup was characteristically muted, stating only that it was closely monitoring the situation, sought to protect Chinese nationals, and urged all parties to peacefully resolve their differences and ensure stability. Ultimately the junta opted to ignore external pressure and remain in power after some token civilianization. Damiba did not leave office after elections, but after another coup led by junior officers just nine months later. This coup was accompanied by mass protests where Russian flags were waved and the French embassy was attacked. The latest coup leader, Captain Ibrahim Traoré, made it clear he "wanted to work with new international partners to push back Islamist groups" but that he was "also open to working with the US or any other country willing to help improve security in the country." It is far from clear that the junta seeks an exclusive alignment with Russia. Yet the very prospect of an alternative source of security assistance nevertheless serves the same purpose it did during the Cold War. By reducing the reliance on one source of succor, alternative sources of support lessen external leverage over the internal political dynamics of the regime. For Burkinabe military rulers, reduced Western pressure over human rights abuses and military rule would surely be a welcome development brought by a decline in American unipolarity.[18]

RUSSIAN REGIME SUPPORT WAS FAIRLY LIMITED AFTER THE COLlapse of the Soviet Union. For much of the early post-Soviet years, Tajikistan was the only state where Moscow made an investment in supporting a particular regime. Things began to change after the Russian invasion of Ukraine in 2014 and the severe decline in relations with the West. Perhaps the most dramatic indication of a shift was the Russian military intervention in September 2015 on behalf of its beleaguered ally in Syria. In the estimation of General Valery Gerasimov, chief of the Russian general staff, Bashar al-Assad's government held just over 10 percent of Syrian territory before the intervention. The Russian intervention helped reverse the tide of the war and solidify the position of the Assad regime.[19]

In more recent years, Russia has aided beleaguered regimes in Belarus (2020) and Kazakhstan (2022). In Belarus, while Russia pledged security assistance, the regime's own security services proved up to the task of repression and remained cohesive.

It is of course possible their resolve was stiffened by the pledge of Russian support five days into the mass protests. Russia played a more minor role in the January 2022 Kazakhstan protests over fuel prices, and the Russian intervention force was quickly withdrawn. In the past few years Russia has also taken on an expanded, though still limited, role in providing security assistance to regimes far outside the former Soviet bloc. This has been done in part through the Wagner Group mentioned above. Some have gone so far as to describe the Wagner Group as an entity that "props up autocrats" in Africa. Wagner played a notable role in the Central African Republic, where Russia has replaced France as the primary patron of the government of President Faustin-Archange Touadéra, who has been in power since March 2016.[20]

Initial Russian support to the CAR began in January 2018, with a deployment of 175 advisers to train military personnel and the provision of small arms and ammunition. This deployment grew to some five hundred advisers in total by early 2021, and in January 2022 the Kremlin acknowledged military advisers remain in the CAR and operate "at various levels." Russian advisers have been involved in training both the state army (Forces armées centrafricaines, FACA) and the Presidential Guard (Garde présidentielle). Already by May 2018 Russian advisers had trained nearly nine hundred FACA and Presidential Guard soldiers. In May 2019, a new elite unit in the Presidential Guard was created after Russian training as the Groupement spécial chargé de la protection républicaine (GSPR). According to the UN, Russian advisers have accompanied FACA in deployments. Russian-trained forces and Wagner personnel, who have been accused of human rights abuses, helped CAR and UN forces repel an attack by rebels on Bangui in January 2021. Russia's influence in Bangui was reinforced by the appointment of an alleged former Russian intelligence officer, Valery Zakharov, as the national security adviser to President Touadéra in April 2018, and Russian personnel acted as his personal guard.[21]

While Russian security assistance has increased, it has several key differences from Soviet-era support. Russian efforts are no longer geared to creating the Soviet model of a partisan army abroad. This is in part because Russia itself has a new security structure. While still carefully structured to prevent a military coup, Russia's security apparatus exhibits several important differences from the Soviet period. Gone are the party committees and political commissars. Officers are not generally members of the ruling party. It was considered highly abnormal when General Andrei Kartapolov announced he would run for office on Putin's United Russia ticket in 2021, and he quickly resigned his commission. While a successor to the Main Political Administration does remain in the Russian army, it is a much pared down entity that does not maintain an extensive web of political commissars and is instead geared toward military-patriotic education. The Russian army is "expert" and no longer "red."[22]

The only major element of the Soviet system that remains is the embedded military counterintelligence service. Shortly after Putin came to power, he strengthened this military counterintelligence department. These officers are embedded directly in the Russian military to monitor the reliability of the armed forces. When Putin briefly ran the Federal Security Service (Federal'naya sluzhba bezopasnosti, FSB) under his predecessor, Boris Yeltsin, he described the military counterintelligence department as a "mini-FSB." In addition to military counterintelligence, the Russian system relies on the creation of a large internal security service responsible for domestic repression and the maintaining of redundant intelligence and security agencies. In 2016, Putin authorized the reorganization of several other internal security forces into a unified command as the National Guard (Rosgvardia), oriented toward managing mass unrest and repressing protest.[23]

Russia has four major intelligence agencies with varying degrees of redundancy. The most important in preventing a coup is the Federal Protective Service (Federal'naya sluzhba okhrani, FSO). The FSO is the successor to the Ninth Directorate of the Soviet KGB and acts as a presidential guard responsible for protecting top regime leadership. It is a large organization with infantry units. It also plays an intelligence role that duplicates some of the functions of other agencies, and has a role in monitoring the military alongside FSB military counterintelligence. The largest Russian security and intelligence service and primary successor to the KGB, the Federal Security Service, has a sweeping internal security mandate. The other two agencies—the Main (Intelligence) Directorate of the General Staff of the Armed Forces (GRU) and the Foreign Intelligence Service (SVR)—also play duplicative roles to one another in foreign intelligence collection.[24]

In short, while the Russian security system hardly resembles the security apparatus of the United States, it does differ in important ways from that of the Soviet Union. Relying more on overlapping intelligence structures than partisan control, the Russian system does not depend on coup prevention through partisan infiltration.

While this book has focused on the Soviet Union and the United States, it is important to note that the People's Republic of China (PRC) engaged in several attempts to prop up friendly dictatorships as well as pursue a broadly interventionist foreign policy in the Cold War. China acted as the principal patron of the Khmer Rouge regime, delivering arms, aid, and advisers. Beijing was also a major supporter of Hanoi during its war against South Vietnam, and Chinese troops were deployed in force to save its ally in Pyongyang during the Korean War. Smaller amounts of Chinese aid reached from Albania to Zambia. After Mao's death, however, Chinese foreign policy entered a period of broad retrenchment and a much less zealous export of revolution. Since Mao, Chinese foreign aid has been far less interventionist in trying to shape the ruling institutions of receiving countries. Instead, most aid has been a "regime-type blind" offer of technical, economic, and military assistance in exchange for diplomatic or economic returns. A Chinese willingness to tolerate human rights abuses among its allies has undoubtedly helped regimes with few friends from engaging in the liberalization necessary to bring Western aid. Nevertheless, there is no strong evidence that China has yet been providing the kind of sensitive internal security assistance characteristic of its earlier Maoist era or of its former Soviet ally.[25]

Despite this relatively hands-off military aid profile, China itself maintains a domestic security apparatus that closely follows the Soviet model of a partisan army. The structure of the Chinese state, party, and security apparatus was itself partly the product of Soviet aid. Soviet advisers helped organize the first Chinese Communist Party (CCP) armed force and arrived in large numbers after the revolution, and Mao looked to the Soviet Union as a model. Nevertheless, the Chinese security apparatus differed in several ways from its Soviet predecessor, most notably in the relatively smaller role played by the secret police and the more important role played by the political commissars and the General Political Department (GPD). Relative to the Red Army commissars after the Russian Civil War, the GPD played a more muscular role in ensuring the loyalty of the army to the party in the Chinese system through its Organization and Security Departments. GPD personnel worked closely with the Political Security Department of the CCP Central Committee, which operated its own covert agents in the military, as well as the Ministry of Public Security and the Ministry of State Security after 1983. While they played important military counterintelligence roles, the Chinese security services were never as large as their KGB counterparts. In short, although China's People's Liberation Army maintained some distinctive qualities from its Soviet predecessor, it was and remains a thoroughly partisan army.[26]

Chinese military aid since the Cold War has come primarily in the sales of weapons to a wide variety of recipients. Chinese security assistance and its global military presence have also expanded considerably in recent years, and China is now the world's fifth-largest arms supplier. The PRC's first overseas base was established in Djibouti in August 2017, and a long-rumored naval facility in Cambodia was recently confirmed by US officials. In the Solomon Islands, Prime Minister Manasseh Sogavare signed a security agreement with China in April 2022. While the text of the agreement was not made public, a leaked early version had included possible deployment of Chinese troops against internal disturbances and the establishment of a Chinese military base on the islands. The Australian prime minister Scott Morrison declared at the time that a Chinese military base in the Solomon Islands would be a "red line" for Australia. The recent increases in China's global military footprint are all relative—historically, China is still nowhere close to the US or the Soviet Union in providing international military assistance. Nevertheless, if trends continue, China will gradually emerge as a major source of military and security aid. It remains to be seen whether the offer of internal police assistance to the Solomon Islands is a harbinger of a greater willingness to provide sensitive internal security assistance and organizational support to particular governments, or whether Chinese military assistance will remain primarily at the level of weapons sales.[27]

A RECENT HISTORY OF REVOLUTIONS DECLARED THAT THE LENINist vanguard party was as "obsolete as the typewriter." Yet not only is the major great power rival to the United States—China— led by a Leninist party with a partisan army, but there have also been several adaptations of the Soviet model in non-leftist regimes. The Iranian revolutionary regime (1979–present) adopted a Soviet-style political-military structure. The Iranian regime built two new security services after the revolution: the conventionally structured Islamic Revolutionary Guards Corps (IRGC, Sepah-e

Pasdaran-e Enghelab) and the Basij paramilitary organization. In order to "monitor the loyalty and performance" of the regular army, the regime established the Organization for Ideology (Sazman-e Ideolog) as an entity independent from the Ministry of Defense and "directed and staffed by clerics loyal to the clerical government and Ayatollah Khomeini." These Sazman officers were attached to "all armed forces units down to the platoon or barracks level." These officers also mirrored the Soviet party committee system by leading Sazman bureaus in their units. In another emulation of the Soviet model, Sazman clerics approved "all officer candidates or applicants for the military academies" and assessed their "political reliability." The IRGC and Basij also featured an "extensive political control structure" that was similar to the political control apparatus attached to the regular army. The Supreme Council of the Revolutionary Guard controlled this apparatus through the Supreme Directorate of Ideological and Political Affairs and operated "much in the same way as the Sazman units in the regular armed forces." Directorate officials were attached to all IRGC and Basij units and were responsible for screening new recruits and monitoring the "activities and decisions of unit commanders" as well as maintaining a network of informers. To dilute the power of the IRGC, a separate Intelligence Ministry was established in 1984.[28]

The Islamic State (IS, or Daesh) (2014–2019) security apparatus also shared many features of the Soviet political-military order. The Public Security Ministry acted as an intelligence and security service. The security service was a "shadowy entity feared even by IS's own cadre." It was apparently founded by Haji Bakr, the nom de guerre of a now-deceased former officer in Saddam Hussein's Air Force Defense Intelligence Service. Its responsibilities included counterintelligence and "rooting out spies and traitors within the territory controlled by the caliphate." This responsibility meant the service spent time "monitoring and reporting on the performance and leadership of combat units" as well as "recruiting and selecting, training, and overseeing the activities of elite forces," "monitoring cadres to root out spies and informants," and "vetting new recruits and IS personnel." It also maintained a dedicated directorate, the Soldier Security Office, for monitoring the IS armed forces in the Soldiery Department. In addition to this large security service, the regular armed forces in the Soldiery Ministry featured embedded clerical control. Political control over the army was achieved through the careful screening of recruits for religious (political) reliability and the "integration of *Shari'i* to the lowest levels to ensure the correct ideological practice in units of the caliphal army." Shari'a advisers were parallel to the amirs who acted as the regular military commanders directing units. They also operated parallel to the deputy amir of battalions, but the overall battalions were led by amirs. The *shari'i* were the individual representatives of the larger Shari'a Committee, which reported to IS leadership. These security structures differed in important ways from the Soviet partisan army. Nevertheless, for repressive regimes, the appeal of an invasive internal security structure to quell incipient acts of military disloyalty has ensured the survival of certain elements of the Soviet structure.[29]

THE END OF THE COLD WAR BROUGHT UNPARALLELED AMERICAN power, a largely retrenched Russia, and a gradual expansion in Chinese military assistance. It also marked the end of the partisan army as a great power export. While a few partisan armies survived the end of the Cold War, others were gradually rendered nonpartisan or collapsed along with their regimes. Of course, the major great power rival to the United States in Beijing itself sustained its party army. As of yet, Chinese foreign policymakers have not returned to a promotion of the Chinese model of political-military relations abroad. Instead, Chinese military aid has been primarily at the level of weapons transfers rather than organizational assistance to transform the security apparatus in friendly governments. The age of communist revolutionaries building their own party armies after successful revolution may indeed be over. Yet the institutions of revolutionary rule—the party, the partisan army, and the internal security service—may not be obsolete. These structures provided considerable advantages to incumbents seeking to inoculate their regimes from the threat of military coups. If coups do rise again and China begins a more thorough provision of internal security assistance, we may again witness adaptations of the Bolshevik model. For now, however, the organizational model of security assistance most frequently exported is that of the United States and its nonpartisan army meant to coexist with democracy. As recent years have shown, these armies may yet again prove highly praetorian. With the decline in American unipolarity may come a concomitant decline in democracy in the developing world. American leverage and preferences for promoting democracy were the catalyst for the dramatic expansion in political liberalization after the end of the Cold War. The US did not get better at training militaries to respect civilian rule. Instead, unipolar American power meant the US could punish coups in countries where it did not have a countervailing geostrategic interest in ensuring alignment. With a return to great power competition, US capacity to insist on democratic rule in geopolitically important states may again decline. The lessons from the first Cold War are not merely for a retrospective analysis of that period of great power competition. They are also of vital importance for the next era of great power rivalry.

CONCLUSION

LEARNING FROM THE PAST

The Cold War was many things—an ideological contest, a bipolar world system, and a period of great power rivalry. It was a time marked by the pursuit of alliances by competing power blocs who sought to sustain the domestic rule of their allies. If friendly governments fell, allies of the rival superpower might emerge in their wake. This contest was rendered more difficult as it was fought in a terrain comprising newly sovereign states and the rise of modern nationalism. Friendly regimes had to be sustained from afar through the provision of aid, arms, and advisers. Naked imperialism and direct colonial rule were increasingly rare and ever more difficult.

Many of the regimes ruling the newly independent states in which this contest unfolded were autocratic. Detractors and supporters of American foreign policy argue that the US frequently propped up tyrants during the Cold War who survived in office thanks only to American aid. As we have seen, the truth is considerably more complicated. The United States did support plenty of friendly dictatorships during the Cold War. Washington provided billions in armaments and budgetary support and deployed thousands of advisers to strengthen ruling regimes. Yet despite—indeed in part *because of*—these investments, US-backed dictatorships were not in fact particularly long-lasting. They survived in office for terms that resembled those of dictators who did not enjoy such windfalls of foreign aid, and half as long as their Soviet-backed counterparts. This was not because American aid simply did not matter at all. It was because the assistance given by the United States to autocratic client regimes, compared with that given by the Soviet Union, had profoundly different consequences for the stability of those regimes.

US aid strengthened militaries in ways that often undermined rather than strengthened authoritarian rule. Increases in military autonomy and capacity elevated a potent internal rival to autocrats and worsened the risk of military coups. By contrast, Soviet aid helped subordinate the army to the ruling regime. As coups d'état are the principal cause of authoritarian breakdown, this difference in strategies of regime support had profound consequences for the durability of foreign-backed authoritarian regimes. Soviet-backed regimes outlasted their American counterparts by a significant margin. This was not because Moscow provided more aid or backed regimes with greater domestic legitimacy or remarkable economic performance. Soviet-backed regimes in fact experienced worse economic outcomes and engaged in highly unpopular economic and social reforms. The Soviet Union was a generous arms supplier, but its increasingly sclerotic economy could never match the United States in financial assistance.

Instead, Soviet clients were so durable because they received help in removing the single most important cause of authoritarian breakdown: military coups. The Soviet Union provided support in building security services that rendered military coups too difficult to carry out. Monitored by party commissars and counterintelligence officers, military officers in Soviet client governments had few opportunities to successfully plot against their regimes. By contrast, the United States and its allies promoted security structures that mirrored their own domestic apparatus and pushed for depoliticized, autonomous, and powerful militaries. While this system works reasonably well in a democracy with a highly legitimate government, in authoritarian regimes both officers and governments weakly or rarely adhered to norms dictating a separation of the military from partisan politics. Although encouraged by American advisers to remain outside of politics and focus on preparing for war, these military officers sat atop powerful institutions they could use to translate political ambition into political office. America's dictators knew this and took every effort to hobble their newly ascendant armies to keep them loyal to the regime. The unintended consequence of this military aid was to exacerbate rather than alleviate internal power struggles within the state security apparatus. This battle between dictators and their armies for political power played out in the shadows until it burst forth in dramatic coups that witnessed the triumph of the army or in purges of the military command that marked victory by the regime. In both cases, the result of US military aid was domestic political unrest and a weakening of state strength. This in turn made regimes more vulnerable to threats from outside the government like communist insurgencies and dragged a reluctant US sponsor into interventions to save the beleaguered government.

In short, it was not the amount of aid or the quality of arms that accounted for the variation in durability of regimes backed by foreign powers. Autocrats who found favor either in Moscow or Washington enjoyed windfalls of both military and economic aid. Instead, it was the *nature* of assistance offered by the superpowers and their advisers that made a difference. Soviet personnel arrived ready and willing to help their allies subordinate the army to the regime and build formidable internal security services that protected their regimes from the principal causes of authoritarian breakdown. American advisers arrived promoting an army insulated from rather than penetrated by politics, but that army consequently posed a potent threat to authoritarian survival. These different models of political-military relations had profoundly divergent consequences for the loyalty of militaries to allied regimes and the survival of dictatorships.

THE CONVENTIONAL WISDOM ABOUT HOW MILITARY AID SHAPES the politics of authoritarian survival undergirds both criticism and praise of American foreign policy. Given what we have learned in this reevaluation, how are we to judge American foreign policy toward friendly dictatorships in the Cold War? Whatever one thinks of the moral dimensions of American Cold War policy toward allied dictatorships, was US policy effective? Did it achieve the goals articulated by its proponents, or was it responsible for the worst excesses as claimed by its opponents? It is worth acknowledging at the outset that US policies toward client dictators were never uncontroversial within or outside the US government. Diplomats, intelligence officers, military commanders, and cabinet officials repeatedly offered misgivings and outright condemnations of US policy. Criticism outside the executive branch was also often withering, with frequent congressional and public denunciations of American foreign policy toward friendly tyrants.

Nevertheless, and despite multiple efforts at reform like President Kennedy's Alliance for Progress or the emphasis on human rights by President Carter, American foreign policy was remarkably uniform in this regard during the Cold War. Kennedy ultimately embraced military juntas in Latin America and Southeast Asia, and Carter came to terms with the shah in Iran as a key ally. Of course, not every dictatorship was deemed worthy of American support, and some regimes that were earlier considered sufficiently important to earn American aid were later shunned, and vice versa. Anastasio Somoza Debayle received the aid his father had long craved, thanks to inroads made by a tiny Marxist-Leninist insurgent group; and Fulgencio Batista found his support evaporate after his American-supplied air force bombed civilians indiscriminately in its fight against its own insurgency. American support for anticommunist tyrants was never total or uniform. Many dictatorships were held at arm's length, neither isolated nor embraced. But successive American administrations did embrace some friendly tyrants. It was not until the cooling of superpower rivalry with the Soviet Union that the US began a more consistent—though never total—sanctioning of foreign autocrats and promotion of democratization.

To assess whether the US succeeded in its goals in the Cold War, it is worth reflecting on what American foreign policy toward friendly autocracies was trying to achieve. The United States sought alignment, stability, military effectiveness, and gradual democratization. It did not always seek all these four outcomes at the same time or with the same degree of intensity. Yet these constituted the broad contours of American policy toward friendly tyrants. On only one of these dimensions—alignment with the United States— was US policy arguably, though not unequivocally, successful. Perhaps concerningly, this is also an outcome the United States may find it has even less success achieving in the next period of great power competition.

Of the twenty-eight US backed regimes that collapsed while still receiving support from the United States, seven realigned toward another great power or to active hostility toward the United States. This means three-quarters of cases where an allied authoritarian government fell, the subsequent regime retained US alignment. This continued alignment after collapse was particularly true for coups d'état. The only instance of realignment after a coup—Laos in 1960—was reversed a few months later by the larger pro-US faction of the armed forces. In part, the dearth of realignment after coups reflected a successful US policy of cultivating support in the armed forces through training and advising armies. This was the explanation most favored by American policymakers. More importantly, however, it reflected a set of shared interests between the United States and many army officers in the developing world.[1]

Military officers in client regimes tended to share with their American patrons a fear of communism. This was not just because as a relatively privileged class they feared social revolution or the triumph of previously repressed peasant and proletarian groups seizing power. It was also because they knew that the communist military model involved embedding political commissars and secret police in their ranks or even replacing them wholesale with a "people's army." Military officers nervously consumed reports of changes in pro-Soviet states in their regions and feared similar transformations if communist groups were to seize power in their own country. They did not have to look far afield to find examples of what communist revolution brought to their fellow officers in other armies. The dissolution of the old army and the creation of the Fuerzas Armadas Revolucionarias in Cuba reverberated across Latin America, and officers from Indonesia to Mali feared their replacement by popular militias or their circumscribed authority under communist military systems. The United States benefited, therefore, from a latent anticommunism in the armed forces, which generated a pro-American orientation among military officers. This was of course recognized by American officials and in part explains the permissive attitude of the US to successful military coups in allied countries. However, this advantage has arguably evaporated in the years since the Cold War.

The sharp decline in communism after the Cold War, with only five ruling communist regimes and no successful communist revolutions, means military officers are not confronted with a plausible prospect of communist takeover. China is of course a communist global power, and the commitment of the regime to party rule and Leninist organizational principles should not be underestimated. Despite increasing personalism and the decline of collective party rule under Xi Jinping, there is certainly no reason to suspect the regime will abandon its system of partisan control of its armed forces and security services. Nevertheless, as we saw in the preceding chapter, there is no evidence that China has yet resuscitated the export of communist institutions abroad.[2]

The other major alternative to liberal institutions in the developing world—Islamism—does not engender the same concern by military officers as communism. The relative paucity of Islamist regimes and the considerable variation in their military structure give the military as an institution less to fear from Islamist takeover. For revolutionary Islamist regimes, there is notable variation in their military structures. While the Islamic State in Syria and Iraq and the Islamic Republic of Iran have or had military organizations that mirrored the Soviet model of political control, the Taliban in Afghanistan do not. Other supposedly Islamist governments vary in their models of political-military relations as well. Military officers are afforded limited autonomy under the highly fragmented Saudi security apparatus, but in Omar al-Bashir's Sudan, the army formed the backbone of the government, particularly after 1999.

The organization of military forces under contemporary autocracies and the nature of regime promotion engaged in by great powers are important because they inform how army officers evaluate the prospect of living under a particular regime. If the United States no longer shares a common enemy with army officers in the developing world, it is less clear that the alignment advantage after coups will continue in the future. While the US still maintains an advantage with contemporary army officers— many have trained in the United States, and the US still has the army with the most international prestige—the growing great power rivalry with China and Russia may prove sharply different from the first Cold War in this regard. On the one hand, the US Army remains the world's premier fighting force, and the US position in the global economy is still dominant. The disastrous Russian military performance in its full-scale invasion of Ukraine in 2022 has dampened the global perception of Russian military prowess. It has also rendered Russia a less credible contemporary patron. China's army is untested since its relatively poor showing in its war with Vietnam in 1979, though it has engaged in a large-scale modernization. While the recent Chinese economic aid blitz has not always proven the blessing its recipients might have hoped, China is a more credible rival economic and security patron than Russia over the long term. However, as neither Moscow nor Beijing are promoting the export of partisan armies like their Soviet and Maoist predecessors, military officers have less to fear from living under their influence. If anything, the willingness by both China and Russia to ignore human rights abuses, naked authoritarianism, and military rule render them an attractive ally for praetorian armies.[3]

This transformation can be seen in Thailand, a longtime US ally. Using survey data from nearly two thousand Thai military officers and officials, two researchers found that while the Thai military establishment is wary of growing Chinese power and values the US security relationship, officers unsurprisingly disliked the US criticism and isolation of the regime after the 2014 coup. While US military supplies did not actually cease with the 2014 coup, they did decline, especially relative to Chinese imports. Sanctions were applied, and other military aid and training programs suspended. Surveyed Thai officers indicated they preferred US military supplies but resented the "unreliability of the US as a supplier" and the conditions imposed on military aid. The researchers further found a relatively limited knowledge of US-Thai military relations during the Cold War among contemporary Thai military officers and that "many Thai military officers see China as a source of protection against external military threats." These attitudinal shifts have been accompanied by relatively denser Sino-Thai military-to-military ties, beginning with joint exercises in 2007 and a $400 million arms deal in 2017.[4]

The Chinese reaction to the 2014 Thai coup was permissive, and Beijing quickly pledged not to "interfere" in an "internal

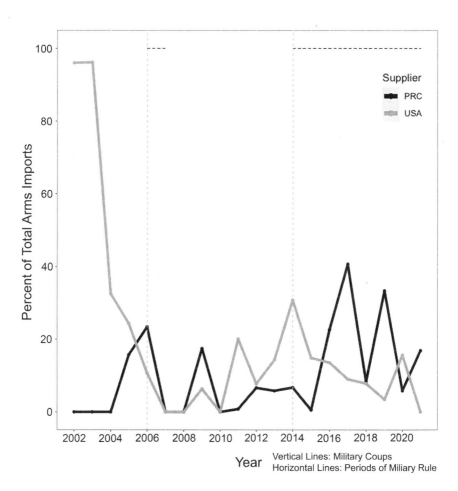

Figure 6. Arms imports to Thailand (2002–2021) (*Source:* Stockholm International Peace Research Institute. Dataset is from the Arms Transfers Database.)

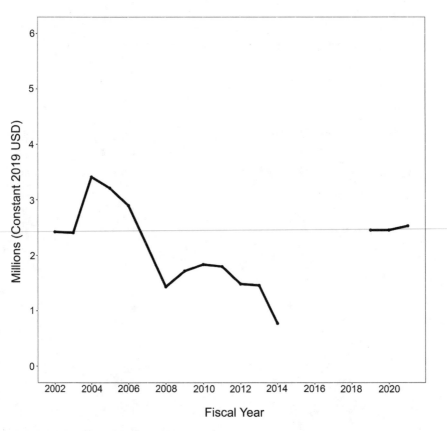

Figure 7. US Military Training (IMET) for Thailand (2002–2021)
(*Source:* USAID, US State Department)

issue" and expressed support for the new junta. While the closeness of Bangkok and Beijing should not be overstated, and there is no reason to suspect Thailand wishes to be dominated by China, it is clear that Thai military officers do not view China as posing a revolutionary challenge and instead see it as a potentially appealing patron. The Communist Party of Thailand has been long defunct, and there has been no effort by Beijing to revive its former client guerrilla movement. The US has responded to this increasing rivalry with China over Bangkok's alignment by resuming military training after the nominal return to democracy in 2019 and continuing military exercises and sales under the current authoritarian regime.[5]

If the US loses its latent advantage among military forces in the developing world, we can expect even greater volatility and instability in allied governments. Coups could bring more wholesale geopolitical realignment and in turn prompt the US or China to more readily back countercoup movements, which risk splitting the military and leading to civil war. During the Cold War, US personnel were sometimes approached by factions of the army to support their plots to reverse recent coups. Most of these were rejected for fears that they would either fracture the army or their failure would lead to the realignment of the otherwise pro-American new military leadership. If coups more readily lead to realignment to a rival superpower, both the US and China might be less hesitant to support countercoups in the future.[6]

The second goal the United States sought to achieve in its support for friendly tyrants was domestic stability. As we have seen, it is far from clear that client autocrats brought the stability they and their supporters promised. Autocrats sought above all else to secure the survival of their regimes, often at considerable cost to stability. Officials were purged and rotated, intra-elite rivalries fostered to balance factions off one another, and institutions were hollowed out to privilege loyalty over competence. These behaviors generated intense conflict within ruling coalitions and opposition outside the government. Client autocrats were repressive, corrupt, and unpopular, and this generally became worse over time. Their meddling in the army led to coups, which hardly ever brought the stability promised by the putschists or hoped for by desperate American officials. Instead, coups brought more coups and a spiral of instability. At times the state grew so weakened that the United States was dragged in to directly defend allies from festering insurgencies that fed on government weakness and repression. Interventions that began as efforts to secure the tenure of friendly regimes through aid, arms, and advisers degenerated into ever greater involvement by the United States on behalf of increasingly hollow clients.

There is no reason to suspect that the dearth of stability promised by aid for autocrats will be limited to the Cold War. Coups declined after the Cold War not because armies lost their praetorian impulses, incumbent regimes engaged in fewer coup-inducing behaviors, or American military aid suddenly succeeded in finally inculcating liberal democratic values. Instead, coups declined because the United States had achieved unparalleled global power after the collapse of its Soviet rival and was in a position where it could punish naked authoritarianism. Coups became rare because the value of holding office declined after a coup: military officers who ousted their governments faced pariah status and sometimes interventions to reverse their coups. As we saw in the preceding chapter, with the return of great power rivalry, the coup will likely return if it hasn't already. External instability is also not obsolete. Civil wars in fact increased after the Cold War. Insurgencies ousted governments as recently as in Afghanistan in August 2021 and nearly did so in 2022 in Ethiopia. There is no reason to think that future clients won't face the threat of civil wars and insurgencies.[7]

Third, the United States sought consistently to promote military effectiveness in autocratic allies. This was predicated on a desire to strengthen indigenous forces so that the US would not be required to deploy its own forces. As we have seen, the United States pursued this goal by promoting the organization of military forces along its own lines. This has been criticized convincingly elsewhere for failing to properly incorporate effective indigenous military structures, for its overreliance on complicated logistics, or its privileging of conventional threats over insurgencies. But perhaps its most important failing was political: autonomous and powerful armies were threats to their own regimes. US-backed dictators sought to undermine, subvert, and hobble these armies, all while the US sought to strengthen them. Sometimes an army overcame a dictator's efforts and ousted its own government. Once in power, military rulers also cultivated factionalism and undermined commanders who were not loyalists. Other times the incumbent dictatorships successfully overcame the threat of coups with a heavy dose of luck and purged disloyal elements after failed coups. The end result of both trajectories was a hollow army. The problem was exacerbated by the influx of resources, which provided opportunities for graft. Officers padded their ranks with phantom soldiers and even sold American-supplied weapons to their ostensible enemies.

It is difficult to build armies abroad. This was of course reinforced recently by the ignominious collapse of the Afghan army in August 2021 after nearly two decades and $88 billion in American aid. The postmortem on the Afghan army was remarkably similar to US statements after its Indochinese allies collapsed in 1975. Much of the retrospective analysis offered that the US "fell victim to the conceit that it could build from scratch an enormous Afghan army and police force with 350,000 personnel that was modeled on the centralized command structures and complex bureaucracy of the Defense Department." The US chairman of the Joint Chiefs of Staff General Mark Milley seconded this analysis a month after the fall, stating that the US-created Afghan security forces, built as "a mirror image" of US forces, were probably "not designed appropriately for the type of mission." Political meddling in the army was also a problem in Kabul. President Ashraf Ghani (2014–2021) interfered in military appointments to place loyalists in key commands and marginalize US-trained officers he did not trust and feared might carry out a coup. Like in Vietnam, Cambodia, and Laos, ghost soldiers were a massive problem that the US government knew about for years. These fictive soldiers were the creatures of creative bookkeeping by corrupt commanders who claimed their presence on the payroll to pocket their pay and equipment. As Chapter 7 made clear, ghost soldiers were not a new problem for American officials. In 2019, the US special inspector general for Afghanistan reconstruction (SIGAR) reported that after Lieutenant General James Rainey started using a new biometric system instead of relying on Afghan field commanders to supply Afghan troops, his command eliminated around fifty thousand ghost soldiers. In mid-2020, by the Afghan government's own estimation up to 70 percent of police personnel in several provinces, including Kandahar and Helmand, were phantoms. While desertions and defections were a major part of this as well, by the time the Afghan army collapsed it was likely one-sixth of its purported strength of three hundred thousand.[8]

Finally, the United States promoted gradual democratization in client regimes. In many cases during the Cold War, these experiments in liberalization were short-lived or reversed. In Thailand, the US played a limited role in democratization from 1973 to 1976 and proved supportive of the coup that ended the brief democratic regime. The US was generally able to push its clients to decorate their regimes with legal window dressing such as constitutions, referenda, legislatures, and even semicompetitive elections. Military officers donned business suits over the field marshal's uniform, but most of these instances of civilianization were more fiction than fact.

They were not, however, meaningless. US clients had to exert effort to win fraudulent elections, manipulate unruly legislatures, and manage the judiciary. When these efforts were particularly ham-fisted, they exposed the weakness and unpopularity of ruling regimes. After the Cold War, many US clients did democratize. In some cases, the US played an active role in supporting the transition to democracy, and in others the role was more passive. Cold War autocracies cast a long shadow over their democratic successors. New democracies inherited powerful praetorian militaries that exacted a heavy toll on accountability and justice for agreeing to return to the barracks. Democracy came, but it was more limited than its advocates had hoped. Dangling the prospect of a coup over the weak new republics, armies largely remained outside efforts at reform. Their security portfolios remained expansive and their commanders largely safe from prosecution for abuses under the previous regime.

The end of the Cold War did not bring the end of military political power. But it did reduce coups and direct military rule in many places. This may change. It is far from clear that US military aid has solved the problem of fostering praetorianism through the new emphasis on curricula on civil-military relations and respect for human rights. While such training has expanded since 1990, it remains a relatively limited facet of American military assistance. How effectively, if at all, such norms are truly internalized by individuals trained by the United States remains to be seen. As recent coups in West Africa by US-trained officers illustrate, we should be skeptical that several hours of training on respecting civilian rule will successfully turn armies away from praetorian impulses. In short, democracy spread through the world after the Cold War not because the US finally learned how to effectively promote it. It spread because of unipolarity in the international system. America was now an unrivaled global power. No longer facing the threat of the Soviet bloc, the US could privilege economic and political liberalization in the developing world. In areas of limited geopolitical importance, this meant that many autocrats and would-be dictators faced the prospect of international isolation if they did not engage in visible democratization.

What about the Soviet Union? It is worth briefly considering whether Moscow achieved its multiple goals in pursuing support for friendly regimes during the Cold War. The Soviet Union pursued objectives largely similar to those of the United States: alignment, stability, and military effectiveness. However, rather than seeking to support liberal democracy abroad, the Soviet Union sought to support socialism and social revolution. The Soviet Union was, with some notable qualifications, more successful in achieving its goals in these areas than the United States. Moscow broadly succeeded in securing alignment and regime stability. Its record on military effectiveness was more mixed, as was its ability to support socialist transformation.

The Soviet Union largely succeeded in securing the alignment of the regimes it supported with aid, arms, and advisers. As its regimes were highly invulnerable to internal rivals, the Soviet Union did not suffer realignments owing to military coups. Several regimes did, however, break with the Soviet Union while still in power. Albania, China, Egypt, and Somalia all realigned away from the Soviet Union. Only Egypt became a US ally, while Somalia and China adopted a more arm's-length alignment with Washington during the Cold War. After Albania broke with Moscow, it went it alone, pursuing a remarkably autarkic foreign policy under an unreformed Stalinist regime. For related reasons, the Soviet Union also broadly succeeded at building stable regimes in allied autocracies. This reflected its own success at regime stability and rested on the vanguard party, the internal security services, and partisan penetration of the army and state. The fact that the Soviet Union eventually collapsed does not negate the fact that its regime was remarkably resilient in the face of repeated and severe self-made and external crises. The parties that Soviet advisers helped establish or expand did not generally provide the check on excessive personal power that Moscow had hoped. They were instead usually full of allies and sycophants and did not provide the pool of replacements Moscow had wished for. These parties did, however, play a key role in ensuring the loyalty of the security apparatus.

It is of course also worth noting that regime stability came at a terrible price. Fear, more than anything else, kept these

Soviet-backed systems in power. Although fear and loyalty are observationally equivalent under authoritarianism, there is considerable evidence that quiescence was bought by fear of retribution rather than regime legitimacy. When given the opportunity, publics in Soviet-backed regimes resisted. Life for political opposition and the everyday public was often miserable in Soviet-backed states. Soviet-backed regimes were highly violent, with opposition groups often imprisoned en masse or executed. Media outlets were shuttered, the clergy either emasculated or violently liquidated, and peasant land seized for the state or collective farms. The repression and authoritarianism of life under Soviet-backed regimes cast a long shadow, even after regimes themselves lost power.[9]

The Soviet record in creating effective militaries abroad was uneven. As we have seen, military performance in Afghanistan and Ethiopia was poor and can be at least partly accounted for by the system of political control embedded in the armed forces. The Soviet Union's own military performance was decidedly mixed. While the Eastern European armies built by Moscow never ultimately faced the test of fighting NATO, US estimates of their likely prowess consistently rated them poorly. US intelligence viewed the Bulgarian army as likely to mutiny in the event of war with the West, and the US military viewed its Czechoslovak counterpart as logistically dependent on Moscow and of "questionable political reliability." The Mongolian People's Revolutionary Army nearly collapsed in the face of its disorganized opposition in 1932, prompting Soviet intervention. Soldiers deserted en masse, preferring to defect rather than fight the rebels. By contrast, the Korean People's Army and especially the People's Army of Vietnam enjoyed much higher military effectiveness.[10]

Just as the US was frequently pessimistic about the prospects for democracy in the postcolonial world during the Cold War, Soviet officials were frequently dismissive of the prospects for socialism in their allied states. Moscow in fact often preached moderation in domestic economic and social policy and repeatedly sought to rein in overly radical clients. Many Soviet clients emulated the agrarian transformations that had taken place in the Soviet Union and experienced similarly horrendous results. Famine, violence, corruption, and inefficiency were the result of state collectivization of agriculture. State control over the economy varied across Soviet clients, and the Soviet Union itself prodded its clients to engage in their own economic reforms along with perestroika in the USSR. The Soviet Union never succeeded in the global revolution envisioned by Lenin and Trotsky, though that revolutionary missionary zeal had faded relatively early in the Soviet Union itself. Moscow was the cradle of socialist revolution, but it did not ultimately upend the global order in the way the first generation of Bolshevik leaders had hoped. Instead, the Soviet Union's international behavior was fairly similar to that of its American rival. Moscow supported friendly socialist movements and regimes and sought to entrench their hold on power by providing aid, arms, and advisers. The only major difference was that Moscow's client regimes were more durable.

IF THE COLD WAR WERE MERELY A HISTORIC PERIOD UNLIKELY TO be echoed or replayed again, this inquiry would be less pressing. The return of great power competition, however, will probably bring with it yet another era in which policymakers and publics alike debate the merits and necessity of aid for friendly tyrants. This new era of great power competition will of course not be exactly like the Cold War. It will probably not offer a sweeping ideological clash, and the global economy and world populations are far more interconnected now than in the early days of the Cold War. Nevertheless, war, dictatorship, and foreign military interventions are not a thing of the past. The benefits of geostrategic alliances and the frailty of the regimes offering such alignment will surely motivate great powers to try to keep friendly regimes in power. Military and economic aid is not an obsolete tool of statecraft, and the political dynamics that shape the survival and demise of modern autocracies have not changed dramatically. No matter how much it appears autocracy has changed in the contemporary era, at its core it remains the same. The loyalty of the security services to ruling authoritarian regimes was, and will continue to be, the single most important factor in ensuring their durability.

The United States of America and the People's Republic of China will surely continue to provide military aid to friendly regimes in an attempt to secure their alignment and entrench their rule. Both will likely continue to support autocratic allies. Whether any renewed period of aid for autocrats will look like the Cold War depends in part on whether policymakers learn lessons from the dynamics of the US-Soviet rivalry.

Military aid for autocrats does not only or always strengthen their rule. It also transforms their rule. If this inquiry into the past of foreign support for friendly dictatorships has taught us anything, it is that the effects of military aid on the survival of authoritarian regimes is not always what either the suppliers or receivers of assistance expect. The intentions of patrons did not always neatly map onto outcomes in clients, and the impact of external assistance is always filtered through the domestic politics of the recipient. Attempts to bolster military capacity often led to a cannibalization of the coercive capacity of the state. The tail frequently wagged the dog in the first Cold War, and it is likely future recipients of American or Chinese aid will seek to extract maximum leverage from their patron to their own benefit. Without understanding how autocracies work, we cannot understand the impact of external military and economic assistance on authoritarian regime survival.

There have been few easy lessons from this study, but it is important that one lesson is not learned. While we have repeatedly highlighted the failure by the United States to build nonpartisan armies abroad during the Cold War, the message of this book is not that partisan armies are good for democracy. As loyal tools of autocratic repression, partisan armies rarely allow for the growth of democracy in the first place. Nonpartisan armies are generally necessary for the emergence and especially the survival of democracy. They are more resistant to attempts to use them as political tools and more capable of remaining outside partisan politics. But a nonpartisan army is not sufficient to guarantee the survival of democracy. To truly resist the use of the armed forces in a slide into authoritarianism requires a healthy civic sphere and a legitimate government. The *civil* side of civil-military relations is as important as the military side. When civilian governments seek to achieve exclusive political power and persecute their rivals, they seek the active support or passive acceptance of the armed forces. When incumbents repeatedly seek to use the army as a political tool, the nonpartisan character of the army can and often does break down. It might hold for a while, but it will not hold forever.

As this book has shown, life under autocracy is often as unpleasant for military officers as it is for civilians. Purges, repression, and war accompany the decamping of the army from the barracks to the corridors of civil power. Autocratic armies are riven by factional politics, and ruling directly does not solve these problems. Military regimes are unstable, highly politicized, corrupt, and only exacerbate the factional politics that justified their intervention in the first place. The army is not the solution for political problems. While they are undoubtedly harder, the solutions to democratic deconsolidation do not come from the barracks.

DISCLAIMER

This book was written while I was a research fellow at the Weiser Center for Emerging Democracies at the University of Michigan. Readers should understand that all statements of fact, opinion, or analysis expressed in this book are those of the author and do not reflect the official positions or views of any US government agency or department. Nothing in the contents should be construed as asserting or implying US government authentication of information or endorsement of the author's views.

ACKNOWLEDGMENTS

This book would not have been possible without the mentorship and friendship of many individuals. My debts are enormous and cannot be adequately paid in such a short set of acknowledgments. First and foremost, this book is the product of a now long-standing relationship with Lucan Way. Lucan has supported this project from its very infancy and has played the role of mentor, collaborator, and friend. He is one of the best political scientists and kindest humans in the business, and it has been one of the great honors of my life to work closely with him over the past nearly ten years. Dan Slater has proven another tremendous mentor, scholar, and friend. He hosted me at the incomparable Weiser Center for Emerging Democracies for two and a half years and has improved my scholarship immeasurably.

Steve Levitsky, Joe Wright, Erica De Bruin, Seva Gunitsky, Sean Yom, Risa Brooks, Noel Anderson, and Eva Bellin deserve special thanks for the roles they played in helping me develop this project over the years. Max Margulies and Dan Mattingly were both gracious enough to labor through early versions of this manuscript, and their feedback strengthened the final version considerably. This book project also benefited from feedback from Laia Balcells, Vanessa van den Boogaard, Sophie Borwein, Noah Buckley, Ajmal Burhanzoi, Killian Clarke, Lindsay Cohn, Jordan Gans-Morse, Stephen Hanson, Kristen Harkness, Yoshiko Herrera, Stathis Kalyvas, Jeff Kopstein, Kevin Luo, Elizabeth Perry, Dan Sherwin, Paul Staniland, Brian Taylor, Jakob Tolstrup, Josh Tucker, and Jason VandenBeukel. Kathleen Collins and Cawo

Abdi deserve special thanks for the role they played in fostering my interest in academic research and their support over many years.

The Weiser Center for Emerging Democracies at the University of Michigan provided the ideal intellectual home to write this book. Special thanks go to Matthew Cebul, Marília Corrêa, Iza Ding, Brendan McElroy, Gitta Kohler, and Derek Groom. WCED also hosted a book workshop in September 2022 where Dan Slater, Lucan Way, Sheena Chestnut Greitens, Erica De Bruin, Erica Frantz, and Megan Stewart provided invaluable feedback.

I would also like to thank David A. Langbart and the staff at the US National Archives in College Park for their help in accessing archival materials. I'd also like to thank audiences at Yale University, Columbia University, the University of Minnesota, the University of Toronto, the University of Michigan, Hamilton College, the American Political Science Association, and the Midwestern Political Science Association for their feedback on versions of this project.

This book would not have been possible without the steadfast support and skill of my indefatigable agent, Julia Eagleton, and the rest of the crew at Janklow & Nesbit. For his incisive editorial comments, I thank Michael Kaler at Basic Books.

I've been so lucky to have a strong network of amazing lifelong friends. The Hotel boys of course deserve a special thanks, and Tanner Uselmann, Zak Black, and Danny Hutton Ferris in particular for listening to me talk about this book for years. My family has been a consistent source of support. My grandparents were a constant source of love and encouragement. My parents, Mark and Lori, imparted a lifelong love for learning and have always been in my corner. My parents-in-law and siblings-in-law have greatly enriched my life. My brothers, Alex and Michael, have provided fun and encouragement for my entire life. My son, Cassius, was born when this book was undergoing its final edits and has already added limitless pleasure to our lives. My greatest debt, of course, goes to my wife, Tayla. She has been my partner through it all and has had to put up with far more talk about this book than any one person deserves. She is my greatest support and the love of my life. It is to her that this book is dedicated.

NOTES

A NOTE ON SOURCES

In the interest of space this manuscript uses shorter-form citations that still allow for the identification of the source of all cited information. Archival records draw on three principal sources: the US National Archives and Records Administration holdings in College Park, Maryland (NARA II), the CIA Freedom of Information Act (FOIA) electronic reading room, and the US Department of State's Foreign Relations of the United States (FRUS) collection. Declassified CIA records are identified by their CREST (CIA Records Search Tool) numbers or their FOIA reference identifiers. Interested readers can find these records at www.cia.gov/readingroom/. FRUS documents are cited according to their collection and document number and can be found at https://history.state.gov/historicaldocuments.

INTRODUCTION

1. Youssef M. Ibrahim, "While Iranians Demonstrate, Americans in Teheran Have Quiet Day," *New York Times*, December 12, 1978, A13.

2. Noam Chomsky, *Deterring Democracy* (Verso, 1991), 14; see also 51–52; telegram from the embassy in Poland to the Department of State, September 22, 1958, *Foreign Relations of the United States* (hereafter *FRUS*), 1958–1960, China, vol. 19, Doc. 120; Edward Miller, *Misalliance: Ngo Dinh Diem, the United States, and the Fate of South Vietnam* (Harvard, 2013), 14; 116 Cong. Rec. 13542 (1970); John Spanier, *American Foreign Policy Since World War II*, 12th ed. (Congressional Quarterly, 1991), 159; Brian Klaas, *The Despot's Accomplice: How the West Is Aiding and Abetting the Decline of Democracy* (Oxford, 2017), 192.

3. Jack A. Goldstone, "Revolutions and Superpowers," in *Superpowers and Revolution*, ed. Jonathan R. Adelman (Praeger, 1986), 38; Gordon Tullock, *Autocracy* (Kluwer Academic, 1987), 132; Dan Connell and Frank Smyth, "Africa's New Bloc," *Foreign Affairs*, March/April 1998; Klaas, *Despot's*

Accomplice, 192; Jeane Kirkpatrick, "Dictatorships and Double Standards," *Commentary* 68, no. 5 (1979): 34–45; Adam Garfinkle, *The Devil and Uncle Sam: A User's Guide to the Friendly Tyrants Dilemma* (Transaction, 1992).

4. Howard J. Wiarda, "Friendly Tyrants and American Interests," in *Friendly Tyrants: An American Dilemma*, ed. Daniel Pipes and Adam Garfinkle (St. Martin's, 1991); Garfinkle, *Devil and Uncle Sam*, 3–8.

5. Odd Arne Westad, *The Global Cold War: Third World Interventions and the Making of Our Times* (Cambridge, 2005), 8–38; Tony Smith, *America's Mission: The United States and the Worldwide Struggle for Democracy in the Twentieth Century* (Princeton, 1994), 5.

6. Steven Levitsky and Lucan Way, *Revolution and Dictatorship: The Violent Origins of Durable Authoritarianism* (Princeton, 2022).

7. Seva Gunitsky, *Aftershocks: Great Powers and Domestic Reforms in the Twentieth Century* (Princeton, 2017).

8. Westad, *Global Cold War*, 25; Chester J. Pach Jr., *Arming the Free World: The Origins of the United States Military Assistance Program, 1945–1950* (UNC Press, 1991).

9. Douglas J. Macdonald, *Adventures in Chaos: American Intervention for Reform in the Third World* (Harvard, 1992), 12.

10. David F. Schmitz, *Thank God They're on Our Side: The United States and Right-Wing Dictatorships, 1921–1965* (UNC Press, 1999), 4, en. 1; Stephen G. Rabe, *The Killing Zone: The United States Wages Cold War in Latin America* (Oxford, 2016), 98.

11. Schmitz, *Thank God*, 126.

12. Macdonald, *Adventures in Chaos*; Schmitz, *Thank God*; Westad, *Global Cold War*; David F. Schmitz, *The United States and Right-Wing Dictatorships, 1965–1989* (Cambridge, 2006).

13. Barbara Geddes, Joseph Wright, and Erica Frantz, "Autocratic Breakdown and Regime Transitions: A New Dataset," *Perspectives on Politics* 12, no. 2 (2014): 313–331; Barbara Geddes, Joseph Wright, and Erica Frantz, *How Dictatorships Work: Power, Personalization, and Collapse* (Cambridge, 2018).

14. CIA, "Chinese Aid in the Third World," 06/30/1972, CIA-RDP08S 02113R000100090001-9; CIA, "Tanzania: Nyerere and Beyond," 11/1982, CIA-RDP83S00855R000200020006-6; CIA, "The Tanzanian Military: Nyerere's Uncertain Shield," 06/1983, CIA-RDP84S00552R000200150003-0; Jeremy Freidman, *Ripe for Revolution: Building Socialism in the Third World* (Harvard, 2021), 126–129, 139–140.

15. CIA, "Stability in Paraguay," 04/09/1970, CIA-RDP85T00875R00 1100090017-9; CIA, "Stroessner's Paraguay," 03/01/1968, CIA-RDP79-00927 A006300040003-8; Paul Lewis, *Paraguay Under Stroessner* (UNC Press, 1980),

64, 82–83, 99, 106, 113; Carlos R. Miranda, *The Stroessner Era: Authoritarian Rule in Paraguay* (Westview, 1990), 133–134; Kirk Tyvela, *The Dictator Dilemma: The United States and Paraguay in the Cold War* (University of Pittsburgh Press, 2019), 14, 21, 27–32, 39–40, 42–43, 54, 61, 63, 65, 69, 105–107.

16. CIA, "Libyan-Soviet Cooperation: The View from Tripoli," 08/1986, CIA-RDP88T00096R000300310001-5.

17. John D. Ciorciari, "China and the Pol Pot Regime," *Cold War History* 14, no. 2 (2014): 216.

18. CIA, "Activities of the Cuban Military in Angola," 07/27/1977, CIA-RDP79R00603A002700040005-7; Valeriy Ivanovich Shariy, "Voennoye vmeshatel'stvo inostrannikh gosudarstv v grazhdanskuyu voynu v Angole, 1975-nachalo 1976 goda," *Voenno-istoricheskiy zhurnal* 4 (April 2008): 19–23. The data on advisory deployments were compiled by the author using the following CIA reports: "Economic Intelligence Statistical Handbook, 1964," 06/1964, CIA-RDP79S01046A001000010002–8; "Intelligence Handbook: Economic Intelligence Statistical Handbook, 1967," 07/1967, CIA-RDP07-00617R000100140001-6; "Economic Intelligence Statistical Handbook, 1969," 07/1969, CIA-RDP07-00617R000100160001-4; "Handbook of Economic Statistics, 1982," 09/1982, CIA-RDP83-00856R000100040001-8; "Handbook of Economic Statistics, 1984," 09/1984, CIA-RDP87T01134R000100040005-0; "Handbook of Economic Statistics, 1985," 09/1985, CIA-RDP87T01134R000100070002-0; "Handbook of Economic Statistics, 1987," 09/1987, CIA-RDP89T01437R000100150002-3; "Handbook of Economic Statistics, 1988," 09/1988, CIA-RDP89T01437R000100140006-0; "Intelligence Handbook: Communist Aid to Less Developed Countries of the Free World, 1974," 03/1975, CIA-RDP79S01091A000400030001-4; "Communist Aid to Less Developed Countries of the Free World, 1975," 07/1976, CIA-RDP08S01350R000602020001-7; "Communist Aid to the Less Developed Countries of the Free World, 1976," 09/1977, CIA-RDP79B00457A000600020001-5; "Soviet Military Policy in the Third World," 10/21/1976, CIA-RDP07S01968R000200450001-2; "Communist Military Transfers and Economic Aid to Non-Communist Less Developed Countries, 1984," 05/1985, CIA-RDP87T01127R000100030009-5; "The Soviet Military Advisory and Training Program for the Third World," 04/1984, CIA-RDP85T00283R000500060003-4; "Insurgency: 1985 in Review," 04/1986, CIA-RDP97R00694R000600020001-2; CIA, "Supporting Allies Under Insurgent Challenge: The Soviet Experience in Africa," 02/1988, CIA-RDP07C00121R001000530001-0; "West Africa: The Socialist Hardcore Looks Westward," 06/1985, CIA-RDP86T00589R000200200005-9.

19. Stephen M. Streeter, *Managing the Counterrevolution: The United States and Guatemala, 1954–1961* (Ohio University Press, 2001), 27–28, 44;

Rabe, *Killing Zone*, 49–50, 55, 57; William I. Hitchcock, *The Age of Eisenhower: America and the World in the 1950s* (Simon & Schuster, 2018), 164, 167; Matilde Zimmermann, *Sandinista: Carlos Fonseca and the Nicaraguan Revolution* (Duke, 2000), 79–82; Morris H. Morley, *Washington, Somoza, and the Sandinistas: State and Regime in U.S. Policy Toward Nicaragua, 1969–1981* (Cambridge, 1994), 37, 48; Michael D. Gambone, *Eisenhower, Somoza, and the Cold War in Nicaragua, 1953–1961* (Praeger, 1997), 88, 90–91, 219–220.

20. For additional statistical analyses see Adam E. Casey, "The Durability of Client Regimes: Foreign Sponsorship and Military Loyalty, 1946–2010," *World Politics* 72, no. 3 (2020): 430–437. For a longer discussion see Adam E. Casey, "The Durability of Client Regimes: Foreign Sponsorship and Autocracies, 1946–2010" (PhD diss., University of Toronto, 2020), 38–65, 189–202.

21. Casey, "Durability of Client Regimes," 431–433, 199–200.

22. Quoted in Lucan Way, "Comparing the Arab Revolts: The Lessons of 1989," *Journal of Democracy* 22, no. 4 (2011): 152–153.

23. Steven Levitsky and Lucan A. Way, *Competitive Authoritarianism: Hybrid Regimes After the Cold War* (Cambridge, 2010); Gunitsky, *Aftershocks*, 218–221.

24. Robert D. Kaplan, "A New Cold War Has Begun," *Foreign Policy*, January 7, 2019; Daniel Bessner, "The Last Thing We Need Is a 'New Cold War' with China," *Jacobin*, April 22, 2020; David E. Sanger, "Washington Hears Echoes of the '50s and Worries: Is This a Cold War with China?," *New York Times*, October 17, 2021; Gabriel Scheinmann, "The U.S. Should Want a Cold War with China," *Wall Street Journal*, February 10, 2022; Robert Daly, "China and the United States: It's a Cold War, but Don't Panic," *Bulletin of the Atomic Scientists*, March 10, 2022; Elliott Abrams, "The New Cold War," *National Review*, March 21, 2022; President Joseph R. Biden Jr., "State of the Union Address," March 1, 2022; "Blinken Warns China Threat Greater Than Russia Long Term," *DW*, May 26, 2022; US Secretary of Defense Lloyd J. Austin, "Remarks at the Shangri-La Dialogue"; "Annual Threat Assessment of the US Intelligence Community," Office of the Director of National Intelligence, April 9, 2021, June 11, 2022; "National Security Strategy," White House, United States Government, October 2022; Chris Buckley and David E. Sanger, "In an Era of Confrontation, Biden and Xi Seek to Set Terms," *New York Times*, November 12, 2022.

25. Robert D. Kaplan, "To Save Democracy, We Need a Few Good Dictators," *Bloomberg*, April 1, 2022; Karen Elliott House, "Biden Needs to Make Up with Saudi Arabia, or China Will Gain," *Wall Street Journal*, March 31, 2022; Dennis Ross, "We Can't Face Down Putin Alone: The U.S. Must

Look Far and Wide for Partners, Including in the Middle East," *Atlantic*, May 6, 2022; Maximilian Hess, "Why the West Should Make Peace with Erdogan Now," *Foreign Policy*, June 22, 2022; "National Security Strategy"; Ted Piccone, "The Awkward Guests: Parsing the Summit for Democracy List," *Brookings Institution*, December 7, 2021; Hillary Clinton, "America's Pacific Century," *Foreign Policy*, October 11, 2011.

26. Nancy A. Youseff, Vivian Salama, and Michael C. Bender, "Trump, Awaiting Egyptian Counterpart at Summit, Called Out for 'My Favorite Dictator,'" *Wall Street Journal*, September 13, 2019; "White House Refuses to Make Egypt 'Coup' Determination," *BBC News*, July 9, 2013; Gregory L. Aftandilian, "Hope Versus Reality: The Efficacy of Using US Military Aid to Improve Human Rights in Egypt," *Parameters* 51, no. 3 (2021): 79–90; David E. Sanger, "Candidate Biden Called Saudi Arabia a 'Pariah.' He Now Has to Deal with It," *New York Times*, February 24, 2021; Peter Baker and Ben Hubbard, "Biden to Travel to Saudi Arabia, Ending Its 'Pariah' Status," *New York Times*, June 2, 2022; David E. Sanger and Peter Baker, "Biden's Goal in the Middle East: Countering China and Russia," *New York Times*, July 17, 2022, A8; John Wagner, Yasmeen Abutaleb, and Karen DeYoung, "Biden to Review U.S. Ties with Saudi Arabia, White House Says," *Washington Post*, October 11, 2022.

27. Ben Blanchard, "Duterte Aligns Philippines with China, Says U.S. Has Lost," Reuters, October 20, 2016; Justin Heifetz, "Tillerson Refuses to Condemn Duterte's War on Drugs," CNN, January 11, 2017; David G. Timberman, "Philippine Politics Under Duterte: A Midterm Assessment," Carnegie Endowment for International Peace, January 10, 2019; "Philippines' Duterte Threatens to End Military Deal with United States," Reuters, January 23, 2020; Sebastian Strangio, *In the Dragon's Shadow: Southeast Asia in the Chinese Century* (Yale, 2020), 250, 253–258, 264–271; David Rising and Jim Gomez, "Marcos Presidency Complicates US Efforts to Counter China," Associated Press, May 10, 2022; Ashley Westerman, "The U.S. and the Philippines Agree to a Larger American Military Presence," NPR, February 2, 2023.

28. Apornrath Phoonphongphiphat, "Thailand's Army Declares Martial Law, Says Not a Coup," Reuters, May 19, 2014; Thomas Fuller, "Thailand's Military Stages Coup, Thwarting Populist Movement," *New York Times*, May 22, 2014; Strangio, *Dragon's Shadow*, 121–127, 140–142; Emma Chanlett-Avery, Ben Dolven, and Kirt Smith, "Thailand: Background and U.S. Relations," June 17 (Congressional Research Service, 2020); "U.S. Security Cooperation with Thailand," April 22, Fact Sheet, Bureau of Political-Military Affairs (US Department of State, 2021); "Thailand," Freedom in the World Report (Freedom House, 2022).

29. Robert D. Schulzinger, *A Time for Peace: The Legacy of the Vietnam War* (Oxford, 2006), 47; Tuong Vu, *Vietnam's Communist Revolution: The Power and Limits of Ideology* (Cambridge, 2017), 270, 259, 266, 279–280; Derek Grossman, *Regional Responses to U.S.-China Competition in the Indo-Pacific: Vietnam* (RAND, 2020), 7, 9, 34–39.

30. Andrei Lungu, "The U.S.-China Clash Is About Ideology After All," *Foreign Policy*, April 6, 2021; Zachary Abuza, "America Should Be Realistic About Its Alliance with Thailand," *War on the Rocks*, January 2, 2020; Thomas Carothers and Benjamin Press, "Navigating the Democracy-Security Dilemma in U.S. Foreign Policy: Lessons from Egypt, India, and Turkey," Carnegie Endowment for International Peace, November 4, 2021; Matthew Yglesias, "The Fight for Democracy Needs Some Hypocrisy," *Bloomberg*, December 12, 2021; Kaplan, "To Save Democracy"; Alex M. Stark, "Who Leads the US' Relationship with Gulf States?," *Inkstick*, April 5, 2022; Dalia Dassa Kaye, "Bowing to the Prince: Why It's a Mistake for Biden to Visit Saudi Arabia," *Foreign Affairs*, June 3, 2022; Kelly Magsamen, Max Bergmann, Michael Fuchs, and Trevor Sutton, "Securing a Democratic World: The Case for a Democratic Values–Based U.S. Foreign Policy," *CAP*, September 5, 2018; President Joseph R. Biden Jr., "Remarks by President Biden at the Summit for Democracy Closing Session," December 10, 2021; Edward Lucas, "Democracies Need a United Strategy Against China," *Foreign Policy*, December 9, 2020; Stephen Wertheim, "Ukraine Doesn't Need a Crusade for Democracy," *Atlantic*, June 11, 2022; Benjamin Denison, "The Folly of a Democracy-Based Grand Strategy," *Defense Priorities*, December 8, 2021.

CHAPTER 1: AUTOCRATS AND ARMIES

1. Quoted in Bradford K. Mudge, *The Eagle and the Lion* (Yale, 2007), 233.

2. Sharan Grewal, "Why Sudan Succeeded Where Algeria Failed," *Journal of Democracy* 32, no. 4 (2021): 104; Brian A. Nelson, *The Silence and the Scorpion: The Coup Against Chávez and the Making of Modern Venezuela* (Nation Books, 2009).

3. Mark R. Beissinger, *The Revolutionary City: Urbanization and the Global Transformation of Rebellion* (Princeton, 2022), 164; quoted in Zoltan Barany, *How Armies Respond to Revolutions and Why* (Princeton, 2016), 141, 138–139, 66; Matthew D. Cebul and Sharan Grewal, "Military Conscription and Nonviolent Resistance," *Comparative Political Studies* 55, no. 13 (2022): 2225; Lucan A. Way, *Pluralism by Default: Weak Autocrats and the Rise of Competitive Politics* (Johns Hopkins, 2015), 153–154; Risa Brooks, "Abandoned at the Palace: Why the Tunisian Military Defected from the Ben Ali Regime in January 2011," *Journal of Strategic Studies* 36, no. 2 (2013): 206–207.

4. Julien Morency-Laflamme, "A Question of Trust: Military Defection During Regime Crises in Benin and Togo," *Democratization* 25, no. 3 (2018): 470–471; Steven R. Ward, *Immortal: A Military History of Iran and Its Armed Forces*, 2nd ed. (Georgetown, 2014), 302, 308; Ben Hubbard and Farnaz Fassihi, "Iran's Loyal Security Forces Protect Ruling System That Protestors Want to Topple," *New York Times*, October 17, 2022.

5. Hannah Beech, "'I Will Die Protecting My Country': In Myanmar, a New Resistance Rises," *New York Times*, March 24, 2021; Aregawi Berhe, *A Political History of the Tigray People's Liberation Front (1975–1991): Revolt, Ideology and Mobilization in Ethiopia* (Tsehai, 2009), 40–41, 54–56, 59–63, 153, 187.

6. Sheena Chestnut Greitens, *Dictators and Their Secret Police: Coercive Institutions and State Violence* (Cambridge, 2016); Barbara Geddes, Joseph Wright, and Erica Frantz, *How Dictatorships Work: Power, Personalization, and Collapse* (Cambridge, 2018), 179; Milan Svolik, *The Politics of Authoritarian Rule* (Cambridge, 2012), 5.

7. Risa A. Brooks, *Political-Military Relations and the Stability of Arab Regimes* (Oxford, 1998), 10, 19–20; Greitens, *Dictators and Their Secret Police*, 24; Alan Cowell, "Failed Mutiny Is Reported in Tanzania," *New York Times*, January 23, 1983; CIA, National Intelligence Daily, 01/26/1983, CIA-RDP85T01094R000100010145-5; CIA, "The Tanzanian Military: Nyerere's Uncertain Shield," 06/1983, CIA-RDP84S00552R000200150003-0; CIA, Africa Review, 06/13/1986, CIA-RDP87T00289R000301420001-9; Maggie Dwyer, *Soldiers in Revolt: Army Mutinies in Africa* (Hurst, 2017).

8. CIA, "Politics in Syria," 05/1979, CIA-RDP80T00942A001000030001-0; CIA, "Syria's Elite Military Units: Keys to Stability and Succession," 02/1987, CIA-RDP88T00096R000500590001-3; Greitens, *Dictators and Their Secret Police*, 27; Kristen A. Harkness, *When Soldiers Rebel: Ethnic Armies and Political Instability in Africa* (Cambridge, 2018), 3, 9–10, 76–77; Geddes et al., *How Dictatorships Work*, 51, 53, 57, 166–167.

9. Eric A. Nordlinger, *Soldiers in Politics: Military Coups and Governments* (Prentice-Hall, 1977), 76; CIA, "Politics in Syria"; CIA, "Saudi Arabia Handbook," 12/1972, CIA-RDP79-00891A001300080001-1; Anthony H. Cordesman, *Saudi Arabia: Guarding the Desert Kingdom* (Westview, 1997), 119, 137, 141, 175–176; Madawi al-Rasheed, *A History of Saudi Arabia*, 2nd ed. (Cambridge, 2010), 41, 56, 65–66, 86–87, 109; CIA, "Syria's Elite Military Units."

10. Erica De Bruin, *How to Prevent Coups d'État: Counterbalancing and Regime Survival* (Cornell, 2020); Geddes et al., *How Dictatorships Work*, 164, 173; UNHRC, "Report of the Detailed Findings of the Commission of Inquiry on Human Rights in Eritrea," A/HRC/29/CRP.1, 06/23/2015, 39–40, 74, 427–434; Nordlinger, *Soldiers in Politics*, 76; Jun Koga Sudduth, "Coup Risk, Coup-Proofing, and Leader Survival," *Journal of Peace Research* 54, no. 1 (2017):

3–15; Geddes et al., *How Dictatorships Work*, 164, 173; CIA, Weekly Summary, 10/04/1963, CIA-RDP79-00927A004200050001-2; Samuel Decalo, *Coups and Army Rule in Africa*, 2nd ed. (Yale, 1990), 55–56.

11. CIA, President's Intelligence Review, 02/04/1964, CIA-RDP78T009 36A002300040001-7; CIA, "Ghana," 11/1966, CIA-RDP79T00826A0032001 00001-9; Simon Baynham, *The Military and Politics in Nkrumah's Ghana* (Westview, 1988), 73, 130, 140, 146–147, 154–155, 183–184.

12. Zoltan Barany, "How Post-colonial Armies Came About: Comparative Perspectives from Asia and Africa," *Journal of Asian and African Studies* 49, no. 5 (2014): 601; Abillah H. Omari, "Civil-Military Relations in Tanzania," in *Ourselves to Know: Civil-Military Relations and Defense Transformation in Southern Africa*, ed. R. Williams, C. Cawthra, and D. Abrahams (Institute for Security Studies, 2003), 93; William Gutteridge, *The Military in African Politics* (Methuen, 1969), 26, 28–29, 41; William Redman Duggan and John R. Civille, *Tanzania and Nyerere: A Study of Ujamaa and Nationhood* (Orbis, 1976), 81; Zoltan Barany, *The Soldier and the Changing State: Building Democratic Armies in Africa, Asia, Europe, and the Americas* (Princeton, 2012), 237. The TPDF was called the United Republic Military Forces until January 8, 1965.

13. Henry Bienen, *Tanzania: Party Transformation and Economic Development*, 2nd ed. (Princeton, 1970), 375; Omari, "Civil-Military Relations in Tanzania," 94; Herman Lupogo, "Tanzania: Civil-Military Relations and Political Stability," *African Security Review* 10, no. 1 (2001): 80; Barany, *Soldier and the Changing State*, 240–241; Henry Bienen, "Public Order and the Military in Africa: Mutinies in Kenya, Uganda, and Tanganyika," in *The Military Intervenes: Case Studies in Political Development*, ed. Henry Bienen (Sage, 1968), 59; CIA, "Tanzania: Nyerere Under Fire," 11/01/1984, CIA-RDP85S00 317R000300070003-8; CIA, "Tanzania: Taking the Left Turn," 05/21/1965, CIA-RDP79-00927A004900030002-6; CIA, "East Africa: Outside Influence and Potential Conflict," 05/07/1975, CIA-RDP79R01142A000500070002-5; CIA, "Tanzanian Military"; CIA, "Kenya-Uganda-Tanzania: Uneasy Neighbors," 06/06/1983, CIA-RDP84S00552R000300070002-9.

14. CIA, "Libya: Will the Revolution Outlast Qadhafi?," 06/1988, CIA-RDP8 9S01450R000400410001-8.

15. Edward N. Luttwak, *Coup d'État: A Practical Handbook*, 2nd ed. (Harvard, 2016), 28–35; Clayton L. Thyne, Jonathan Powell, Sarah Parrott, and Emily VanMeter, "Even Generals Need Friends: How Foreign and Domestic International Reactions to Coups Influence Regime Survival," *Journal of Conflict Resolution* 62, no. 7 (2018): 1407–1408.

16. Victor T. Le Vine, "Insular Problems of an Inland State," *Africa Report* 10 (November 1965): 17–23.

17. George Weeks, "Armies of Africa," *Africa Report* 9 (January 1964): 6; Pierre Kalck, *Central African Republic: A Failure in De-colonisation* (Praeger, 1971), 71, 107, 121–123, 139–141, 154; Frances Terry McNamara, *France in Black Africa* (NDU Press, 1989), 143–145; Brian Titley, *Dark Age: The Political Odyssey of Emperor Bokassa* (McGill-Queens, 1997), 23–24, 31.

18. "News in Brief," *Africa Report* 11 (February 1966): 26; Kalck, *Central African Republic*, 153; Titley, *Dark Age*, 24, 27–28.

19. Titley, *Dark Age*, 25–30.

20. Samuel Decalo, *The Stable Minority: Civilian Rule in Africa, 1960–1990* (Florida Academic, 1998), 162–163; Alain Rouvez, *Disconsolate Empires: French, British and Belgian Military Involvement in Post-Colonial Sub-Saharan Africa* (University Press of America, 1994), 172; Timothy Stapleton, "Central African Republic: Coups, Mutinies, and Civil War," *Oxford Research Encyclopedias: Politics* (Oxford, 2019).

21. Titley, *Dark Age*, 127–131; Thomas O'Toole, "Made in France: The Second Central African Republic," *Proceedings of the Meeting of the French Colonial Historical Society* 6/7 (1982): 143; CIA, "Central African Republic: On a Tightrope," 12/05/1983, CIA-RDP85T00287R000500160001-1.

22. Titley, *Dark Age*, 160; "CAR: Insecure Beginnings," *West Africa*, November 12, 1979b, 2117; "CAR: French Troops for Dacko's Security," *West Africa*, October 22, 1979d, 1968; "African Update," *Africa Report* 25 (January–February 1980): 35; "African Update," *Africa Report* 26 (November–December 1981): 32; International Crisis Group, "Central African Republic: Anatomy of a Phantom State," *Africa Report* 136 (December 13, 2007): 7.

23. "Unhappy Anniversary in Bangui," *West Africa*, January 28, 1980, 144; CIA, "National Intelligence Daily," 03/21/1981, CIA-RDP83T00296 R000200010055-4; Frank K. Prial, "Army Topples Leader of Central African Republic," *New York Times*, September 2, 1981, A7; "African Update," *Africa Report*, 1981, 32; Prial, "Army Topples Leader"; CIA, "Central African Republic"; Titley, *Dark Age*, 152, 158–161.

24. CIA, "Angola," 05/15/1961, CIA-RDP64B00346R000500080025-6, CIA, "Special Report: Status of the Angolan Insurgency," 02/03/1967, CIA-RDP79-00927A005600070003-3; John A. Marcum, *The Angolan Revolution*, vol. 1 (MIT, 1969), 124–130; CIA, "Special Report: The Angolan Insurgency: Ten Years Later," 10/22/1971, CIA-RDP79-00927A009200010002-0; John A. Marcum, *The Angolan Revolution*, vol. 2 (MIT, 1978), 40, 168–169, 174, 197.

25. CIA, "The Angolan Rebellion and White Unrest," 04/05/1963, CIA-RDP79-00927A004000030002-5; Marcum, vol. 1, 27–28, 33, 35–36, 43, 229; CIA, "Soviet and Cuban Aid to the MPLA in Angola from March through December 1975," 01/24/1976, FOIA no. 0000681964; Arthur J. Klinghoffer,

The Angolan War: A Study in Soviet Policy in the Third World (Westview, 1980), 9–10; Rachel Warner, "Historical Setting," in *Angola: A Country Study*, ed. Thomas Collelo (Library of Congress, 1991), 26–27; Norrie MacQueen, *The Decolonization of Portuguese Africa* (Longman, 1997), 19; Marcum, vol. 2, 29–30, 40, 202; Lawrence W. Henderson, *Angola: Five Centuries of Conflict* (Cornell, 1979), 177, 249; Keith Somerville, *Angola: Politics, Economics and Society* (Lynne Rienner, 1986), 31; Warner, "Historical Setting," 35; John P. Cann, *Counterinsurgency in Africa: The Portuguese Way of War, 1961–1974* (Greenwood, 1997), 7.

26. CIA, "Angola: Short-Term Military and Political Prospects," 11/26/1975, CIA-RDP81-00261R000300090019-4; CIA, "Angola's Potential Leaders," 12/1975, CIA-RDP86T00608R000200010064-0; Marcum, vol. 2, 252–253, 258; Henderson, *Angola*, 243–247, 252–254; Somerville, *Angola*, 42–45; Joseph P. Smaldone, "National Security," in *Angola: A Country Study*, ed. Thomas Collelo (Library of Congress, 1991), 210; Warner, "Historical Setting," 35–36; Piero Gleijeses, *Visions of Freedom: Havana, Washington, Pretoria, and the Struggle for Southern Africa, 1976–1991* (UNC Press, 2013), 71–72.

27. Henderson, *Angola*, 252, 254–255; Gleijeses, *Visions of Freedom*, 28.

28. David Birmingham, *Frontline Nationalism in Angola and Mozambique* (James Currey, 1992), 49; Henderson, *Angola*, 252, 254–255; Gleijeses, *Visions of Freedom*, 28, 34, 71; CIA, "Activities of the Cuban Military in Angola"; see also CIA, "Soviet and Cuban Aid to the MPLA in Angola During January 1976," 02/03/1976, FOIA no. 0000307945; CIA, "Soviet and Cuban Aid to the MPLA in Angola During February 1976," 03/26/1976, FOIA no. 0000681967; CIA, "Soviet Military Support to Angola: Intentions and Prospects," 10/24/1985, CIA-RDP87T00573R000801010002-2; CIA, "Angola: Implications of Government Military Offensive," 10/07/1985, CIA-RDP85T01058R000100470001-4; Valeriy I. Shariy, "Voennoye vmeshatel'stvo inostrannikh gosudarstv v grazhdanskuyu voynu v Angole, 1975-nachalo 1976 goda," *Voenno-istoricheskiy zhurnal* 4 (April 2008): 21–22; Smaldone, "National Security," 212, 247–428; Christopher Andrew and Vasili Mitrokhin, *The World Was Going Our Way: The KGB and the Battle for the Third World* (Basic Books, 2005), 454.

29. Paul Fauvet, "Angola: The Rise and Fall of Nito Alves," *Review of African Political Economy* 9 (May–August 1977): 88–104.

30. Fauvet, "Angola: The Rise and Fall of Nito Alves"; CIA, "Assessment of Developments in Angola," 06/10/1977, CIA-RDP79R00603A0027000500 08-3; Bonnie J. Schultz and Robert Rundblad, "African Update," *Africa Report* 22, no. 4 (1977): 40; CIA, "Angola: Prospects for MPLA-UNITA Reconciliation," 02/1985, CIA-RDP86T00589R000100080004-5; Edward George, *The Cuban Intervention in Angola, 1965–1991: From Che Guevara to Cuito Cuanavale* (Cass, 2005), 127–131; Gleijeses, *Visions of Freedom*, 73–74; Paulo Ingles, "The MPLA

Government and Its Post-Liberation Record in Angola," in *National Liberation Movements as Government in Africa*, ed. Redie Bereketeab (Routledge, 2018), 53.

CHAPTER 2: TWO REVOLUTIONS

1. Odd Arne Westad, *The Global Cold War: Third World Interventions and the Making of Our Times* (Cambridge, 2005), 8–72.

2. The literature on both the American and the Russian revolutions is voluminous. For recent work on the Russian Revolution see Sheila Fitzpatrick, *The Russian Revolution*, 4th ed. (Oxford, 2017); Laura Engelstein, *Russia in Flames: Revolution, Civil War, 1914–1921* (Oxford, 2018); Steven Levitsky and Lucan A. Way, *Revolution and Dictatorship: The Violent Origins of Durable Authoritarianism* (Princeton, 2022), 45–84. On the American Revolution see Marc Egnal, *A Mighty Empire: The Origins of the American Revolution*, 2nd ed. (Cornell, 2010); Justin du Rivage, *Revolution Against Empire: Taxes, Politics, and the Origins of American Independence* (Yale, 2018).

3. Edward M. Coffman, *The Regulars: The American Army, 1898–1941* (Belknap, 2004), 203, 4, 144, 256.

4. Bernard Bailyn, *The Ideological Origins of the American Revolution*, 50th anniv. ed. (Belknap, 2017), 63.

5. John Rhodehamel, *George Washington: The Wonder of the Age* (Yale, 2017), 187; Richard H. Kohn, "The Inside History of the Newburgh Conspiracy: America and the Coup d'État," *William and Mary Quarterly* 27, no. 2 (1970): 188–220; Robert K. Wright, *The Continental Army* (US Army, 1983), 171–183; Rhodehamel, *George Washington*, 184–189.

6. Edward M. Coffman, *The Old Army: A Portrait of the American Army in Peacetime, 1784–1898* (Oxford, 1986), 3–4; Max Farrand, ed., *The Records of the Federal Convention of 1787*, vol. 1 (Yale, 1911), 465; Gian Gentile, Jameson Karns, Michael Shurkin, and Adam Givens, *The Evolution of U.S. Military Policy from the Constitution to the Present*, vol. 1 (RAND, 2020), 10.

7. Coffman, *Old Army*, 38.

8. Stephen Skowronek, *Building a New American State: The Expansion of National Administrative Capacities, 1877–1920* (Cambridge, 1982), 213–216, 236, 242–243, 246; Coffman, *Old Army*, 3–12, 43, 49, 96–97, 215, 225, 269–270, 280–281; Coffman, *Regulars*, 4, 143, 234; Gentile et al., *Evolution of U.S. Military Policy*, 11, 20, 61–62.

9. Samuel P. Huntington, *The Soldier and the State: The Theory and Politics of Civil-Military Relations* (Belknap, 1957), pt. 2; Coffman, *Old Army*, 38–39, 83, 97, 267, 272–273; Coffman, *Regulars*, 1, 4, 191, 245; Jason K. Dempsey, *Our Army: Soldiers, Politics, and American Civil-Military Relations* (Princeton, 2010), 11–15; Gentile et al., *Evolution of U.S. Military Policy*, 10–11, 55; Eric A.

Nordlinger, *Soldiers in Politics: Military Coups and Governments* (Prentice-Hall, 1977), 12–15; Morris Janowitz, *The Military in the Political Development of New Nations: An Essay in Comparative Analysis* (Chicago, 1964), 2–3; Samuel E. Finer, *The Man on Horseback: The Role of the Military in Politics* (Praeger, 1962), 25; Amos Perlmutter, *The Military and Politics in Modern Times: On Professionals, Praetorians, and Revolutionary Soldiers* (Yale, 1977), 2–3.

10. Barry M. Stentiford, *Army Expansions: Augmenting the Regular Army During War* (Combat Studies Institute Press, 2021), 154–158; Coffman, *Old Army*, 271–273; Michael D. Pearlman, *Truman and MacArthur: Policy, Politics, and the Hunger for Honor and Renown* (Indiana, 2008).

11. Leon Trotsky, *Military Writings* (Merit, 1969), 45; Mark von Hagen, *Soldiers in the Proletarian Dictatorship: The Red Army and the Soviet Socialist State, 1917–1930* (Cornell, 1990), 15, 20–21; Walter Görlitz, *History of the German General Staff* (Praeger, 1957), 2–3, 16–17; Huntington, *Soldier and the State*, 7, 11, 19, 21; Perlmutter, *Military and Politics*, 9–11, 24, 42–43; Brian M. Downing, *The Military Revolution and Political Change: Origins of Democracy and Autocracy in Early Modern Europe* (Princeton, 1992), 65–74; Roger R. Reese, *Red Commanders: A Social History of the Soviet Army Officer Corps, 1918–1991* (Kansas, 2005), 17–18; A. James McAdams, *Vanguard of the Revolution: The Global Idea of the Communist Party* (Princeton, 2017), 42–44, 46–47.

12. V. I. Lenin, *Gosudarstvo i revolyutsiya* ("Zhizhn i Znaniye," 1918), pt. 2; Stephen Kotkin, *Stalin*, vol. 1 (Penguin, 2014), 324; Kurt Weyland, *Assault on Democracy: Communism, Fascism, and Authoritarianism During the Interwar Years* (Cambridge, 2021); Engelstein, *Russia in Flames*, 290; A. J. Ryder, *The German Revolution of 1918: A Study of German Socialism in War and Revolt* (Cambridge, 1967), 143–144; György Borsányi, *The Life of a Communist Revolutionary, Béla Kun* (Columbia, 1993), 136.

13. Brian D. Taylor, *Politics and the Russian Army: Civil-Military Relations, 1689–2000* (Cambridge, 2003), 117; Reese, *Red Commanders*, 18; Joshua Rubenstein, *Leon Trotsky: A Revolutionary Life* (Yale, 2011), 109; Peter Whitewood, *The Red Army and the Great Terror* (Kansas, 2015), 19; Roman Kolkowicz, *The Soviet Military and the Communist Party* (Princeton, 1967), 38; Dale R. Herspring, *Russian Civil-Military Relations* (Indiana, 1996), 56.

14. Quoted in David R. Jones, "Armies and Revolution: Trotsky's Pre-1917 Military Thought," *Naval War College Review* 27, no. 1 (1974): 91; Leon Trotsky, "The Creation of the Workers' and Peasants' Red Army," July 10, 1918, *Military Writings*, vol. 1.

15. Leon Trotsky, "Labor, Discipline, Order," speech to a Moscow City Conference of the Communist Party, March 27, 1918, reproduced in *A*

Documentary History of Communism in Russia: From Lenin to Gorbachev, ed. Robert V. Daniels, 3rd ed. (University Press of New England, 1993), 73; Trotsky, "Creation of the Workers' and Peasant's Red Army."

16. Leon Trotsky, "Our Policy in Creating the Army," March 1919, *Military Writings*, vol. 1.

17. Herspring, *Russian Civil-Military Relations*, 59; Taylor, *Politics and the Russian Army*, 141; Fitzpatrick, *Russian Revolution*, 77; William E. Odom, *The Collapse of the Soviet Military* (Yale, 1998), 36; Kolkowicz, *Soviet Military and the Communist Party*, 46, 83, fn. 35, 123; Roger R. Reese, *The Soviet Military Experience: A History of the Soviet Army, 1917–1991* (Routledge, 2000), 79; John Erickson, *The Soviet High Command: A Military-Political History, 1918–1941* (Cass, 2001), 197.

18. John A. Lynn, *The Bayonets of the Republic: Motivation and Tactics of the Army of Revolutionary France* (Illinois, 1984), 83–85; Timothy J. Colton, *Commissars, Commanders, and Civilian Authority: The Structure of Soviet Military Politics* (Harvard, 1979), 308, en. 7; Rubenstein, *Trotsky*, 109.

19. Vasili Stepanovich Khristoforov, *Istoriya sovetskikh organov gosbezopasnosti, 1917–1991 gg.* (RGGU, 2015), 33; Amy W. Knight, "Internal Security," in *Soviet Union: A Country Study*, ed. Raymond E. Zickel, 2nd ed. (Library of Congress, 1991), 755–760; Decree on the Establishment of the Extraordinary Commission to Fight Counter-revolution, reproduced in *A Documentary History of Communism in Russia: From Lenin to Gorbachev*, ed. Robert V. Daniels, 3rd ed. (University Press of New England, 1993), 70–71.

20. Lynn, *Bayonets of the Republic*, 79; Christopher Andrew, *The Secret World: A History of Intelligence* (Yale, 2018), 321–323, 425–426; Boris Georgievich Kolokolov, *Zhandarm c tsarem v golovye: Zhiznenniy put' rukovoditelya lichnoy okhrani Nikolaya I* (Molodaya gvardiya, 2009), 70–71.

21. While the special departments were not under a unified command until February 1919, they were first established in December 1918. See Khristoforov, *Istoriya*, 33.

22. Kolkowicz, *Soviet Military and the Communist Party*, 41, 87–89; Colton, *Commissars*, 225–226; Knight, "Internal Security," 769, 776; Odom, *Collapse*, 33; Vyacheslav P. Artemiev, "OKR State Security in the Soviet Armed Forces," *Military Review*, September 1963, 25, 22; Marc Jansen and Nikita Petrov, *Stalin's Loyal Executioner: People's Commissar Nikolai Ezhov, 1895–1940* (Hoover, 2002), 69–70; CIA, "Soviet Security Organs," 12/11/1952, CIA-RDP82-00047R000200240003-9; Amy Knight, "The KGB and Civil-Military Relations," in *Soldiers and the Soviet State: Civil-Military Relations from Brezhnev to Gorbachev*, ed. Timothy J. Colton and Thane Gustafson (Princeton, 1990), 96–97.

23. Colton, *Commissars*, 51; Odom, *Collapse*, 36–37; Reese, *Soviet Military*, 11, 79–80; Erickson, *Soviet High Command*, 198.

24. Huntington, *Soldier and the State*; Nordlinger, *Soldiers in Politics*, 15; Finer, *Man on Horseback*, 3; Janowitz, *Military*, 2–3; Perlmutter, *Military and Politics*, 205; Odom, *Collapse*, 23–27, 39–48.

25. McAdams, *Vanguard*, 154; Nordlinger, *Soldiers in Politics*, 17; Jean Lachapelle, Steven Levitsky, Lucan A. Way, and Adam E. Casey, "Social Revolution and Authoritarian Durability," *World Politics* 72, no. 4 (2020): 557–600.

26. Barbara Geddes, Joseph Wright, and Erica Frantz, *How Dictatorships Work: Power, Personalization, and Collapse* (Cambridge, 2018), 156; Levitsky and Way, *Revolution and Dictatorship*; Robert Conquest, *The Great Terror: A Reassessment*, 3rd ed. (Oxford, 2008), 182, 184, 205–206; Alexander Hill, *The Red Army and the Second World War* (Cambridge, 2016), 690.

CHAPTER 3: EXPORTING REVOLUTION

1. Paul Rood, "Historical Setting," in *Finland: A Country Study*, ed. Eric Solsten and Sandra W. Meditz (Library of Congress, 1990), 29–31; Marko Tikka, "Warfare and Terror in 1918," in *The Finnish Civil War 1918: History, Memory, Legacy* (Brill, 2014), 91, 95–96, 105; Risto Alapuro, *State and Revolution in Finland*, 2nd ed. (Brill, 2019), 152.

2. A. J. Ryder, *The German Revolution of 1918: A Study of German Socialism in War and Revolt*, 200–203, 213; Stephen Kotkin, *Stalin*, vol. 1 (Penguin, 2014), 324–325; György Borsányi, *The Life of a Communist Revolutionary, Béla Kun* (Columbia, 1993), 25, 154, 181; Miklos Molnar, *From Béla Kun to János Kádár: Seventy Years of Hungarian Communism* (Berg, 1990), 28, 18–19; A. James McAdams, *Vanguard of the Revolution: The Global Idea of the Communist Party* (Princeton, 2017), 120, 122–123; Kurt Weyland, *Assault on Democracy: Communism, Fascism, and Authoritarianism During the Interwar Years* (Cambridge, 2021), 90–95.

3. Stanley G. Payne, *The Spanish Civil War, the Soviet Union, and Communism* (Yale, 2004), 161, 164; Stanley G. Payne, *The Spanish Civil War* (Cambridge, 2012), 33, 82, 120; Michael Alpert, *The Republican Army in the Spanish Civil War, 1936–1939* (Cambridge, 2013), 174; William W. Whitson, *The Chinese High Command: A History of Communist Military Politics, 1927–71* (Praeger, 1973), 16, 27; C. Martin Wilbur and Julie Lien-ying How, *Missionaries of Revolution: Soviet Advisers and Nationalist China, 1920–1927* (Harvard, 1989), 5; Xiaobing Li, *A History of the Modern Chinese Army* (Kentucky, 2007), 46–47.

4. Robert Rupen, *How Mongolia Is Really Ruled: A Political History of the Mongolian People's Republic: 1900–1978* (Hoover, 1979), 29; Robert Rupen, "The Mongolian Army," in *Communist Armies in Politics*, ed. Jonathan R. Adelman (Westview, 1982), 171; Ilya I. Kuznetsov, "The Soviet Military Advisers in Mongolia, 1921–39," *Journal of Slavic Military Studies* 12, no. 4 (1999): 118, 122, 126; S. K. Roshchin, *Politicheskaya istoriya Mongolii (1921–1940 gg.)* (I. V. RAN, 1999), 14, 106; James Palmer, *The Bloody White Baron* (Faber and Faber, 2008), 177–178, 206; Christopher Kaplonski, *The Lama Question: Violence, Sovereignty, and Exception in Early Socialist Mongolia* (University of Hawai'i Press, 2014), 48; Kotkin, *Stalin*, 203, 402–403; Willard Sunderland, *The Baron's Cloak: A History of the Russian Empire in War and Revolution* (Cornell, 2014), 193–194, 203–204; S. L. Kuzmin and Zh. Oyuunchimeg, *Vooruzhennoye vosstaniye v Mongolii v 1932 g.* (MBA, 2015), 22, fn. 70.

5. Seva Gunitsky, *Aftershocks: Great Powers and Domestic Reforms in the Twentieth Century* (Princeton, 2017), 157–159.

6. Philip Selznick, *The Organizational Weapon: A Study of Bolshevik Strategy and Tactics* (RAND, 1952); Steven Levitsky and Lucan A. Way, *Competitive Authoritarianism: Hybrid Regimes After the Cold War* (Cambridge, 2010); Dan Slater, *Ordering Power: Contentious Politics and Authoritarian Leviathans in Southeast Asia* (Cambridge, 2010); Milan Svolik, *The Politics of Authoritarian Rule* (Cambridge, 2012); Barbara Geddes, Joseph Wright, and Erica Frantz, *How Dictatorships Work: Power, Personalization, and Collapse* (Cambridge, 2018); Steven Levitsky and Lucan A. Way, *Revolution and Dictatorship: The Violent Origins of Durable Authoritarianism* (Princeton, 2022).

7. CIA, "Soviet Policy in Africa South of the Sahara," 02/28/1969, CIA-RDP79-00927A006900050003-1; Christopher Clapham, *Africa and the International System: The Politics of State Survival* (Cambridge, 1996), 38, 139; Christopher Andrew and Vasili Mitrokhin, *The World Was Going Our Way: The KGB and the Battle for the Third World* (Basic Books, 2005), 425–428, 436–437; Vladislav Zubok, *A Failed Empire: The Soviet Union in the Cold War from Stalin to Gorbachev* (UNC Press, 2009), 248; Sergey Mazov, *A Distant Front in the Cold War: The USSR in West Africa and the Congo, 1956 1964* (Woodrow Wilson Center, 2010), 2, 253, 257; CIA, "Soviet Pressure on Iraq," 08/09/1963, CIA-RDP79-00927A004100090002-8; Aleksandr Fursenko and Timothy Naftali, *Khrushchev's Cold War: The Inside Story of an American Adversary* (W. W. Norton, 2006), 158–159; CIA, "The Soviet Response to Instability in West Africa," 09/1985, CIA-RDP86T00591R000300440002-2; A. L. Adamishin et al., *Istoriya vneshney politiki SSSR: Tom vtoroy, 1945–1980* (Nauka, 1981), 538.

8. Roderick Macfarquhar, *The Origins of the Cultural Revolution*, vol. 2 (Columbia, 1983), 17–18; Valerie Bunce, "The Empire Strikes Back: The

Evolution of the Eastern Bloc from a Soviet Asset to a Soviet Liability," *International Organization* 39, no. 1 (1985): 1–46. On the long-term issues with the Soviet economy and its economic institutions see János Kornai, *The Socialist System: The Political Economy of Communism* (Princeton, 1992); Vladislav M. Zubok, *Collapse: The Fall of the Soviet Union* (Yale, 2021).

9. On the stagnation of the party see Ken Jowitt, *New World Disorder: The Leninist Extinction* (California, 1992); Levitsky and Way, *Revolution and Dictatorship*.

10. John Connelly, *From Peoples into Nations: A History of Eastern Europe* (Princeton, 2020), 501, 505–506, 531; Molly Pucci, *Security Empire: The Secret Police in Communist Eastern Europe* (Yale, 2020), 12–14, 290–291.

11. CIA, "Military Reliability of the Soviet Union's Warsaw Pact Allies," 06/28/1983, CIA-RDP86T00302R000100110001-1; CIA, "Bulgaria: Military— National Militia," 12/04/1950, CIA-RDP80-00809A000600140099-8; CIA, "Report on the Bulgarian Army," 05/29/1951, CIA-RDP82-00457R0077001700 03-3; CIA, "Leadership of the Bulgarian Army," 05/31/1957, CIA-RDP80T00 246A034800420001-9.

12. US Central Intelligence Group (CIG), "Hungarian State Defense Department," 12/30/1947, CIA-RDP82-00457R001200090005-8; CIA, "Hungarian Ministry of Defense, Organization and Personnel," 09/22/1948, CIA-RDP82-00457R001900100001-3; CIA, "Organization of the Secret Police," 02/02/1950, CIA-RDP82-00457R004200580007-9; CIA, "The Position of the AVH," 06/14/1954, CIA-RDP80-00809A000500820146-6; Bennett Kovrig, *Communism in Hungary: From Kun to Kádár* (Hoover, 1979), 265; Bradley R. Gitz, *Armed Forces and Political Power in Eastern Europe: The Soviet/ Communist Control System* (Greenwood, 1992), 17.

13. US CIG, "The Polish Army," IR, 10/21/1947, CIA-RDP81-01035 R000100020021-7; CIA, "Morale and General Conditions in the Army," 05/10/1948, CIA-RDP82-00457R001500260009-2; CIA, "Withdrawal of Soviet Officers from Poland," 06/08/1953, CIA-RDP80-00810A001400280003-3; CIA, "KBW and UB School at Szcytno," 07/21/1954, CIA-RDP80-00810A00 4200740004-0; CIA, "Morale, Benefits, and Restrictions in the Polish Army," 05/26/1955, CIA-RDP82-0004R000500130001-1; CIA, "Political Attitude and Reliability of the Polish Armed Forces," 03/19/1959, CIA-RDP80T00246A0479 00010001-9; A. Ross Johnson, *The Warsaw Pact: Soviet Military Policy in Eastern Europe* (RAND, 1981), 8; Norman Naimark, *Stalin and the Fate of Europe: The Postwar Struggle for Sovereignty* (Belknap, 2019), 199; Molly Pucci, *Security Empire: The Secret Police in Communist Eastern Europe* (Yale, 2020), 5, 31, 34–37, 40–45, 72–75.

14. US CIG, "Korea," 01/02/1948, CIA-RDP78-01617A001400030001-2;

CIA, "The Current Situation in Korea," 03/18/1948, CREST no. CIA-RDP78-01617A003100100001-5; CIA, "Review of the World Situation," 07/19/1950, CIA-RDP86B00269R000300040004-0; CIA, "North Korean Officers," 02/29/1951, CIA-RDP82-00457R007100280005-2; CIA, "Formation of a New Internal Intelligence Organization in North Korea," 01/10/1952, CIA-RDP82-00457 R010000120009-2; CIA, "Political Department of the North Korean Army General Headquarters," 12/29/1952, CIA-RDP82-00457R015700140007-0; CIA, "Relative Soviet and Chinese Influence in North Korea," 07/29/1953, CIA-RDP80R01443R000100280021-9; Bruce Cumings, *The Origins of the Korean War*, vol. 1 (Princeton, 1981), 121; Andrei N. Lankov, *From Stalin to Kim Il Sung: The Formation of North Korea, 1945–1960* (Hurst, 2002), 18, 21–29, 56–57; Charles K. Armstrong, *The North Korean Revolution, 1945–1950* (Cornell, 2003), 216–217, 231–232.

15. CIA, "People's Police Organization," 09/02/1952, CIA-RDP80-00926A005200030003-0; CIA, "Organization of the East Germany Ministry of National Defense," 12/17/1958, CIA-RDP80T00246A046100070001-2; Norman Naimark, *The Russians in Germany: A History of the Soviet Zone of Occupation, 1945–1949* (Belknap, 1995), 356, 362–363, 367, 371; Gary Bruce, "The Prelude to Nationwide Surveillance in East Germany: Stasi Operations and Threat Perceptions, 1945–1953," *Journal of Cold War History* 5, no. 2 (2003): 12–13, 16–17; Pucci, *Security Empire*, 118–150.

16. CIA, "Organization of the SNB Border Guard," 12/19/1949, CIA-RDP82-00457R0032004900008-2; CIA, "Czechoslovakia: Miscellaneous Military, Economic, and Political Information," 02/15/1949, CIA-RDP82-00 457R002300660009-9; CIA, "Czech Military Manpower," 12/20/1951, CIA-RD P80-00809A000600010141-0; CIA, "Competence and Political Reliability of Czechoslovak Army Officers," 05/26/1952, CIA-RDP82-00457R0122 00210005-2; CIA, "Czechoslovakia: Political Orientation of the Army," 04/16/1953, CIA-RDP80-00810A000900050008-9; CIA, "State Security (StB) Intelligence School in Brno," 05/28/1953, CIA-RDP80-00810A0013001000 08-8; CIA, "Organization of the SNB and the StB on the Regional Level," 04/27/1953, CIA-RDP80-00810A000900100010-0; CIA, "Czechoslovakia: Political Control Procedures," 02/04/1958, CIA-RDP80T00246A0400003200 01-1; US Army, "Order of Battle Handbook: Czechoslovak Army," 08/01/1958, accessed via CIA-RDP81-01043R00280014007-5; Condoleezza Rice, *The Soviet Union and the Czechoslovak Army, 1948–1983: Uncertain Allegiance*, 2nd ed. (Princeton, 2014), 4, 34–39, 41, 47–48, 53–56; David R. Shearer and Vladimir Khaustov, *Stalin and the Lubianka: A Documentary History of the Political Police and Security Organs in the Soviet Union, 1922–1953* (Yale, 2015), 283–284; Pucci, *Security Empire*, 6, 13, 77–79, 80–81, 84, 86, 91–92.

17. Dennis Deletant, *Romania Under Communism: Paradox and Degeneration* (Routledge, 2019), 5–15, 26–33, 42, 49–58.

18. US CIG, "Organization and Activities of the Cell and Sector Organizations in the Rumanian Communist Party," 07/28/1947, CIA-RDP82-0 0457R000700710009-1; CIA, "Organizational Structure of Rumanian Army Units," 12/29/1950, CIA-RDP82-00457R006800420005-3; CIA, "The Rumanian Army," 04/04/1951, CIA-RDP82-00457R007400150005-3; CIA, "Rumanian and Soviet Troops in Rumania," 01/08/1951, CIA-RDP82-00457R0067 00280007-5; CIA, "Political Indoctrination in Rumania," 09/02/1952, CIA-RD P80-00809A00600030034-1; Florin Şperlea, *From the Royal Armed Forces to the Popular Armed Forces: Sovietization of the Romanian Military (1948–1955)* (Columbia, 2009), 21, 27–28, 39–41, 44, 53, 128, 141, 157, 183–187, 195, 198, 200–201, 209; Deletant, *Romania Under Communism*, 51.

19. CIA, "Military Units of the Ministry of Interior," 07/29/1962, CIA-RDP80T00246A063600280001-5.

20. CIA, "The Rumanian Security Service," 12/12/1955, CIA-RDP80-00810 A008600180010-0; Dennis Deletant, *Ceaușescu and the Securitate: Coercion and Dissent in Romania, 1965–1989* (M. E. Sharpe, 1995), xiv, 4; Deletant, *Romania Under Communism*, 5, 51, 54, 90–94; Katherine Verdery, "Comparative Surveillance Regimes," in *Spaces of Security: Ethnographies of Securityscapes, Surveillance, and Control*, ed. Mark Maguire and Setha Low (NYU, 2019), 64. Data on other informer-to-population ratios come from Sheena Chestnut Greitens, *Dictators and Their Secret Police: Coercive Institutions and State Violence* (Cambridge, 2016), 9.

21. CIA, "Military Assistance by the Soviet Bloc to the Underdeveloped Countries of the Free World," 01/1959, CIA-RDP79R01141A001300080002-6; CIA, "Soviet Military Aid," 12/20/1963, CIA-RDP79-00927A004300040003-0; CIA, "Soviet Military Aid Diplomacy in the Third World," 09/1971, CIA-RDP 85T00875R001700020037-8; CIA, "Soviet Military Policy in the Third World," 12/21/1976, CIA-RDP07S01968R000200450001-2; CIA, "The Soviet Military Advisory and Training Program for the Third World," 04/1984, CIA-RDP85T00283R000500060003-4; CIA, "Soviet Arms: The Third World Attraction and Soviet Benefits," 02/1985, CIA-RDP97R00694R0004004400 01-8; Antonio Giustozzi and Artemy M. Kalinovsky, *Missionaries of Modernity: Advisory Missions and the Struggle for Hegemony in Afghanistan and Beyond* (Hurst, 2016).

22. CIA, "East European Military, Security, and Intelligence Advisory and Training Programs for LDCs," 09/1984, CIA-RDP85S00315R000100130002-6; CIA, "Soviet Military Policy in the Third World."

23. UK Foreign Office, "South Arabia Cairo Talks," October 6, 1967, Jedda to Foreign Office, Tel. no. 689, FCO 8/356, p. 146; CIA, "The Yemens: A

Handbook," 12/01/1984, CIA-RDP85T00314R000100010001-0; CIA, Central Intelligence Bulletin, 08/30/1967, CIA-RDP79T00975A010200260001-9; CIA, "The Situation in Yemen and South Yemen and the Soviet Role," 12/08/1967, CIA-RDP79T00826A003000400001-8; Noel Brehony, *Yemen Divided: The Story of a Failed State in South Arabia* (I. B. Tauris, 2011), 11–12, 18, 20–27, 31.

24. Yevgeny Primakov, *Konfidentsial'no: Blizhniy Vostok na stsenye i za kulisami (vtoraya polovina XX—nachalo XXI veka)* (Rossiiskaya gazeta, 2006), 91; CIA, "Sources of Opposition to South Yemeni President Ismail," 02/04/1980, CIA-RDP85T00287R000100130001-8.

25. CIA, "Sources of Opposition to South Yemeni President Ismail"; CIA, "Yemens: A Handbook"; CIA, "North and South Yemen: Comparative Military Capabilities," 10/20/1987, CIA-RDP88T00096R000800980002-6; CIA, NIC Outlook, 01/1986, CIA-RDP90R00038R000500580001-7; CIA, "South Yemen—USSR: Outlook for the Relationship," 04/05/1984, FOIA no. 0000681975; E. G. Ishchenko, *Ekonomichiskoye sotrudnichestvo SSSR so stranami sotsialistichestoy oriyentatsii* (Nauka, 1989); Primakov, *Konfidentsial'no*, 89–90; CIA, "The USSR and the Coup in South Yemen: Power Politics in the Third World," 04/03/1986, CIA-RDP86T01017R000504980001-4.

26. Ishchenko, *Ekonomichiskoye sotrudnichestvo.*

27. Primakov, *Konfidentsial'no*, 89–90; Andrew and Mitrokhin, *World Was Going Our Way*, 215; CIA, "South Yemen—USSR: Outlook for the Relationship"; CIA, "Yemens: A Handbook."

28. Primakov, *Konfidentsial'no*, 91; Andrew and Mitrokhin, *World Was Going Our Way*, 215, 218.

29. CIA, "Short-Term Prospects for the African Nationalist Movements in Angola and Mozambique," 07/01/1964, CIA-RDP79R01012A026200010006-6; CIA, "Anti-Portuguese Campaign in Africa Shifts to Mozambique," 12/18/1964, CIA-RDP79-00927A004700060002-5; CIA, "Mozambique," 08/1973, CIA-RDP01-00707R000200100010-4; Malyn Newitt, *A Short History of Mozambique* (Hurst, 2017), 138–142, 146, 152; CIA, "Soviet Military Advisory and Training Program for the Third World"; CIA, "Mozambique: Machel's Embattled Regime," 04/01/1982, CIA-RDP83B00225R000100160001-3; CIA, "The Situation in Mozambique: Short-Term Prospects," 04/21/1983, CIA-RDP86T00303R000100100001-1; Valeriy Ivanovich Shariy, "Podderzhka SSSR natsional'no-osvoboditel'nogo dvizheniya stran Afriki v 1960–1970-e godi," *Voenno-istoricheskiy zhurnal* (May 2008): 67.

30. Valeriy Ivanovich Shariy, "Pomosh' SSSR v sozdanii vooruzhyonnikh sil Narodnoy Respubliki Mozambik, 1965–1991 gg.," *Voenno-istoricheskiy zhurnal* 11 (November 2008): 19; CIA, "Sub-Saharan Africa: A Growing Soviet Military Presence," 01/12/1985, CIA-RDP91T01115R000100 390002-1; CIA, "Mozambique: Short-Term Prospects," 06/01/1986, CIA-RDP87

T00573R000801050001-9; CIA, "Supporting Allies Under Insurgent Challenge: The Soviet Experience in Africa," 02/1988, CIA-RDP07C00121R0010005300 01-0; CIA, "The Soviets in Mozambique: Is the Payoff Worth the Price?," 02/01/1988, CIA-RDP07C00121R001000690001-3; Andrew and Mitrokhin, *World Was Going Our Way*, 455.

CHAPTER 4: BOLSTERING COUNTERREVOLUTION

1. Seva Gunitsky, *Aftershocks: Great Powers and Domestic Reforms in the Twentieth Century* (Princeton, 2017), 159–160. The US military in 1945 had 12.1 million personnel, compared to 1.18 million personnel in the UK, China, Canada, Australia, and France combined. Data on military personnel come from Correlates of War National Material Capabilities dataset v6.0.

2. Jennifer M. Miller, *Cold War Democracy: The United States and Japan* (Harvard, 2019), 41, 72, 75, 105–110; Alan McPherson, *Intimate Ties, Bitter Struggles: The United States and Latin America Since 1945* (Potomac Books, 2006), 24.

3. *FRUS*, 1958–1960, East Asia–Pacific Region; Cambodia; Laos, vol. 16, Doc. 36; CIA, "The Meaning of Militarism in Latin America," 10/21/1963, CIA-RDP79T00429A001300050016-4.

4. *FRUS*, 1964–1968, vol. 24, Africa, Doc. 260; Christopher Heurlin, "Authoritarian Aid and Regime Durability: Soviet Aid to the Developing World and Donor-Recipient Institutional Complementarity and Capacity," *International Studies Quarterly* 64, no. 4 (2020): 973; *FRUS*, 1969–1976, vol. E-12, Documents on East and Southeast Asia, 1973–1976, Doc. 380.

5. Tony Smith, *America's Mission: The United States and the Worldwide Struggle for Democracy in the Twentieth Century* (Princeton, 1994), 183; William I. Hitchcock, *The Age of Eisenhower: America and the World in the 1950s* (Simon & Schuster, 2018), 153.

6. Ethan B. Kapstein, *Seeds of Stability: Land Reform and U.S. Foreign Policy* (Cambridge, 2017), 30; Douglas J. Macdonald, *Adventures in Chaos: American Intervention for Reform in the Third World* (Harvard, 1992); Smith, *America's Mission*, 188; *FRUS*, 1955–1957, vol. 19, National Security Policy, Doc. 6; "Counter-insurgency Operations: A Handbook for the Suppression of Communist Guerrilla / Terrorist Operations," United States Army, May 22, 1961, Papers of John F. Kennedy, President's Office Files, JFKPOF-080-014.

7. GAO, "U.S. Security and Military Assistance: Programs and Related Activities," GAO/ID–82–40, 06/01/1982.

8. Hitchcock, *Age of Eisenhower*, 161.

9. Daniel Ritter, *The Iron Cage of Liberalism: International Politics and*

Unarmed Revolutions in the Middle East and North Africa (Oxford, 2015), 18; Uk Heo and Terence Roehrig, *The Evolution of the South Korea–United States Alliances* (Cambridge, 2018), 90.

10. Timothy N. Castle, *At War in the Shadow of Vietnam: U.S. Military Aid to the Royal Lao Government, 1955–1975* (Columbia, 1993), 19; Hitchcock, *Age of Eisenhower*, 501; Thomas L. Ahern Jr., *Undercover Armies: CIA and Surrogate Warfare in Laos, 1961–1973* (Center for the Study of Intelligence, 2006), 8–11.

11. Roger L. Nichols, *Indians in the United States and Canada: A Comparative History* (Nebraska, 1998); Richard W. Maass, *The Picky Eagle: How Democracy and Xenophobia Limited U.S. Territorial Expansion* (Cornell, 2020).

12. Carolina Galicia Hernandez, "The Extent of Civilian Control of the Military in the Philippines: 1946–1976" (PhD diss., SUNY Buffalo, 1979), 62, 99–100, 106–108, 111–114, 119, 122–123, 126–127, 134, 169, 171; Stanley Karnow, *In Our Image: America's Empire in the Philippines* (Random House, 1989), 13, 15.

13. Marvin Goldert, *The Constabulary in the Dominican Republic and Nicaragua: Progeny and Legacy of the United States Intervention* (Florida, 1962), 3–21; Dan Gardner Munro, *The United States and the Caribbean Republics, 1921–1933* (Princeton, 1974), 65.

14. Telegram from American Legation to Washington, DC, January 19, 1916, File No. 838.51/466, *Papers Relating to the Foreign Relations of the United States*, Doc. 373; Munro, *United States and the Caribbean Republics*, 73–76; "Agreement Between the United States and Nicaragua Establishing the 'Guardia Nacional de Nicaragua,'" December 22, 1927, *Papers Relating to the Foreign Relations of the United States*, Doc. 452; Acting Secretary of State to the Minister in Nicaragua, December 28, 1933, *FRUS*, Diplomatic Papers, the American Republics, vol. 5; Goldert, *Constabulary*, 22–46; John A. Booth, *The End and the Beginning: The Nicaraguan Revolution* (Westview, 1982), 43, 47–48.

15. Se-Jin Kim, *The Politics of Military Revolution in Korea* (UNC, 1971), 15; Robert K. Sawyer, *Military Advisors in Korea: KMAG in Peace and War* (Center of Military History, 1988), 3; Quee-Yong Kim, *The Fall of Syngman Rhee* (California, 1983), 11; Young Ick Lew, *The Making of the First Korean President: Syngman Rhee's Quest for Independence, 1875–1948* (University of Hawai'i Press, 2014), 98, 267; Heo and Roehrig, *Evolution of the South Korea–United States Alliances*, 55, 81–82; Lorenz M. Lüthi, *Cold Wars: Asia, the Middle East, Europe* (Cambridge, 2020), 98.

16. W. D. Reeve, *The Republic of Korea: A Political and Economic Study* (Oxford, 1963), 24; Kim, *Fall of Syngman Rhee*, 12; Gregg Brazinsky, *Nation Building in South Korea: Koreans, Americans, and the Making of a Democracy*

(UNC, 2007), 2; Lew, *Making of the First Korean President*, 268–271; Odd Arne Westad, *The Cold War: A World History* (Basic Books, 2017), 161, 163; Heo and Roehrig, *Evolution of the South Korea–United States Alliances*, 83.

17. Brazinsky, *Nation Building*, 9; Heo and Roehrig, *Evolution of the South Korea–United States Alliances*, 85–86.

18. Sawyer, *Military Advisors in Korea*, 9, 11–15, 17, 20–24, 26, 32; Bryan R. Gibby, *The Will to Win: American Military Advisors in Korea, 1946–1953* (Alabama, 2012), 3–4, 11.

19. Sawyer, *Military Advisors in Korea*, 20, 26, 36, 39–40.

20. Sawyer, 34–38, 45, 58, 65.

21. Sawyer, 41, 49, 56, 61, 67, 79–81, 86, 90, 93.

22. Sawyer, 140, 150; Robert D. Ramsey, "Advising Indigenous Forces: American Advisors in Korea, Vietnam, and El Salvador," Global War on Terrorism Occasional Paper No. 18 (Combat Studies Institute, 2006), 5; Brazinsky, *Nation Building*, 9; Gibby, *Will to Win*, 2; Heo and Roehrig, *Evolution of the South Korea–United States Alliances*, 49.

23. Memorandum by the Director of the Executive Secretariat (Scott) to the Secretary of State, October 28, 1952, *FRUS*, 1952–1954, Korea, vol. 15, pt. 2, Doc. 781; Heo and Roehrig, *Evolution of the South Korea–United States Alliances*, 1–3, 64, 66; Lüthi, *Cold Wars*, 98; William H. Gleysteen, *Massive Entanglement, Marginal Influence: Carter and Korea in Crisis* (Brookings, 1999), 3, 9–10.

24. John Adams Wickham, *Korea on the Brink: From the "12/12" Incident to the Kwangju Uprising, 1979–1980* (National Defense University Press, 1999), 24; Brazinsky, *Nation Building*, 9.

25. Antonio Giustozzi and Artemy M. Kalinovsky, *Missionaries of Modernity: Advisory Missions and the Struggle for Hegemony in Afghanistan and Beyond* (Hurst, 2016), 112; Joseph Sassoon, *Saddam Hussein's Ba'th Party: Inside an Authoritarian Regime* (Cambridge, 2012), 98–97, 143–145; "Report to the National Security Council Pursuant to NSC Action 1290-d," Operations Coordinating Board, 11/23/1955, Dwight D. Eisenhower Presidential Library; Jay Taylor, *The Generalissimo: Chiang Kai-shek and the Struggle for Modern China* (Belknap, 2011), 306; Sheena Greitens, *Dictators and Their Secret Police: Coercive Institutions and State Violence* (Cambridge, 2016), 98, 110.

26. On Afghanistan see Giustozzi and Kalinovsky, *Missionaries of Modernity*, 90, 241, 296–297, 330–334; Antonio Giustozzi, *The Army of Afghanistan: A Political History of a Fragile Institution* (Hurst, 2015), 127; Thomas Gibbons-Neff, Fahim Abed, and Sharif Hassan, "The Afghan Military Was Built over 20 Years. How Did It Collapse So Quickly?," *New York Times*, August 13, 2021; Craig Whitlock, "Afghan Security Forces' Wholesale Collapse

Was Years in the Making," *Washington Post*, August 16, 2021; Rachel Tecott, "Why America Can't Build Allied Armies," *Foreign Affairs*, August 26, 2021; Jennifer Griffin and Caitlin McFall, "Milley: Afghan Forces 'Not Designed Appropriately' to Secure Nation in 'Lessons Learned' Following Withdrawal," *Fox News*, September 4, 2021.

27. Erica De Bruin, "Will There Be Blood? Explaining Violence During Coups d'État," *Journal of Peace Research* 56, no. 6 (2019): 797–811; CIA, "Postcoup Prospects in Liberia," 12/22/1980, CIA-RDP97S00289R000100190007-2; J. Gus Liebenow, *Liberia: The Quest for Democracy* (Indiana, 1987), 208, 303.

CHAPTER 5: COMMISSARS AND COUPS

1. Vasilii Stepanovich Khristoforov, *Afganistan: Voenno-politicheskoye prisutstviye SSSR, 1979–1989* (RAN: IRI, 2016), 53–54; V. G. Korgun, *Istoriya afganistana XX vek* (IV RAN, 2004), 373–374; Anthony Arnold, *Afghanistan's Two-Party Communism: Parcham and Khalq* (Hoover, 1983), 44, 47, 51.

2. Khristoforov, *Afganistan: Voenno-politicheskoye prisutstviye SSSR*, 55, 61, 217; Leonid Mikhailovich Mlechin, *Istoriya vneshney razvedki: Kar'eri i sud'bi* (Litres, 2019), 351–352.

3. Arnold, *Afghanistan's Two-Party Communism*, 57; Korgun, *Istoriya afganistana*, 404; Antonio Giustozzi, *Army of Afghanistan: A Political History of a Fragile Institution* (Hurst, 2015), 24–29; Khristoforov, *Afganistan: Voenno-politicheskoye prisutstviye SSSR*, 61–62.

4. CIA, NIDC, 04/28/1978, CIA-RDP79T00975A030600010102-8; Vasiliy Mitrokhin, "The KGB in Afghanistan," CWIHP Working Paper no. 40, 2nd ed. (July 2009), 26; Leonid Mikhailovich Mlechin, *Brezhnev* (Prospekt, 2006), 443–444; Vasilii Stepanovich Khristoforov, *Afganistan: Pravyashchaya partiya i armiya, 1978–1989* (Granitsa, 2009), 20; Khristoforov, *Afganistan: Voenno-politicheskoye prisutstviye SSSR*, 62; Mlechin, *Istoriya vneshney razvedki*, 349.

5. Khristoforov, *Afganistan: Pravyashchaya partiya i armiya*, 20–22; Mlechin, *Brezhnev*, 444; Khristoforov, *Afganistan: Voenno politicheskoye pri sutstviye SSSR*, 64, 296.

6. Fred Halliday and Zahir Tanin, "The Communist Regime in Afghanistan 1978–1992: Institutions and Conflicts," *Europe-Asia Studies* 50, no. 8 (1998): 1366; Barnett R. Rubin, *The Fragmentation of Afghanistan: State Formation and Collapse in the International System*, 2nd ed. (Yale, 2002), 114; Giustozzi, *Army of Afghanistan*, 45–46; Antonio Giustozzi and Artemy M. Kalinovsky, *Missionaries of Modernity: Advisory Missions and the Struggle for Hegemony in Afghanistan and Beyond* (Hurst, 2016), 196, 203–204; CIA, "Developments

in Afghanistan," 03/07/1986, CIA-RDP89T01363R000200240004-2; CIA, "Afghanistan: Regime Military and Political Capabilities After the Soviet Withdrawal," 09/20/1988, CIA-RDP89S01450R000500510001-6; Elizabeth Leake, *Afghan Crucible: The Soviet Invasion and the Making of Modern Afghanistan* (Oxford, 2022), 94, 99; CIA, "Afghanistan: Regime Military and Political Capabilities After the Soviet Withdrawal"; Olga Oliker, *Building Afghanistan's Security Forces in Wartime* (RAND, 2011), 25, 28; Khristoforov, *Afganistan: Voenno-politicheskoye prisutstviye SSSR*, 219, 36, 295, 306, 312.

7. Khristoforov, *Afganistan: Voenno-politicheskoye prisutstviye SSSR*, 218–219, 224, 227; Giustozzi, *Army of Afghanistan*, 104, 43; CIA, "Afghanistan: Party Factionalism and Fratricide," 03/01/1984, CIA-RDP85T00314 R000100020001-9; CIA, "The Soviet Invasion of Afghanistan: Five Years After," 05/01/1985, CIA-RDP86T00587R000200200003-3; Leake, *Afghan Crucible*, 69.

8. Leake, *Afghan Crucible*, xix, 44; Korgun, *Istoriya afganistana*, 404; Rubin, *Fragmentation of Afghanistan*, 115; Vassily Klimentov, "'Communist Muslims': The USSR and the People's Democratic Party of Afghanistan's Conversion to Islam, 1978–1988," *Journal of Cold War Studies* 24, no. 1 (2022): 6–7; Mlechin, *Istoriya vneshney razvedki*, 352–354; Khristoforov, *Afganistan: Pravyashchaya partiya i armiya*, 21; Giustozzi and Kalinovsky, *Missionaries of Modernity*, 194.

9. Leake, *Afghan Crucible*, 48–63; CIA, NIDC, 08/07/1978, CIA-RDP79 T00975A030800010012-6; Halliday and Tanin, "Communist Regime in Afghanistan," 1375; Korgun, *Istoriya afganistana*, 404; Khristoforov, *Afganistan: Voenno-politicheskoye prisutstviye SSSR*, 66.

10. Rubin, *Fragmentation of Afghanistan*, 115; Klimentov, "Communist Muslims," 9–10; Leake, *Afghan Crucible*, 63.

11. Rubin, *Fragmentation of Afghanistan*, 112; Khristoforov, *Afganistan: Pravyashchaya partiya i armiya*, 28; Khristoforov, *Afganistan: Voenno-politicheskoye prisutstviye SSSR*, 217.

12. Giustozzi, *Army of Afghanistan*, 23; Rubin, *Fragmentation of Afghanistan*, 114; Khristoforov, *Afganistan: Voenno-politicheskoye prisutstviye SSSR*, 63, 213.

13. CIA, NIDC, 08/01/1978, CREST no. CIA-RDP79T00975A0308000 10002-7.

14. CIA, NIDC, 08/16/1978, CREST no. CIA-RDP79T00975A0309000 10024-2; Khristoforov, *Afganistan: Voenno-politicheskoye prisutstviye SSSR*, 24, 63; M. Hassan Kakar, *Afghanistan: The Soviet Invasion and the Afghan Response, 1979–1982* (California, 1995), 62–63; CIA, NIDC, 08/18/1978, CIA-RDP79T00975A030800010032-4; CIA, NIDC, 08/07/1978.

15. Artemy M. Kalinovsky, *The Long Goodbye: The Soviet Withdrawal from Afghanistan* (Harvard, 2011), 20–21; Khristoforov, *Afganistan: Pravyashchaya*

partiya i armiya, 24, 32, 34, 38; Leake, *Afghan Crucible*, 6; Giustozzi, *Army of Afghanistan*, 30–33, 108.

16. Mlechin, *Brezhnev*, 436; Leake, *Afghan Crucible*, 69; Kalinovsky, *Long Goodbye*, 22, 25.

17. Khristoforov, *Afganistan: Pravyashchaya partiya i armiya*, 169; Leake, *Afghan Crucible*, 69; Mlechin, *Istoriya vneshney razvedki*, 359–364.

18. Khristoforov, *Afganistan: Pravyashchaya partiya i armiya*, 30; CIA, "Afghanistan: Resisting Sovietization," 11/14/1984, CIA-RDP85T00314R000 400020005-2; CIA, "The Afghan Air Force: New Planes, Old Problems, Little Impact," 05/1986, CIA-RDP88T00096R000200260002-1; Leake, *Afghan Crucible*, 98.

19. CIA, "Afghanistan: Regime Military and Political Capabilities After the Soviet Withdrawal"; Gordon Lubold and Yaroslav Trofimov, "Afghan Government Could Collapse Six Months After U.S. Withdrawal, New Intelligence Assessment Says," *WSJ*, June 23, 2021; SIGAR (US special inspector general for Afghanistan reconstruction), "Collapse of the Afghan National Defense and Security Forces: An Assessment of the Factors That Led to Its Demise," SIGAR 22-22-IP Evaluation Report, May 2022.

20. Rubin, *Fragmentation of Afghanistan*, 109; Kalinovsky, *Long Goodbye*, 178–179.

21. Giustozzi, *Army of Afghanistan*, 38–39, 55, 91; Khristoforov, *Afganistan: Voenno-politicheskoye prisutstviye SSSR*, 313.

22. Khristoforov, *Afganistan: Pravyashchaya partiya i armiya*, 288; John F. Burns, "In Power Still, Afghan Can Thank His 4-Star Aide," *New York Times*, May 10, 1990, A4; Rubin, *Fragmentation of Afghanistan*, 151; Giustozzi, *Army of Afghanistan*, 45.

23. CIA, "Ethiopia and the Horn of Africa," 05/07/1976, CIA-RDP85 T00353R000100280001-5; Fantahun Ayele, *The Ethiopian Army: From Victory to Collapse, 1977–1991* (Northwestern, 2014), 205–206.

24. Ayele, *Ethiopian Army*, 207–208; Christopher Clapham, *Transformation and Continuity in Revolutionary Ethiopia* (Cambridge, 1988), 56, 61; Clifford Krauss, "Ethiopia's Dictator Flees; Officials Seeking U.S. Help," *New York Times*, May 22, 1991, A1; Andargachew Tiruneh, *The Ethiopian Revolution, 1974–1987: A Transformation from an Aristocratic to a Totalitarian Autocracy* (Cambridge, 1993), 77–79, 190; Sergei Yakovlevich Sinitsin, *Missiya v Efiopii* (XXI Vek-soglasiye, 2001), 209; Messay Kebede, *Ideology and Elite Conflicts: Autopsy of the Ethiopian Revolution* (Lexington, 2011), 266–271.

25. Clapham, *Africa and the International System*, 61; Sinitsin, *Missiya v Efiopii*, 188; CIA, "Intelligence Assessment of Ethiopia," 10/16/1974, FOIA no. LOC-HAK-53-2-3-7.

26. Sinitsin, *Missiya v Efiopii*, 192; CIA, "Ethiopia and the Horn of Africa," 05/07/1976, CIA-RDP85T00353R000100280001-5; Clapham, *Transformation and Continuity*, 61.

27. CIA, "Ethiopia: Assessment of Key Issues," 06/16/1977, CIA-RDP79 R00603A002700020003-1; Ayele, *Ethiopian Army*, 104–105, 113–114, 210.

28. CIA, "Sub-Saharan Africa: A Growing Soviet Military Presence," 01/12/1985, CIA-RDP91T01115R000100390002-1.

29. CIA, "Ethiopia: The Northern Insurgencies," 10/01/1984, CIA-RDP85 S00317R000300050001-2; Jeffrey A. Lefebvre, *Arms for the Horn: U.S. Security Policy in Ethiopia and Somalia, 1953–1991* (Pittsburgh, 1991), 32, 42.

30. CIA, "The USSR and the Third World," 09/19/1984, CIA-RDP87 T00126R000600630007-8; CIA, "Supporting Allies Under Insurgent Challenge: The Soviet Experience in Africa," 02/1988, CIA-RDP07C00121R001000 530001-0"; Berouk Mesfin, "The Role of Military Power in Ethiopia's National Security (1974–1991)" (MA thesis, Addis Ababa University, 2002), 47–48; Berouk Mesfin, "The Architecture and Conduct of Intelligence in Ethiopia (1974–1991)," *International Journal of Ethiopian Studies* 5, no. 1 (2010): 46–47; Ayele, *Ethiopian Army*, 77.

31. Mesfin, "Role of Military Power," 49–50, 79–80, 84; Mesfin, "Architecture," 48, 50–51; Ayele, *Ethiopian Army*, 77, 86, 95–96.

32. CIA, "Ethiopia: The Impact of Soviet Military Assistance," 01/06/1983, FOIA no. 0000496797; CIA, "Ethiopia: Institutionalizing a Marxist-Leninist State," 04/01/1986, CIA-RDP88T00768R000100110001-3; Clapham, *Transformation and Continuity*, 70, 75–77; Edmond J. Keller, *Revolutionary Ethiopia: From Empire to People's Republic* (Indiana, 1988), 236–239; Steven Saxonberg, *Transitions and Non-transitions from Communism: Regime Survival in China, Cuba, North Korea, and Vietnam* (Cambridge, 2013), 47.

33. CIA, "Ethiopia: The Northern Insurgencies"; CIA, "Ethiopia: Institutionalizing a Marxist-Leninist State"; Mesfin, "Role of Military Power," 77; Ayele, *Ethiopian Army*, 77–78.

34. Ayele, *Ethiopian Army*, 77; Mesfin, "Role of Military Power," 83–84, 142; CIA, "Supporting Allies Under Insurgent Challenge"; CIA, "Ethiopia: Institutionalizing a Marxist-Leninist State."

35. CIA, "Ethiopia: The Northern Insurgencies"; CIA, Africa Review, 07/26/1985, CIA-RDP87T00289R000100380001-7; CIA, "Supporting Allies Under Insurgent Challenge"; Tiruneh, *Ethiopian Revolution*, 344–345; Gebru Tareke, *The Ethiopian Revolution: War in the Horn of Africa* (Yale, 2009), 257–258; Ayele, *Ethiopian Army*, 221, 78, 213.

36. CIA, National Intelligence Daily, 05/18/1989, accessed via Wilson Center Digital Archive; Abebe Andualem, "Mengistu Crushes Coup Attempt; Most Generals Killed," Associated Press, May 19, 1989; CIA,

"Ethiopia's President Mengistu: The Morning After," 06/16/1989, CIA-RDP91 B01306R001400030002-2; Tiruneh, *Ethiopian Revolution*, 345–356; Mesfin, "Architecture," 50–51.

CHAPTER 6: NONPARTISAN PRAETORIANS

1. Douglas C. Dacy, *Foreign Aid, War, and Economic Development: South Vietnam, 1955-1975* (Cambridge, 1985), 20; William Rosenau, *US Internal Security Assistance to South Vietnam: Insurgency, Subversion, and Public Order* (Routledge, 2005), 41; Michael G. Kort, *The Vietnam War Reexamined* (Cambridge, 2018), 1–2, 100; Seth Jacobs, *Cold War Mandarin: Ngo Dinh Diem and the Origins of America's War in Vietnam, 1950-1963* (Rowman & Littlefield, 2006), 8; James M. Carter, *Inventing Vietnam: The United States and State Building, 1954-1968* (Cambridge, 2008), 122–123.

2. Jacobs, *Cold War Mandarin*, 8; Carter, *Inventing Vietnam*, 23–24; Jessica M. Chapman, *Cauldron of Resistance: Ngo Dinh Diem, the United States, and 1950s Southern Vietnam* (Cornell, 2013), 40–41, 47–48; William I. Hitchcock, *The Age of Eisenhower: America and the World in the 1950s* (Simon & Schuster, 2018), 180; Xiaobing Li, *Building Ho's Army: Chinese Military Assistance to North Vietnam* (Kentucky, 2019), 44–45; Christopher Goscha, *The Road to Dien Bien Phu* (Princeton, 2022), 30.

3. Thomas L. Ahern Jr., "The CIA and the Government of Ngo Dinh Diem," *Studies in Intelligence* 37 (Winter 1993): 41; Jacobs, *Cold War Mandarin*, 20; Chapman, *Cauldron of Resistance*, 61; Andrew J. Gawthorpe, *To Build as Well as Destroy: American Nation Building in South Vietnam* (Cornell, 2018), 29–30.

4. CIA, "Situation in Vietnam," 10/06/1954, CIA-RDP80R01443R000 300070002-1; CIA, "Possible Developments in South Vietnam," 04/26/1955, CIA-RDP79R01012A005900010001-7; Ahern, "CIA and the Government of Ngo Dinh Diem," 41; Mark Moyar, *Triumph Forsaken: The Vietnam War, 1954-1965* (Cambridge, 2006), 43; Chapman, *Cauldron of Resistance*, 15–16, 61 65, 76; Geoffrey C. Stewart, *Vietnam's Lost Revolution: Ngo Dinh Diem's Failure to Build an Independent Nation, 1955-1963* (Cambridge, 2017), 42; Kort, *Vietnam War Reexamined*, 98.

5. CIA, "Possible Developments in South Vietnam"; Thomas L. Ahern Jr., *CIA and the House of Ngo: Covert Action in South Vietnam, 1954-63* (Center for the Study of Intelligence, 2000), 34; Rosenau, *US Internal Security Assistance*, 31; Jacobs, *Cold War Mandarin*, 61; Chapman, *Cauldron of Resistance*, 15–16, 65, 76.

6. CIA, "Situation in Vietnam"; CIA, "Possible Developments in South Vietnam"; Dennis J. Duncanson, *Government and Revolution in Vietnam*

(Oxford, 1968), 228; Ronald H. Spector, *Advice and Support: The Early Years, 1941–1960: The United States Army in Vietnam* (Center of Military History, 1985), 272; Ahern, *CIA and the House of Ngo*, 45; Moyar, *Triumph Forsaken*, 43; Chapman, *Cauldron of Resistance*, 74–76, 184; Stewart, *Vietnam's Lost Revolution*, 42; Gawthorpe, *Build as Well as Destroy*, 19.

7. Spector, *Advice and Support*, 233–237; Chapman, *Cauldron of Resistance*, 80–83, 94, 109; Hitchcock, *Age of Eisenhower*, 203, 442.

8. CIA, "Probable Developments in Vietnam to July 1956," 10/11/1955, CIA-RDP79R01012A005900030001-5; Moyar, *Triumph Forsaken*, 46–47; Chapman, *Cauldron of Resistance*, 81–83.

9. Ahern, *CIA and the House of Ngo*, 40–43, 67–69; Rosenau, *US Internal Security Assistance*, 31; Moyar, *Triumph Forsaken*, 6, 46–53; Chapman, *Cauldron of Resistance*, 142.

10. CIA, "Political Opposition to the Diem Government," 04/05/1963, CIA-RDP79T00429A001100030006-6; Ahern, *CIA and the House of Ngo*, 37; Rosenau, *US Internal Security Assistance*, 31–32; Jacobs, *Cold War Mandarin*, 75; Moyar, *Triumph Forsaken*, 49; Chapman, *Cauldron of Resistance*, 3, 116, 151, 174; Gawthorpe, *Build as Well as Destroy*, 29.

11. Edward Miller, *Misalliance: Ngo Dinh Diem, the United States, and the Fate of South Vietnam* (Harvard, 2013), 149; Moyar, *Triumph Forsaken*, 45; Dulles is quoted in Spector, *Advice and Support*, 228; Walter C. Ladwig, *The Forgotten Front: Patron-Client Relationships in Counterinsurgency* (Cambridge, 2017), 149.

12. Spector, *Advice and Support*, 131, 133–134, 153, 221; Jacobs, *Cold War Mandarin*, 8.

13. Spector, *Advice and Support*, 155–157, 221, 252; Chapman, *Cauldron of Resistance*, 64.

14. CIA, "Probable Developments in Vietnam to July 1956"; Spector, *Advice and Support*, 225, 228–229, 239, 263; Rosenau, *US Internal Security Assistance*, 34; Jacobs, *Cold War Mandarin*, 42.

15. Dispatch from the Ambassador in Vietnam (Durbrow) to the Department of State, December 7, 1959, *FRUS*, 1958–1960, Vietnam, vol. 1, Doc. 163; CIA, "Report on General Taylor's Mission to South Vietnam," 11/03/1961, CIA-RDP86B00269R000200030001-5; Spector, *Advice and Support*, 241, 242, 278–279, 282; Mara Karlin, *Building Militaries in Fragile States: Challenges for the United States* (Pennsylvania, 2018), 78–79; Lindsey A. O'Rourke, *Covert Regime Change: America's Secret Cold War* (Cornell, 2018), 175.

16. CIA, "Probable Developments in Vietnam to July 1956"; CIA, "Cast of Characters in South Vietnam," 08/28/1963, CIA-RDP79T00429A001200020021-2; Spector, *Advice and Support*, 320–323; Rosenau, *US Internal Security Assistance*, 57, 65; Carter, *Inventing Vietnam*, 70.

17. CIA, "South Vietnam," 05/16/1961, CIA-RDP64B00346R0005000
80015-7; CIA, "Report on General Taylor's Mission to South Vietnam"; CIA,
"Cast of Characters in South Vietnam"; Spector, *Advice and Support*, 316, 320;
Rosenau, *US Internal Security Assistance*, 40–41, 46, 55, 124; Ahern, *CIA and
the House of Ngo*, 60; Edward Miller, "A House Divided: Ngo Dinh Nhu, the
Can Lao Party, and the Internal Politics of the Diem Regime, 1954–1960,"
in *American Experience in Southeast Asia, 1945–1975* (Washington, DC:
Department of State, 2010), 14–16; Miller, *Misalliance*, 135, 223.

18. Rosenau, *US Internal Security Assistance*, 37, 40, 47, 54–57, 67; Spector,
Advice and Support, 321–322; Carter, *Inventing Vietnam*, 67–68.

19. CIA, "Report on General Taylor's Mission to South Vietnam"; Rosenau,
US Internal Security Assistance, 41, 53, 62, 65; Carter, *Inventing Vietnam*, 69.

20. Rosenau, *US Internal Security Assistance*, 66; Carter, *Inventing Vietnam*,
10; Ahern, *CIA and the House of Ngo*, 140–142.

21. CIA, "The Consequences of the Attempted Coup in South Vietnam,"
11/22/1960, CIA-RDP79R00904A000500020009-8; Jacobs, *Cold War Mandarin*, 119; CIA, "South Vietnam," 05/16/1961, CIA-RDP64B00346R0005000
80015-7.

22. CIA, "The Situation in South Vietnam," 09/12/1963, CIA-RDP79T
00429A001400060002-4; Jacobs, *Cold War Mandarin*, 160.

23. Jacobs, *Cold War Mandarin*, 1; Ahern, *CIA and the House of Ngo*,
210–214; Miller, *Misalliance*, 320–324.

24. Carter, *Inventing Vietnam*, 153; Gawthorpe, *Build as Well as Destroy*, 57.

25. Daniel Fineman, *A Special Relationship: The United States and Military Government in Thailand, 1947–1958* (University of Hawai'i Press, 1997),
12, 18, 22, 24, 40–42.

26. CIA, "Peking's Support of Insurgencies in Southeast Asia," 04/1973,
CIA-RDP85T00875R001000010052-9.

27. Fineman, *Special Relationship*, 49–50, 56–57, 73–74, 90, 106, 116, 118,
132, 145; Telegram from Turner (Chargé in Thailand) to US Secretary of State,
10/22/1951, *FRUS*, Asia and the Pacific, vol. 6, pt. 2, Doc. 89; General Orders
No. 1, "Redesignation of MAAG Thailand," February 9, 1954, JUSMAGTHAI,
Bangkok, Thailand, General Orders, 1952-7/1976, RG 472.

28. Memorandum from Walter S. Robertson, Assistant Secretary of State,
to Secretary of State Dulles, July 3, 1957, Secret, NND 877412, General Records
of the Department of State, RG 59, Central Decimal File (CDF) 1955–1959;
"State of Emergency, March 2–14, 1957," Despatch from US Embassy Thailand
to Secretary of State, April 22, 1957, Secret, NND 877412, General Records of
the Department of State, RG 59, CDF 1955–1959; Despatch from First Secretary
Douglas N. Batson (US Embassy Thailand) to State Department (Washington),

July 26, 1957, Confidential, NND 877412, General Records of the Department of State, RG 59, CDF 1955–1959.

29. Telegram from Ambassador Bishop (Thailand) to Secretary of State Dulles (Washington), 12:48PM, March 3, 1957, Unclassified, NND 877412, General Records of the Department of State, RG 59, CDF 1955–1959; Ambassador Bishop (Thailand) to Secretary of State Dulles (Washington), 8:00AM, March 5, 1957, Secret, NND 877412, General Records of the Department of State, RG 59, CDF 1955–1959; Telegram from Ambassador Bishop (Thailand) to Secretary of State Dulles (Washington), 9:00PM, March 5, 1957, Secret, NND 877412, General Records of the Department of State, RG 59, CDF 1955–1959; Telegram from Counselor Wilson (US Embassy Thailand) to Secretary of State Dulles (Washington), 12:57PM, March 13, 1957, Confidential, NND 877412, General Records of the Department of State, RG 59, CDF 1955–1959; Telegram from Ambassador Bishop (Thailand) to Secretary of State Dulles (Washington), 7:24AM, March 20, 1957, Secret, NND 877412, General Records of the Department of State, RG 59, CDF 1955–1959; "State of Emergency, March 2–14, 1957," Despatch from US Embassy Thailand to Secretary of State, April 22, 1957, Secret, NND 877412, General Records of the Department of State, RG 59, CDF 1955–1959; Telegram from US Ambassador Bishop (Thailand) to Secretary of State Dulles (Washington), 12:30PM, March 6, 1957, Secret, NND 877412, General Records of the Department of State, RG 59, CDF 1955–1959.

30. CIA, "Thailand's Ability to Withstand Communist Pressures or Attacks," 05/19/1953, CIA-RDP79S01011A001000070010-1; Memorandum from Walter S. Robertson, Assistant Secretary of State, to Secretary of State Dulles, July 3, 1957, Secret, NND 877412, General Records of the Department of State, RG 59, CDF 1955–1959; Telegram from US Embassy Thailand to Secretary of State, May 18, 1957, Secret, NND 877412, General Records of the Department of State, RG 59, CDF 1955–1959.

31. Telegram from Ambassador Bishop (Thailand) to Secretary of State Dulles (Washington), 1:05PM, September 17, 1957, Secret, NND 877412, General Records of the Department of State, RG 59, B3909, F729.00/8–557, CDF 1955–1959; Telegram from Ambassador Bishop (Thailand) to Secretary of State Dulles (Washington), 3:57PM, September 17, 1957, Unclassified, NND 877412, General Records of the Department of State, RG 59, B3909, F729.00/8–557, CDF 1955–1959; Telegram from Murphy (Department of State) to United States Mission to United Nations, 5:32PM, September 17, 1957, Secret, NND 877412, General Records of the Department of State, RG 59, B3909, F729.00/8–557, CDF 1955–1959; Telegram from ALUSNA Bangkok to Secretary of State, September 17, 8:22PM, Confidential, NND 877412, General Records of the Department of State, RG 59, B3909, F729.00/8–557, CDF 1955–1959.

32. Telegram from Ambassador Bishop (Thailand) to Secretary of State Dulles (Washington), 3:57PM, September 17, 1957, Unclassified, NND 877412, General Records of the Department of State, RG 59, B3909, F729.00/8-557, CDF 1955–1959; Tillman Durdin, "Thailand Is Calm After Army Coup," *New York Times*, September 18, 1957, A1.

33. Telegram No. 3725 from Ambassador Bishop to Secretary of State, 4:00AM, June 18, 1957, Secret, NND 877412, RG59, B3911, F792.00(W)/6-457, File No. 792.00(W)/6-1857, CDF 1955–1959; Telegram from Bishop (US Embassy Bangkok) to Secretary of State, May 30, 1957, Secret, NND 877412, General Records of the Department of State, RG 59, CDF 1955–1959; Telegram from Ambassador Bishop (Thailand) to Secretary of State Dulles (Washington), 1:33PM, August 23, 1957, Secret, NND 877412, General Records of the Department of State, RG 59, CDF 1955–1959; Telegram from Ambassador Bishop (Thailand) to Secretary of State Dulles (Washington), 8:49PM, August 31, 1957, Secret, NND 877412, General Records of the Department of State, RG 59, CDF 1955–1959; Telegram from Ambassador Bishop (Thailand) to Secretary of State Dulles (Washington), 12:35PM, September 14, 1957, Secret, NND 877412, General Records of the Department of State, RG 59, CDF 1955–1959; Telegram from Ambassador Bishop (Thailand) to Secretary of State Dulles (Washington), 6:06PM, September 16, 1957, Secret, NND 877412, General Records of the Department of State, RG 59, CDF 1955–1959.

34. Telegram from Ambassador Bishop (Thailand) to Secretary of State Dulles (Washington), 1:05PM, September 17, 1957, Secret, NND 877412, General Records of the Department of State, RG 59, B3909, F729.00/8-557, CDF 1955–1959; Telegram from Ambassador Bishop (Thailand) to Secretary of State Dulles (Washington), 7:48AM, September 17, 1957, Secret, NND 877412, General Records of the Department of State, RG 59, B3909, F729.00/8-557, CDF 1955–1959; "Threat to Present Thai Government," Memorandum of Conversation between Floyd L. Whittington, Counselor of Embassy for Economic Affairs, and Captain Somwang Sarasas, Managing Director of Thai Shale and Oil Co., Ltd., July 13, 1960, Secret, NND 959312, General Records of the Department of State, RG 59, Bureau of Far Eastern Affairs, Office of Southeast Asian Affairs, Thailand Files, 1960–1963.

35. Telegram from Bern (US Embassy Thailand) to Secretary of State (Washington), 7:20AM, September 17, 1957, Unclassified, NND 877412, General Records of the Department of State, RG 59, B3909, F729.00/8-557, CDF 1955–1959; Telegram from Ambassador Bishop (Thailand) to Secretary of State Dulles (Washington), 8:33AM, September 17, 1957, Unclassified, NND 877412, RG59, B3909, F792.00/8-557, CDF 1955–1959; Telegram from Ambassador Bishop (Thailand) to Secretary of State Dulles (Washington), 6:25AM,

September 20, 1957, Confidential, NND 877412, RG59, B3909, F792.00/8-557, CDF 1955–1959.

36. Telegram from Ambassador Bishop (Thailand) to Secretary of State Dulles (Washington), 9:58AM, September 17, 1957, Secret, NND 877412, General Records of the Department of State, RG 59, CDF 1955–1959; Telegram from Ambassador Bishop (Thailand) to Secretary of State Dulles (Washington), 1:05PM, September 17, 1957, Secret, NND 877412, General Records of the Department of State, RG 59, B3909, F729.00/8-557, CDF 1955–1959; Telegram from Ambassador Bishop (Thailand) to Secretary of State Dulles (Washington), 3:00PM, September 20, 1957, Secret, NND 877412, RG59, B3909, F792.00/8-557, CDF 1955–1959.

37. "Possibility of Field Marshal Sarit's Accession to Power," Instruction from Secretary of State John Foster Dulles to US Embassy, Thailand, September 3, 1957, Secret, NND 877412, General Records of the Department of State, RG 59, CDF 1955–1959.

38. "Possibility of Field Marshal Sarit's Accession to Power," Instruction from Secretary of State John Foster Dulles to US Embassy, Thailand, September 3, 1957, Secret, NND 877412, General Records of the Department of State, RG 59, CDF 1955–1959.

39. Telegram from Deputy Under Secretary of State for Political Affairs Robert D. Murphy (Washington) to US Embassy Thailand, 8:00PM, September 18, 1957, Secret, NND 877412, RG59, B3909, F792.00/8-557, CDF 1955–1959.

40. Telegram from Ambassador Bishop (Thailand) to Secretary of State Dulles (Washington), 4:31AM, September 19, 1957, Secret, NND 877412, RG59, B3909, F792.00/8-557, CDF 1955–1959; Telegram from Ambassador Bishop (Thailand) to Secretary of State Dulles (Washington), 1:05PM, September 19, 1957, Secret, NND 877412, RG59, B3909, F792.00/8-557, CDF 1955–1959; "Recognition of New Thai Government," Memo for Secretary of State Dulles from G. Frederick Reinhardt, Counselor, September 19, 1957, Confidential, NND 877412, RG59, B3909, F792.00/8-557, CDF 1955–1959; Telegram from Secretary of State Dulles to US Embassy Bangkok, 7:48PM, October 1, 1957, Confidential, NND 877412, RG59, B3909, F792.00/8-557, CDF 1955–1959; Telegram from Secretary of State Dulles (Washington) to US Embassy Thailand, September 24, 1957, Secret, NND 877412, RG59, B3909, F792.00/8-557, NARA II, CDF 1955–1959.

41. Telegram from Ambassador Bishop (Thailand) to Secretary of State Dulles (Washington), December 30, 1957, Confidential, NND 877412, General Records of the Department of State, RG 59, CDF 1955–1959; "Status Report: Implementation of NSC Action 1290-D/Thailand," JUSMAGTHAI and US Embassy, November 23, 1957, NND 877412, General Records of the Department

of State, RG 59, CDF 1955–1959; "Sarit Visit, May 1958: Background Information Regarding U.S. Thai Relations," Briefing Paper, Secret, NND 877412, General Records of the Department of State, RG 59, CDF 1955–1959.

42. "Comments on MSP for Thailand for FY 1961," Ambassador U. Alexis Johnson to Department of State, September 15, 1959, Confidential, NND 877412, General Records of the Department of State, RG 59, CDF 1955–1959; "U.S. Aid Programs in Thailand," Briefing Paper prepared ahead of the State Visit of the King and Queen of Thailand to Washington, June 28–July 2, 1960, Secret, NND 959312, General Records of the Department of State, RG 59, Bureau of Far Eastern Affairs, Office of Southeast Asian Affairs, Thailand Files, 1960–1963.

43. "Developments in Thailand," 1st Half FY72, July 1–December 31, 1971, Secret, Declass, December 31, 1980, NND 974377, USMACTHAI/ JUSMAGTHAI, Bangkok, Thailand, RG 472; Message from USARMA Bangkok Thailand to DA WASH DC, November 24, 1960, Secret, NND 959312, General Records of the Department of State, RG 59, Bureau of Far Eastern Affairs, Office of Southeast Asian Affairs, Thailand Files, 1960–1963.

44. CIA, "Thailand's Military: The Power Brokers' Role in Transition," 10/1985, CIA-RDP86T00590R000300510002-5; Message from USARMA Bangkok Thailand to DA WASH DC, December 3, 1960, Secret, NND 959312, General Records of the Department of State, RG 59, Bureau of Far Eastern Affairs, Office of Southeast Asian Affairs, Thailand Files, 1960–1963.

CHAPTER 7: HOLLOW ARMIES

1. Ith Sarin, "Life in the Bureaus (Offices) of the Khmer Rouge: 3 June 1972 to 15 January 1973," in *Communist Party Power in Kampuchea: Documents and Discussion*, Data Paper no. 1066, ed. Timothy Carney (Cornell, 1973), 48; Chenyi Wang, "The Chinese Communist Party's Relationship with the Khmer Rouge in the 1970s: An Ideological Victory and a Strategic Failure," Working Paper no. 88 (Cold War International History Project, 2018), 18; Ben Kiernan, *How Pol Pot Came to Power: Colonialism, Nationalism, and Communism in Cambodia, 1930–1975*, 2nd ed. (Yale, 2004); Ben Kiernan, *The Pol Pot Regime: Race, Power, and Genocide in Cambodia under the Khmer Rouge, 1975–79*, 3rd ed. (Yale, 2008); Steven Levitsky and Lucan Way, *Revolution and Dictatorship: The Violent Origins of Durable Authoritarianism* (Princeton, 2022), 256–264.

2. Timothy Carney, "The Unexpected Victory," in *Cambodia 1975–1978: Rendezvous with Death*, ed. Karl D. Jackson (Princeton, 1989), 31; Wilfred P. Deac, *Road to the Killing Fields: The Cambodian War of 1970–1975* (Texas

A&M, 1997), 108; Elizabeth Becker, *When the War Was Over: Cambodia and the Khmer Rouge Revolution*, 2nd ed. (PublicAffairs, 1998), 17, 133.

3. Telegram from Ambassador John G. Dean to Secretary of State Kissinger, 08/14/1974, *FRUS*, January 1973–July 1975, vol. 10, Vietnam, Doc. 137.

4. Becker, *When the War Was Over*, 33–36, 43, 73, 76–77.

5. Sak Sutsakhan, *The Khmer Republic at War and the Final Collapse* (US Army Center of Military History, 1980), 33; Justin J. Corfield, "Khmers Stand Up! A History of the Cambodian Government, 1970-1975," Monash Papers on Southeast Asia No. 32 (Centre of Southeast Asian Studies, Monash University, 1994), 24, 38; David P. Chandler, *A History of Cambodia*, 4th ed. (Westview, 2008), 234, 245.

6. Carney, "Unexpected Victory," 31; Corfield, "Khmers," 56.

7. Christopher Goscha, *The Road to Dien Bien Phu* (Princeton, 2022), 30.

8. Becker, *When the War Was Over*, 45, 47–48, 51, 53, 65, 69–71, 78–83, 90–94, 97; Kiernan, *Pol Pot Regime*, xi, 11, 13, 126; Xiaobing Li, *Building Ho's Army: Chinese Military Assistance to North Vietnam* (Kentucky, 2019), 28.

9. Becker, *When the War Was Over*, 74–75, 89, 98–99, 104–106, 109–110; CIA, "The Cambodian Insurgency: From Shadow to Substance," 02/12/1973, CIA-RDP85T00875R001100160034-2; Kiernan, *Pol Pot Regime*, xi, 14; Carney, "Unexpected Victory," 13; Chandler, *History of Cambodia*, 245.

10. Marie Alexandrine Martin, *Cambodia: A Shattered Society* (California, 1994), 122; Deac, *Road to the Killing Fields*, 59; Chandler, *History of Cambodia*, 248.

11. Kenneth Conboy, *The Cambodian Wars: Clashing Armies and CIA Covert Operations* (Kansas, 2013), 6–9; Becker, *When the War Was Over*, 119; Corfield, "Khmers," 13, 21–22, 32; Chandler, *History of Cambodia*, 238.

12. David Chandler, *The Tragedy of Cambodian Politics: Politics, War, and Revolution Since 1945* (Yale, 1991), 197–198; Corfield, "Khmers," 53–54; Martin, *Cambodia*, 122; Deac, *Road to the Killing Fields*, 58–59; Chandler, *History of Cambodia*, 249.

13. Chandler, *Tragedy*, 198; Martin, *Cambodia*, 123; Kiernan, *How Pol Pot Came to Power*, 301; Chandler, *History of Cambodia*, 249; Conboy, *Cambodian Wars*, 10–11.

14. Chandler, *Tragedy*, 198; Corfield, "Khmers," 77, 79; Martin, *Cambodia*, 124; Chandler, *History of Cambodia*, 250.

15. Kiernan, *How Pol Pot Came to Power*, 302; Chandler, *History of Cambodia*, 251; Conboy, *Cambodian Wars*, 15.

16. William Shawcross, *Sideshow: Kissinger, Nixon, and the Destruction of Cambodia*, rev. ed. (Cooper Square, 2002), 118–122; Corfield, "Khmers," 53; Martin, *Cambodia*, 122, 135; Chandler, *History of Cambodia*, 248; Deac, *Road to the Killing Fields*, 66–67; Kiernan, *How Pol Pot Came to Power*, 301.

17. "The 9/11 Commission Report: Final Report of the National Commission on Terrorist Attacks upon the United States," 2004, 353–357.

18. *FRUS*, 1969–1976, vol. 6, Vietnam, January 1969–July 1970, Doc. 205; *FRUS*, 1969–1976, vol. 6, Doc. 208; US Department of State Cable, 09/07/1968, DNSA Collection: Vietnam War II, 1969–1975.

19. Shawcross, *Sideshow*, 128.

20. *FRUS*, 1969–1976, vol. 6, Doc. 205; *FRUS*, 1969–1976, vol. 6, Doc. 250.

21. Conboy, *Cambodian Wars*, 17; *FRUS*, 1969–1976, vol. 6, Doc. 208; United States Embassy Cambodia Cable, 04/24/1970, DNSA Collection: Vietnam War II, 1969–1975.

22. Shawcross, *Sideshow*, 131.

23. Senator Javits (R-NY), speech at the University of Richmond, April 27, 1970, printed in the Congressional Record April 30, 1970.

24. Shawcross, *Sideshow*, 145.

25. Robert B. Semple Jr., "Nixon Sends Combat Forces into Cambodia to Drive Communists from Staging Zone," *New York Times*, May 1, 1970, A1; 116 Cong. Rec. 13499 (1970).

26. Shawcross, *Sideshow*, 153, 164; David F. Schmitz, *The United States and Right-Wing Dictatorships, 1965–1989* (Cambridge, 2006), 120–121.

27. Shawcross, *Sideshow*, 185; Deac, *Road to the Killing Fields*, 106–107; United States Embassy Cambodia Cable, 04/28/1970, DNSA Collection: Vietnam War II, 1969–1975.

28. Shawcross, *Sideshow*, 235, emphasis in original; Becker, *When the War Was Over*, 14, 119.

29. Sutsakhan, *Khmer Republic at War*, 87; Craig R. Whitney, "Cambodia Seems Adrift After Two Years as Republic: A Demoralized Cambodia Losing Confidence in Her Leadership and Institutions," *New York Times*, June 6, 1972.

30. CIA, President's Daily Brief, 06/09/1972, FOIA no. DOC_0005993345.

31. CIA, "Political Developments in Phnom Penh," 10/26/1971, CIA-RD P85T00875R001100100127-5; CIA, "Central Intelligence Bulletin," 06/17/1972, CIA-RDP79T00975A022100080001-7; Senator McGee (D-WY), June 21, 1972, 118 Cong. Rec., 21825 (1972); Deac, *Road to the Killing Fields*, 112.

32. Sutsakhan, *Khmer Republic at War*, 32, 38–39; Deac, *Road to the Killing Fields*, 71; Memorandum from NSC staff Morris, Lord, and Lake to Kissinger, 04/22/1970, accessed in *FRUS*, 1969–1976, vol. 6, Doc. 250; Ralph Blumenthal, "Cambodia's Army: A Force Long Used to Make Roads, Not War," *New York Times*, May 2, 1970.

33. Sutsakhan, *Khmer Republic at War*, 39–45; Carney, "Unexpected Victory," 13; Chandler, *History of Cambodia*, 247. On the Vietnamese army see Douglas Pike, *PAVN: People's Army of Vietnam* (Presidio, 1986); Lien-Hang T.

Nguyen, *Hanoi's War: An International History of the War for Peace in Vietnam* (UNC, 2012); Li, *Building Ho's Army*; Goscha, *Road to Dien Bien Phu*.

34. *FRUS*, 1969–1976, vol. 7, Vietnam, July 1970–January 1972, Doc. 91; Laurence Stern, "Cambodian Experience Turns Sour," *Washington Post*, May 8, 1972; CIA, "Developments in Indochina," 09/27/1973, CIA-RDP85 T00875R001100010069-0; Shawcross, *Sideshow*, 132.

35. Department of Defense, "Military Assessment in Cambodia," Memo from F. J. West, Col. M. J. Brady, and Col. T. Owens for Secretary of Defense, 05/14/1971, accessed via CIA-RDP78T02095R000500230001-9; Deac, *Road to the Killing Fields*, 82.

36. Taylor Owen and Ben Kiernan, "Bombs over Cambodia," *Walrus*, October 2006, 62–69; Chandler, *History of Cambodia*, 252.

37. Carney, "Unexpected Victory," 31; Department of Defense, "Military Assessment"; Deac, *Road to the Killing Fields*, 82.

38. Cable from Ladd (US Embassy Phnom Penh) to Haig (NSC), 05/10/1971, accessed via CREST FOIA no. LOC-HAK–449–6–14–2.

39. Senator Symington (D-MO), June 21, 1972, 118 Cong. Rec. 21827 (1972); Deac, *Road to the Killing Fields*, 103; Conboy, *Cambodian Wars*, 59.

40. Carney, "Unexpected Victory," 13; Chandler, *History of Cambodia*, 247; CIA, "Khmer Communist Combat Forces in Cambodia," 11/1971, CIA-RD P85T00875R001700020071-0; CIA, "Factions Among the Khmer Insurgents," 03/01/1973, CIA-RDP80T01719R000400140002-4; Sarin, "Life in the Bureaus," 54; Ith Sarin, "Nine Months in the Maquis," in *Communist Party Power in Kampuchea: Documents and Discussion*, Data Paper no. 1066, ed. Timothy Carney (Cornell, 1973), 38; Becker, *When the War Was Over*, 109, 111, 133–134; Kiernan, *Pol Pot Regime*, 16, 38, 70, 75, 86–91, 314–315; Andrew Mertha, *Brothers in Arms: Chinese Aid to the Khmer Rouge, 1975–1979* (Cornell, 2014), 30; *FRUS*, 1969–1976, vol. 7, Doc. 9.

41. Sutsakhan, *Khmer Republic at War*, 69–79; Cable from Brig. Gen. Alexander M. Haig (NSC) to Fredd Ladd (US Embassy Phnom Penh), 12/07/1971, accessed via CREST FOIA no. LOC-HAK-450-7-9-5; *FRUS*, 1969–1976, vol. 10, Doc. 99; Chandler, *Tragedy*, 360, en. 89.

42. Shawcross, *Sideshow*, 228; Deac, *Road to the Killing Fields*, 110; *FRUS*, 1969–1976, vol. 10, Doc. 92; Chandler, *Tragedy*, 205, 223.

43. Becker, *When the War Was Over*, 16; Shawcross, *Sideshow*, 314, 316.

44. Becker, *When the War Was Over*, 124; Shawcross, *Sideshow*, 185–186, 315.

45. Deac, *Road to the Killing Fields*, 172; Carney, "Unexpected Victory," 35; Martin, *Cambodia*, 141.

46. *FRUS*, 1969–1975, vol. 10, Doc. 137; *FRUS*, 1969–1976, vol. 10, Doc. 100; *FRUS*, 1969–1976, vol. 10, Doc. 37.

47. CIA, "The Cambodian Political Situation," 03/26/1973, FOIA no. LOC-HAK-32-2-12-0; State Department, "Possibilities of a Military Power Play in Phnom Penh," Telegram from US Embassy Phnom Penh to Secretary of State, 09/10/1973, accessed via CREST, FOIA no. LOC-HAK-39-3-24-9.

48. CIA, "Cambodian Political Situation."

49. Becker, *When the War Was Over*, 15; CIA, "Cambodia: The Prospects for Compromise," 02/26/1973, CIA-RDP79R00967A0016000100 15-8; CIA, President's Daily Brief, 06/25/1973, FOIA no. 0005993858; CIA, "Lon Non: Cambodia's Prime Troublemaker," 03/16/1973, CIA-RDP85 T00875R001100160041-4.

50. CIA, "Lon Non"; CIA, "Cambodian Political Situation"; State Department, "Possibilities of a Military Power Play."

51. Martin, *Cambodia*, 134; Shawcross, *Sideshow*, 232; CIA, "Cambodian Suggestions," Memo for Henry A. Kissinger from CIA, 06/28/1973, CIA-RDP80T01719R000400320005-1, "Remedial Actions to Improve the Performance and Negotiating Position of the GKR," Annex III accessed via CIA-RDP80T01719R000400320007-9; CIA, "Cambodia: The Prospects for Compromise."

52. State Department, "Possibilities of a Military Power Play."

53. CIA, "Lon Non"; CIA, "Cambodian Political Situation"; *FRUS*, 1969–1967, vol. 10, Doc. 36.

54. *FRUS*, 1969–1976, vol. 10, Doc. 99.

55. *FRUS*, 1969–1976, vol. 10, Doc. 106.

56. State Department, "Possibilities of a Military Power Play"; *FRUS*, 1969–1976, vol. 10, Doc. 92.

57. CIA, "Cambodian Suggestions," Annex III.

58. *FRUS*, 1969–1967, vol. 10, Doc. 36; CIA, President's Daily Brief, 03/10/1975, FOIA no. DOC_0006014741.

59. *FRUS*, 1969–1976, vol. 10, Doc. 100.

60. *FRUS*, 1969–1976, vol. 10, Doc. 182.

61. Martin, *Cambodia*, 131.

CHAPTER 8: AFTER THE COLD WAR

1. G. John Ikenberry, *Liberal Leviathan: The Origins, Crisis, and Transformation of the American World Order* (Princeton, 2011), 42–45, 119–120; Vladislav M. Zubok, *Collapse: The Fall of the Soviet Union* (Yale, 2021), 159; William E. Odom, *The Collapse of the Soviet Military* (Yale, 1998), 272; Doyle McManus, "Soviet Troops to Leave Cuba, Gorbachev Says," *Los Angeles Times*, September 12, 1991; Ivan Safronov and Elena Yernenko, "Imeyushchiy ushi da vdnov' uslishit: Rossiya vozvrashchayet na Kubu svoy tsentr radioperekhvata,"

Kommersant, July 16, 2014; "Otryad boyevikh korabley Rossii pribil s vizitom v port Kamran'," TASS, June 25, 2022. Data on troop deployments come from Michael A. Allen, Michael E. Flynn, Carla Martinez Machain, and Andrew Stravers, *Beyond the Wire: US Military Deployments and Host Country Public Opinion* (Oxford, 2022). Data on military training come from Theodore McLauchlin, Lee J. M. Seymour, and Simon Pierre Boulanger Martel, "Tracking the Rise of United States Foreign Military Training: IMTAD-USA, a New Dataset and Research Agenda," *Journal of Peace Research* 59, no. 2 (2022): 286.

2. Steven Levitsky and Lucan A. Way, *Competitive Authoritarianism: Hybrid Regimes After the Cold War* (Cambridge, 2010), 17–18.

3. Levitsky and Way, 17–18; Lorenz M. Lüthi, *Cold Wars: Asia, the Middle East, Europe* (Cambridge, 2020), 563–565; Mark Peceny and William Stanley, "Counterinsurgency in El Salvador," *Politics and Society* 38, no. 1 (2010): 84; Michaeh K. McKoy and Michael K. Miller, "The Patron's Dilemma: The Dynamics of Foreign-Supported Democratization," *Journal of Conflict Resolution* 56, no. 5 (2013): 922–923; Russell Crandall, *America's Dirty Wars: Irregular Warfare from 1776 to the War on Terror* (Cambridge, 2014), 334; Morris H. Morley and Chris McGillion, *Reagan and Pinochet: The Struggle over U.S. Policy Toward Chile* (Cambridge, 2015), 319; Matthew Y. H. Wong, "Chinese Influence, U.S. Linkages, or Neither? Comparing Regime Changes in Myanmar and Thailand," *Democratization* 26, no. 3 (2019): 369; Colin M. Waugh, *Charles Taylor and Liberia: Ambition and Atrocity in Africa's Lone Star State* (Zed, 2011), 131; Gerard Prunier, *Africa's World War: Congo, the Rwandan Genocide, and the Making of a Continental Catastrophe* (Oxford, 2009), 138; Jason Brownlee, *Democracy Prevention: The Politics of the U.S.-Egyptian Alliance* (Cambridge, 2012), 68, 75–76, 81; Sean L. Yom, *From Resilience to Revolution: How Foreign Interventions Destabilize the Middle East* (Columbia, 2016), 206–207; Aqil Shah, *The Army and Democracy: Military Politics in Pakistan* (Harvard, 2014), 189.

4. Archie Brown, *The Rise and Fall of Communism* (Ecco, 2009), 523; Mark Kramer, "The Demise of the Soviet Bloc," *Journal of Modern History* 83, no. 4 (2011): 812, 842, 851–852; Zoltan Barany, *How Armies Respond to Revolutions and Why* (Princeton, 2016), 102, 105, 117–118, 120, 126–127; Zubok, *Collapse*, 90–92; William Taubman, *Gorbachev: His Life and Times* (W. W. Norton, 2017), 465–466; Telegram from the Romanian Embassy in Moscow to the Ministry of Foreign Affairs (Bucharest), December 22, 1989, Archives of the Ministry of Foreign Affairs—Arhivele Ministerului Afacerilor Externe (AMAE), telegram, folder Moscow/1989, vol. 10, 324–325, translated for CWIHP by Mircea Munteanu, History and Public Policy Program Digital Archive, Woodrow Wilson International Center for Scholars; Peter Siani-Davies, *The Romanian Revolution of December 1989* (Cornell, 2005), 9.

5. CIA, NID, 07/26/1990, FOIA no. 0005301308; Richard F. Starr, *Foreign*

Policies of the Soviet Union (Hoover, 1991), 180; Vladislav Zubok, *A Failed Empire: The Soviet Union in the Cold War from Stalin to Gorbachev* (UNC Press, 2009), 308; Andargachew Tiruneh, *The Ethiopian Revolution, 1974–1987: A Transformation from an Aristocratic to a Totalitarian Autocracy* (Cambridge, 1993), 358, 365; Noel Brehony, *Yemen Divided: The Story of a Failed State in South Arabia* (I. B. Tauris, 2011), 168–169; CIA, "Soviet Troop Withdrawal from Mongolia," 04/20/1987, CIA-RDP91B00874R000300190006-4; William Finnegan, *A Complicated War: The Harrowing of Mozambique* (California, 1992), 130; Margaret Hall and Tom Young, *Confronting Leviathan: Mozambique Since Independence* (Hurst, 1997), 139, 204.

6. Tony Smith, *America's Mission: The United States and the Worldwide Struggle for Democracy in the Twentieth Century* (Princeton, 1994), 315; Levitsky and Way, *Competitive Authoritarianism*.

7. Carla Martinez Machain, "Exporting Influence: U.S. Military Training as Soft Power," *Journal of Conflict Resolution* 65, no. 2–3 (2021): 313; Renanah Miles Joyce, "Soldiers' Dilemma: Foreign Military Training and Liberal Norm Conflict," *International Security* 46, no. 4 (2022): 54; GAO, "International Military Education and Training," Report to Congressional Committees, October 2011, GAO-12-123; GAO, "US Security and Military Assistance: Programs and Related Activities," GAO/ID-82-40, June 1, 1982; Emily M. Morgenstern and Nick M. Brown, "Foreign Assistance: An Introduction to U.S. Programs and Policy," R40213 (Congressional Research Service, 2022), 10–11; *Foreign Military Training Report*, fiscal years 2020 and 2021, Joint Report to Congress, vol. 1, Department of Defense and Department of State, October 18, 2021; GAO, "International Military Education and Training," 10, 13–14; GAO, "Security Assistance: U.S. Agencies Should Improve Oversight of Human Rights Training for Foreign Security Forces," Report to Congressional Committees, August 2019, GAO-19-554; Jesse Dillon Savage and Jonathan D. Caverley, "When Human Capital Threatens the Capitol: Foreign Aid in the Form of Military Training and Coups," *Journal of Peace Research* 54, no. 4 (2017): 542–557; Wayne Sandholtz, "United States Military Assistance and Human Rights," *Human Rights Quarterly* 38, no. 4 (2016): 1070–1101. McLauchlin et al., "Tracking the Rise," find in a recent analysis that only the IMET program is associated with coup risk (293).

8. Craig Whitlock, "Coup Leader in Burkina Faso Received U.S. Military Training," *Washington Post*, November 3, 2014; Arshad Mohammed and Humeyra Pamuk, "Exclusive: U.S. Halts Nearly $160 Million Aid to Burkina Faso After Finding Military Coup Occurred," Reuters, February 19, 2022; Alexis Arieff, "Burkina Faso: Conflict and Military Rule," Congressional Research Service, IF10434, October 17, 2022; Marie-Soleil Frère and Pierre Englebert, "Burkina Faso: The Fall of Blaise Compaoré," *African Affairs* 114, no.

455 (2015): 298; Kristen A. Harkness, "Security Force Assistance in Cameroon: How Building Enclave Units Deepens Autocracy," *International Affairs* 98, no. 6 (2022): 2108, 2110–2111, 2114–2115.

9. Paul D. Williams, "Building the Somali National Army: Anatomy of a Failure, 2008–2018," *Journal of Strategic Studies* 43, no. 3 (2020): 367, 374; *East Africa Counterterrorism Operations, North and West Africa Counterterrorism Operations*, Lead Inspector General Report to the United States Congress, July 1–September 30, 2020; Thomas H. Henriksen, *America's Wars: Interventions, Regime Change, and Insurgencies After the Cold War* (Cambridge, 2022), 196; Max Bearak, "As U.S. Forces Leave, Somalia's Elite Fighting Unit Fears Becoming a Political Pawn," *Washington Post*, December 29, 2020; Falastine Iman, "US to Review Support for Elite Somali Military Unit," *Voice of America* (hereafter *VOA*), October 26, 2021; Anita Powell and Jeff Seldin, "Biden Approves 'Small, Persistent' US Military Presence in Somalia," *VOA*, May 16, 2022; Harkness, "Security Force Assistance," 2116–2117.

10. John J. Chin, David B. Carter, and Joseph G. Wright, "The Varieties of Coups d'État: Introducing the Colpus Dataset," *International Studies Quarterly* 65, no. 4 (2021): 1046; Nikolay Marinov and Hein Goemans, "Coups and Democracy," *British Journal of Political Science* 44, no. 4 (2014): 799–825.

11. Ludovic Ouhonyioué Kibora and Mamadou Traoré, "Towards Reforming the Burkinabé Security System?," Foundation pour la Recherche Stratégique, September 2017; Nadoun Coulibaly and Mathieu Bonkoungou, "Soldiers Crush Protests as Military Seizes Power in Burkina Faso," Reuters, September 16, 2015; "Security Council Press Statement on Situation in Burkina Faso," September 17, 2015, SC/12051-AFR/3211; Simon Allison, "How the People of Burkina Faso Foiled a Military Coup," *Guardian*, September 25, 2015; "Burkina Faso a Test for the AU's Impact on Crises," PSC Report, ISS, November 2, 2015; Dan Joseph, "Burkina Faso Coup Leader Apologizes, Pledges to Step Down," *VOA*, September 21, 2015.

12. Adam Nossiter, "Soldiers Overthrow Mali Government in Setback for Democracy in Africa," *New York Times*, March 22, 2012; Lydia Polgreen, "Mali Coup Leaders Suffer Sanctions and Loss of Timbuktu," *New York Times*, April 2, 2012; "Ecowas Threatens Mali Coup Leaders with New Sanctions," *BBC News*, May 14, 2012.

13. Peter Baker, "A Coup? Or Something Else? $1.5 Billion in U.S. Aid Is on the Line," *New York Times*, July 4, 2013.

14. Eric Nagourney, "Mali Military Coup: Why the World Is Watching," *New York Times*, August 19, 2020; Hannah Beech, "Myanmar Coup Puts the Seal on Autocracy's Rise in Southeast Asia," *New York Times*, July 12, 2021; David Lewis, "Military Detain Mali's President, Prime Minister, and Defence

Minister," Reuters, May 24, 2021; Abdourahmane Diallo, Ruth Maclean, and Mady Camara, "Special Forces Colonel Says He Has 'Seized' Guinea's President," *New York Times*, September 5, 2021; Max Bearak, "Sudan's Military Detains Prime Minister and Dissolves Government in Coup," *Washington Post*, October 25, 2021; Sam Mednick, Stephanie Busari, and Niamh Kennedy, "Burkina Faso's Military Seizes Power in a Coup, Detains President and Dissolves Government," *CNN*, January 24, 2022; Thiam Ndiaga and Anne Mimault, "Burkina Faso President Resigns on Condition Coup Leader Guarantees His Safety," Reuters, October 3, 2022; Omar Hama Saley, Elian Peltier, and Declan Walsh, "Military in Niger Announces Coup After Soldiers Detain President," *New York Times*, July 26, 2023; "Chad's President Idriss Déby Dies After Clashes With Rebels," *BBC News*, April 20, 2021; Mahamat Ramadane, "About 50 Killed in Chad Protests, Government Says," Reuters, October 21, 2022; "Niger Foils 'Coup Attempt' Days Before Presidential Inauguration," *France 24*, March 31, 2021; Declan Walsh, "Sudan Leaders Say They Thwarted Coup Attempt by Loyalists of Former Dictator," *New York Times*, September 21, 2021; Alberto Dabo, "Guinea-Bissau President: Failed Coup May Have Been Linked to Drug Trade," Reuters, February 1, 2022; "Mali's Military Junta Says It Foiled Attempted Coup," *France 24*, May 17, 2022; "Madagascar Makes 21 Further Arrests over Suspected Coup Plot," Reuters, August 2, 2021; "Updated Version on the Alleged Coup Plot," Office of the President, Republic of the Gambia, December 21, 2022; Adam E. Casey, "Something's Happening in Armenia. But Is It a Coup?," *Washington Post*, March 2, 2021; "Head of Sierra Leone Army Calls on Soldiers to Remain Loyal to Government Amid Rumors of Attempted Coup," *Sierra Leone Telegraph*, August 6, 2023.

15. Benoit Faucon, Summer Said, and Joe Parkinson, "Military Coups in Africa at Highest Level Since End of Colonialism," *Wall Street Journal*, November 4, 2021; Danielle Paquette, "Mali Coup Leader Was Trained by U.S. Military," *Washington Post*, August 21, 2020; Stephanie Savell, "U.S. Security Assistance to Burkina Faso Laid the Groundwork for a Coup," *Foreign Policy*, February 3, 2022; Declan Walsh and Eric Schmitt, "U.S. Forces Were Training the Guinean Soldiers Who Took Off to Stage a Coup," *New York Times*, September 10, 2021. Data on coups until 2019 are from Chin et al., "Varieties." Other coups were cataloged by the author using sources cited above, and the rate is given relative to the previous three years.

16. "Chad After Idriss Déby: African Union Urges End to Military Rule," *BBC News*, April 24, 2021; John Irish and Tangi Salaün, "With Eye to Islamist Fight, France Backs Chad Military Takeover," Reuters, April 22, 2021.

17. "Who Is Burkina Faso Coup Leader Lt-Col Damiba?," *BBC News*, January 26, 2022; "ECOWAS Due to Discuss Response to Burkina Faso Coup,"

Al Jazeera, January 28, 2022; "W. Africa Bloc Suspends Post-coup Burkina," *France 24*, January 28, 2022; Sam Mednick, "African Union Suspends Burkina Faso After Coup Last Week," *AP News*, January 31, 2022; "France, UN Join West African States in Denouncing Burkina Faso Army Takeover," *France 24*, January 25, 2022; Sam Mednick, "Hundreds March in Burkina Faso to Show Support for New Junta," *AP News*, January 25, 2022.

18. "Coup d'état au Burkina Faso: Le parrain du groupe Wagner salue une 'nouvelle ère de décolonisation,'" *Le Monde*, January 26, 2022; Cora Engelbrecht, "Putin Ally Acknowledges Founding Wagner Mercenary Group," *New York Times*, September 26, 2022; Kimberly Marten, "Russia's Use of Semi-state Security Forces: The Case of the Wagner Group," *Post-Soviet Affairs*, 35, no. 3 (2019): 195–197; Ellen Nakashima, John Hudson, and Paul Sonne, "Mercenary Chief Vented to Putin over Ukraine War Bungling," *Washington Post*, October 25, 2022; Andrey Pertsev, "Prigozhin stal lyubimchikom Putina i napisal zayavleniye v prokuraturu na Beglova. Nachinaetsya obeshchanniy 'raskol elit'?" *Meduza*, November 1, 2022; Jeff Seldin, "US Aware of Allegations of Russian Links to Burkinabe Coup," *VOA*, January 27, 2022; "Burkina Faso Military Coup: How the World Reacted," *Al Jazeera*, January 25, 2022; Ned Price, "The Situation in Burkina Faso," press statement, US State Department, October 1, 2022; Ivan Zhukovskiy, "V Burkina-Faso vtoroy raz za god vlast' zakhvatila voyennaya khunta," *Gazeta*, October 1, 2022; Clea Caulcutt, "French Symbols Targeted After Burkina Faso Coup," Politico, October 2, 2022; Mayeni Jones, "Why Russia Is Cheering on the Burkina Faso Coup," *BBC News*, October 9, 2022.

19. Kathleen A. Collins, *Clan Politics and Regime Transition in Central Asia* (Cambridge, 2006), 204, 293; Jesse Driscoll, *Warlords and Coalition Politics in Post-Soviet States* (Cambridge, 2015), 120, 127, 148–149, 152–153; Samuel Charap, Elina Treyger, and Edward Geist, *Understanding Russia's Intervention in Syria* (RAND, 2019), 4.

20. "Lukashenko zayavil, shto Rossiya okazhet pomosh' pri vneshney ugroze bezopasnosti Belorussii," TASS, August 15, 2020; Vladimir Soldatkin, "Putin Throws $1.5 Billion Lifeline to Belarus Leader," Reuters, September 14, 2020; "Russia-Led Bloc Starts Kazakhstan Pullout After Possible Coup Bid Crushed," Reuters, January 13, 2022; Declan Walsh, "Shadow Soldiers for Putin Across Africa," *New York Times*, June 4, 2022, A6.

21. "Rossiya otpravila v TsAR voyennikh sovetnikov i oruzhiye," *Kommersant*, March 23, 2018; "Rossiya i TsAR podpisali mezhpravitel'stvennoye soglasheniye o voyennom sotrudnichestvye," TASS, August 21, 2018; "V MID zayavili, shto instruktori RF prodolzhayut svoyu rabotu v TsAR na zakonnikh osnovaniyakh," TASS, April 8, 2021; "Peskov: V TsAR yest' voyenniye sovetniki

iz RF, no Moskva ne vmeshivayetsya v dela etoy strani," TASS, January 20, 2022; La garde présidentielle se dote d'une nouvelle unité spéciale," Agence Centrafricaine de Presse, May 3, 2019; "Midterm Report of the Panel of Experts on the Central African Republic Extended Pursuant to Security Council Resolution 2399 (2018)," United Nations Security Council, S/2018/729, July 23, 2018, 7, 30–31, 131; Marten, "Russia's Use of Semi-state Security Forces," 196; "Central African Republic: Abuses by Russia-Linked Forces," Human Rights Watch, May 3, 2022; "Rebels Launch Attacks on Central African Republic's Capital," *Al Jazeera*, January 13, 2021; Bram Posthumus, "Analysis: The Curious Case of Russia in the Central African Republic," *Al Jazeera*, May 20, 2022; Yuri Safronov and Irek Murtazin, "Nam nuzhen svoy TsAR? V bogatoy zolotom i brilliantami Tsentral'noafrikanskoy Respublikye v posledniye mesyatsi idyet peredel vliyaniya: Rossiya vistesnyaet Frantsiyu," *Novaya Gazeta*, August 2, 2018; "EUTM RCA: European Training Mission in Central African Republic— Military Mission," press release, November 30, 2020.

22. Adam E. Casey, "Putin Has Coup-Proofed His Regime," *Foreign Policy*, March 23, 2020; "Zamministra oboroni Kartapolov pokinet post v sluchae izbraniya v Dumu," Interfax, May 5, 2021; Vladimir Mukhin, "Predvibornoe nastuplenie edinorossov vozglavyat generali," *Rossiyskaya Gazeta*, April 29, 2021; Aleksey Nikol'skiy, "Minoboroni ishchet novogo nachal'nika Glavnogo voenno-politicheskogo upravleniya," *Vedemosti*, September 23, 2021.

23. "Den' rossiyskoy voennoy kontrrazvedki," *RIA Novosti*, December 19, 2021; "Glava voennoy kontrrazvedki: 'SMERSH' rabotal dazhe na Alyaske," TASS, December 18, 2018; "Putin postavil vo glave Natsio-nal'noy gvardii svoego bivshego okhrannika," *Forbes*, April 5, 2016.

24. Mark Galeotti, "What Turkey Can Learn From Russia About Coup-Proofing the Military," War on the Rocks, August 2, 2016; Andrei Soldatov and Irina Borogan, *The New Nobility: The Restoration of Russia's Security State and the Enduring Legacy of the KGB* (PublicAffairs, 2010); "FSO, otvechayushchaya za bezopasnost' pervikh lits Rossii, 20 let nazad poluchila nineshnee nasvanie," TASS, June 18, 2016; Andrew S. Bowen, "Russian Military Intelligence: Background and Issues for Congress," Congressional Research Service, R46616, November 15, 2021; Andrei Soldatov and Irina Borogan, "Putin's New Police State," *Foreign Affairs*, July 27, 2022.

25. Jeremy Friedman, *Shadow Cold War: The Sino-Soviet Competition for the Third World* (UNC, 2015); Andrew Mertha, *Brothers in Arms: Chinese Aid to the Khmer Rouge, 1975–1979* (Cornell, 2014); on China–North Korea see Charles K. Armstrong, *Tyranny of the Weak: North Korea and the World, 1950–1992* (Cornell, 2013); on China–North Vietnam see Xiaobing Li, *Building Ho's Army: Chinese Military Assistance to North Vietnam* (Kentucky, 2019);

Elidor Mëhilli, *From Stalin to Mao: Albania and the Socialist World* (Cornell, 2017); CIA, "The New Look in Chinese Communist Aid to Sub-Saharan Africa," 09/1968, CIA-RDP85T00875R001600010058-7; Chen Jian, "China and the Cold War After Mao," in *The Cambridge History of the Cold War*, vol. 3, *Endings*, ed. Melvyn P. Leffler and Odd Arne Westad (Cambridge, 2010), 181–200; Julia Bader, "China, Autocratic Patron? An Empirical Investigation of China as a Factor in Autocratic Survival," *International Studies Quarterly* 59, no. 1 (2015): 23–33.

26. William W. Whitson, *The Chinese High Command: A History of Communist Military Politics, 1927–71* (Praeger, 1973), 17, 28–31, 43–44, 56, 61, 64, 67–68, 91; CIA, "Post-Mao Party-Military Relations: The Role of the General Political Department," 12/1976, CIA-RDP79T00889A000900080001-2; CIA, "China: Reorganization of Security Organs," 08/01/1983, CIA-RDP85T00287R000401310001-4; Xiaobing Li, *A History of the Modern Chinese Army* (Kentucky, 2007), 45–46, 52–73; Michael Schoenhals, *Spying for the People: Mao's Secret Agents, 1949–1967* (Cambridge, 2012), 17, 24, 84; Daniel Mattingly, "How the Party Commands the Gun: The Foreign-Domestic Threat Dilemma in China," *American Journal of Political Science* (2022), https://doi.org/10.1111/ajps.12739.

27. Department of Defense, "Military and Security Developments Involving the People's Republic of China," Annual Report to Congress, 2022, 134–138, 143–145, 152, 164; Ellen Nakashima and Cate Cadell, "China Secretly Building PLA Naval Facility in Cambodia, Western Officials Say," *Washington Post*, June 6, 2022; Damien Cave, "Why a Chinese Security Deal in the Pacific Could Ripple Through the World," *New York Times*, April 20, 2022; Daniel Hurst and Katharine Murphy, "Morrison Silent on 'Red Line' for China as Labor Continues Attack over Handling of the Pacific," *Guardian*, April 26, 2022; Phillip C. Saunders, "China's Global Military-Security Interactions," in *China and the World*, ed. David Shambaugh (Oxford, 2020), 204.

28. Mark R. Beissinger, *The Revolutionary City: Urbanization and the Global Transformation of Rebellion* (Princeton, 2022), 13; CIA, "The Iranian Revolutionary Guard," 01/1980, CIA-RDP81B00401R000500100018-0; CIA, "The Iranian Armed Forces: Clerical Control and Military Effectiveness," 09/1984, CIA-RDP85T00314R000300010003-6; CIA, "Iran's Revolutionary Guard: Armed Pillar of the Islamic Republic," 01/1987, CIA-RDP06T00412R000606580001-5.

29. Anne Speckhard and Ahmet S. Yayla, "The ISIS Emni: Origins and Inner Workings of ISIS's Intelligence Apparatus," *Perspectives on Terrorism* 11, no. 1 (2017): 2–4, 7; Asaad Almohammad and Charlie Winter, "From Directorate of Intelligence to Directorate of Everything: The Islamic State's Emergent Amni-Media Nexus," *Perspectives on Terrorism* 13, no. 1 (2019):

41–43; Daniel Milton, "Structure of a State: Captured Documents and the Islamic State's Organizational Structure" (United States Military Academy, 2021), 18–19, 21; Craig Whiteside, Anas Elallame, Moorthy Muthuswamy, and Aram Shabanian, "The ISIS Files: The Islamic State's Department of Soldiers" (George Washington University, 2021), 5, 7–8, 12, 30; Jamie Allinson, *The Age of Counter-revolution: States and Revolutions in the Middle East* (Cambridge, 2022), 225.

CONCLUSION

1. The seven realignments were Cambodia 1975, Cuba 1959, Iran 1979, Nicaragua 1979, Laos 1960, Laos 1975, and South Vietnam 1975.

2. The remaining regimes led by a communist party are China, Cuba, Laos, North Korea, and Vietnam. There are several other regimes still led by Leninist parties that were never officially declared communist, including Angola and Mozambique, as well as parties that at one time embraced a Marxist-Leninist designation but have since jettisoned the affiliation, such as Cambodia, Eritrea, Namibia, and Uganda. The former Marxist-Leninist ruling party in Nicaragua, the FSLN, returned to power in 2007 via elections but is no longer a revolutionary leftist party. While Maoist rebels in Nepal successfully entered government and have competed in elections following a peace deal in 2006, it was not a revolutionary seizure of power. The royal army remained intact, and very few of the former rebels were integrated into the military. On the differences between revolutions and other seizures of power see Jean Lachapelle, Steven Levitsky, Lucan A. Way, and Adam E. Casey, "Social Revolution and Authoritarian Durability," *World Politics* 72, no. 4 (2020).

3. Carla Martinez Machain, "Exporting Influence: U.S. Military Training as Soft Power," *Journal of Conflict Resolution* 65, no. 2–3 (2021): 313; Renanah Miles Joyce, "Soldiers' Dilemma: Foreign Military Training and Liberal Norm Conflict," *International Security* 46, no. 4 (2022): 49; Kosal Path, *Vietnam's Strategic Thinking During the Third Indochina War* (Wisconsin, 2020), 95; Xiaobing Li, *The Dragon in the Jungle: The Chinese Army in the Vietnam War* (Oxford, 2020), 262; David Shambaugh, *Modernizing China's Military: Progress, Problems, and Prospects* (California, 2003); M. Taylor Fravel, *Active Defense: China's Military Strategy Since 1949* (Princeton, 2019), 217–222.

4. John Blaxland and Greg Raymond, "Tipping the Balance in Southeast Asia? Thailand, the United States, and China" (Australian National University, 2017), 14, 12, 15; Gregory Raymond, *Thai Military Power: A Culture of Strategic Accommodation* (NIAS, 2018), 88–90; Gregory Raymond and John Blaxland, *The US-Thai Alliance and Asian International Relations: History, Memory*

and Current Developments (Routledge, 2021), 67–68, 86–89, 92, 103, 114–115; Juarawee Kittisilpa and Amy Sawitta Lefevre, "Thai-U.S. Security Ties Still Feel Chill of 2014 Coup," Reuters, February 9, 2016; Jack Detsch, "Washington Worries China Is Winning Over Thailand," *Foreign Policy*, June 17, 2022.

5. Sebastian Strangio, *In the Dragon's Shadow: Southeast Asia in the Chinese Century* (Yale, 2020), 123; "Readout of Secretary of Defense Lloyd J. Austin III Meeting with Thailand Prime Minister and Minister of Defense Prayut Chan-o-cha," Department of Defense, June 13, 2022. On why 2019 did not actually mark a return to democracy see Duncan McCargo, "Democratic Demolition in Thailand," *Journal of Democracy* 30, no. 4 (2019): 119, 131.

6. On how coups can lead to civil wars see Philip Roessler, *Ethnic Politics and State Power in Africa: The Logic of the Coup–Civil War Trap* (Cambridge, 2016); Erica De Bruin, *How to Prevent Coups d'État: Counterbalancing and Regime Survival* (Cornell, 2020).

7. Nikolay Marinov and Hein Goemans, "Coups and Democracy," *British Journal of Political Science* 44, no. 4 (2014); Noel Anderson, "Competitive Intervention, Protracted Conflict, and the Global Prevalence of Civil War," *International Studies Quarterly* 63 (2019): 692–693.

8. Jonathan Landay and Idrees Ali, "Taliban Surge Exposes Failure of U.S. Efforts to Build Afghan Army," Reuters, August 15, 2021; Matthieu Aikins, "Inside the Fall of Kabul," *New York Times Magazine*, December 10, 2021; Craig Whitlock, "Afghan Security Forces' Wholesale Collapse Was Years in the Making," *Washington Post*, August 16, 2021; see also Kori Schake, "Why the Afghan Army Folded," *Atlantic*, August 17, 2021; Jennifer Griffin and Caitlin McFall, "Milley: Afghan Forces 'Not Designed Appropriately' to Secure Nation in 'Lessons Learned' Following Withdrawal," *Fox News*, September 4, 2021; SIGAR, "Collapse of the Afghan National Defense and Security Forces: An Assessment of the Factors That Led to Its Demise," SIGAR 22-22-IP Evaluation Report, May 2022; Quarterly Report to the United States Congress, Special Inspector General for Afghanistan Reconstruction, July 30, 2020, 4–5; Thomas Gibbons-Neff, Fahim Abed, and Sharif Hassan, "The Afghan Military Was Built over 20 Years. How Did It Collapse So Quickly?," *New York Times*, August 13, 2021.

9. Timur Kuran, "Now Out of Never: The Element of Surprise in the East European Revolution of 1989," *World Politics* 44, no. 1 (1991): 7–48; Arturas Rozenas and Yuri M. Zhukov, "Mass Repression and Political Loyalty: Evidence from Stalin's 'Terror by Hunger,'" *American Political Science Review* 133, no. 2 (2019): 569–583; Marc Morjé Howard, *The Weakness of Civil Society in Post-Communist Europe* (Cambridge, 2003); Grigore Pop-Eleches and Joshua A. Tucker, *Communism's Shadow: Historical Legacies and Contemporary Political Attitudes* (Princeton, 2017).

10. Roger R. Reese, *Why Stalin's Soldiers Fought: The Red Army's Military Effectiveness in World War II* (Kansas, 2011); Jason Lyall, *Divided Armies: Inequality and Battlefield Performance in Modern War* (Princeton, 2020), 363–403; Jason Lyall and Yuri Zhukov, "Fratricidal Coercion in Modern War," November 4, 2021, http://dx.doi.org/10.2139/ssrn.3956923; CIA, "Report on the Bulgarian Army," 05/29/1951, CIA-RDP82-00457R007700170003-3; US Army, "Order of Battle Handbook: Czechoslovak Army," 08/01/1958, accessed via CIA-RDP81-01043R00280014007-5; S. L. Kuzmin and Zh. Oyuunchimeg, *Vooruzhennoye vosstaniye v Mongolii v 1932 g.* (MBA, 2015), 169; CIA, "Communist Capabilities and Probable Courses of Action in Korea Through Mid-1952," 12/07/1951, CREST no. CIA-RDP79R01012A001700010001-3; Caitlin Talmadge, *The Dictator's Army: Battlefield Effectiveness in Authoritarian Regimes* (Cornell, 2015), 84–85, 96–97, 117–118, 129–130.

INDEX

Tayla Smith

Adam E. Casey is an analyst in the United States government. His writing has appeared in the *Washington Post*, *Foreign Affairs*, and *Foreign Policy*, and his research has been cited by the *New York Times*, the *Economist*, and *Bloomberg*, among others. He received his PhD in political science from the University of Toronto. A native of Minnesota, he lives in Maryland.